Schlechty, Phi
C., 1937-
  Creating great
schools

D0403565

Creating Great Schools

Creating Great Schools

Six Critical Systems at the Heart
of Educational Innovation

Phillip C. Schlechty

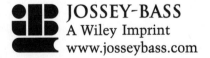

JOSSEY-BASS
A Wiley Imprint
www.josseybass.com

Published by Jossey-Bass
A Wiley Imprint
989 Market Street, San Francisco, CA 94103-1741   www.josseybass.com

Jossey-Bass books and products are available through most bookstores. To contact Jossey-Bass directly call our Customer Care Department within the U.S. at 800-956-7739, outside the U.S. at 317-572-3986, or fax 317-572-4002.

Jossey-Bass also publishes its books in a variety of electronic formats. Some content that appears in print may not be available in electronic books.

Excerpt on p. 6 reprinted with the permission of Simon & Schuster from *Left Back* by Diane Ravitch.

Library of Congress Cataloging-in-Publication Data

Schlechty, Phillip C., date
    Creating great schools : six critical systems at the heart of educational innovation / Phillip C. Schlechty.— 1st ed.
        p. cm. — (The Jossey-Bass education series)
    Includes bibliographical references and index.
    ISBN 0-7879-7690-3 (alk. paper)
    1. School management and organization—United States—Philosophy.   2. Educational change—United States—Philosophy.   I. Title.   II. Series.
    LB2805.S343 2005
    371.2—dc22   2004019207

Printed in the United States of America
FIRST EDITION
HB Printing   10 9 8 7 6 5 4 3

The Jossey-Bass Education Series

Contents

Introduction

Strategies to make bad schools adequate are not necessarily the same as strategies to make good schools great.

Most reformers are concerned with fixing bad schools. My concern in this book is different. My focus is on creating great schools.

There are certainly many more good schools than some policymakers and critics seem to believe. Further, I am not convinced that current efforts to fix bad schools are likely to produce the results intended. Indeed, I fear that the assumptions on which some of these efforts are based are so faulty that if educators continue to act on them they are in danger of making many schools worse rather than better.

A Look Back

When America's schools were created it was never intended that all students would learn at high levels. Educators, civic leaders, parents, and nonparents alike assumed that a relatively few students would learn at high levels, many students would learn a good deal, some students would learn a bit, and others would learn enough to know how to respond to authority in order to carry out tasks assigned to unskilled workers in a factory system of production.

Consequently, America's schools were designed to produce compliance and attendance. Today the expectation is radically different. Educators, civic leaders, parents, and nonparents expect that all students will learn at high levels and that what they learn will be related to matters once reserved for the elite—that is, all children are to be provided a high-quality academic education. If this is to happen we need schools that nurture engagement rather than simply producing compliance and attendance and harvesting whatever engagement should happen to occur.

Even at its best the present system of schooling will not produce high-order learning among most students. And it is high-order learning that is required for effective living in the twenty-first century.

High-order learning occurs only when students are engaged. If schools are to ensure that all—or nearly all—students learn at high levels, they will need innovations that go well beyond the kind of innovation based on research because we presently lack adequate examples of systems that purposefully nurture engagement.

The unfortunate fact is that our educational system is working as it was designed to work, but the way it was designed to work is not adequate to our present needs and expectations.

Designing for Invention

The purpose of this book is to help leaders design school systems that invite inventions, as opposed to systems that mandate implementation of programs that will serve only to shore up for a brief time a system of schooling that must either be changed in fundamental ways or die.

Systemic changes, unlike the innovations that give rise to the need for them, cannot be introduced through programs and projects. Systemic changes require more than training and more than corrective feedback, coaching, and support. Systemic changes require education and reeducation; what Fullan refers to as *reculturing*.[1] Such changes cannot be successfully implemented without strong moral leadership as well as great technical skill.

Two Types of Innovations

In recent years my thinking regarding the relationship between innovation and social systems has been reignited and given clearer focus by the work of Clayton Christensen as represented in his

---

[1]See M. Fullan, *Leading in a Culture of Change* (San Francisco: Jossey Bass, 2001).

book *The Innovator's Dilemma*. Christensen distinguishes between two types of innovations: those that are sustaining and those that are disruptive.[2]

Innovations that are sufficiently congruent with the existing social systems that they have little impact on either the structure or the culture of those systems are *sustaining* innovations. Such innovations are neither more nor less than extensions of the present systems. They are intended to improve effectiveness and efficiency and to make it possible for the present systems to perform *up to capacity*. For example, PowerPoint is an electronic elaboration of the slate board and the overhead projector. Using PowerPoint does not, however, alter the role of the teacher or any other structural aspect of the school. It simply makes it easier for teachers to do what they have always done, albeit perhaps somewhat more effectively and efficiently.

Disruptive innovations, if they are to be employed effectively, require dramatic alterations in both the structure and the culture of the organization. Such alterations require changes in beliefs, values, and commitments as well as changes in rules, roles, and relationships. More important, such innovations require changes in the way vital organizational functions are carried out: for example, in the way people and programs are evaluated, in the way new members are recruited and inducted, and so on. This is what is meant by *systemic change:* the alteration of rules, roles, and relationships and of the culture in which they are embedded so that people can carry out critical functions of the organization (for example, evaluation or recruitment) in dramatically different ways.

---

[2]In *Teaching and Social Behavior: Toward an Organizational Theory of Instruction* (Needham Heights, Mass.: Allyn & Bacon, 1976), I developed the concept of *structural fit* to explain why many of the inquiry-oriented curriculum projects of the 1960s failed on implementation. I argued that the pedagogical assumptions on which these materials were based were not congruent, did not *fit*, with the authority principles on which the typical high school was (and is) based, with the result that the materials were rejected by the system or their uses were modified so that practices never really changed. I find Clayton M. Christensen's ideas of sustaining and disruptive innovations a more economical way of expressing the concerns I addressed in my earlier book; see C. M. Christensen, *The Innovator's Dilemma* (Boston: Harvard Business School Press, 1997).

Six Critical Systems

In complex social organizations like schools, rules, roles, and relationships (structure) tend to become organized around functions critical to the operation of the enterprise. The norms that define this structure are expressions of an organization's culture, and it is these cultural expressions that are referred to when the term *social systems* is used. Among the more critical organizational social systems are

- *Recruitment and induction systems:* the systems through which new members are identified and attracted to the organization and brought to understand and embrace the norms and values they must understand and embrace to be full members of the organization
- *Knowledge transmission systems:* the formal and informal systems of education, training, and socialization through which organizational members are brought to know and understand what they need to know and understand to uphold organizational norms and to function effectively in the organization
- *Power and authority systems:* the systems that legitimize the use of sanctions, define the proper exercise of power, and determine status relationships
- *Evaluation systems:* the systems through which measures of merit and worth are assigned, status is determined, honor is bestowed, and the method and timing of negative sanctions are set
- *Directional systems:* the systems through which goals are set, priorities are determined, and when things go awry, corrective actions are initiated
- *Boundary systems:* the systems that define who and what are inside the organization, and are therefore subject to the control of the organization, and who and what are outside the organization, and are therefore beyond the reach of the systems that make up the organization

Viewed collectively, the structure and the culture of an organization make up what classical sociologists sometimes refer to as the *normative order.* It is this order that is at stake when leaders set about the business of changing systems. And because so much is at stake, resistance is likely to be met at every turn.

Those who lead systemic change need to be armed with every bit of insight available. Even with the most powerful understandings, leading systemic change is a daunting task. I hope this book will make the task less daunting by demystifying some of the ideas leaders need to master to understand the social systems they propose to change.

Leaving no child behind is a noble sentiment, but ensuring that every child is empowered to get ahead is an even nobler goal.

The Organization of This Book

Part One (Chapters One through Three) addresses in broad terms what systemic change means. Chapter One discusses the reasons underlying my belief that such change is much needed in American education. My argument is straightforward. As schools are now organized, their core business is to produce attendance and compliance and to harvest existing engagement. If schools are to serve the needs of twenty-first-century America, they must instead focus on nurturing engagement. In this chapter I distinguish between compliance produced through engagement and compliance produced by extrinsic rewards or the threat of punishment, and I show how compliance that results from engagement produces a type and level of learning different from the learning produced by compliance that results from other means. Finally, I argue that schools can make the nurturance of engagement their core business only by dramatically changing the systems that define behavior in schools.

Proceeding from the observation that the six critical systems outlined previously are held together by a complex set of norms and values expressed in rules, roles, and relationships, Chapter Two describes the nature of normative systems generally and illustrates how these norms operate in the context of schools and school districts. At the end of this chapter I present a set of questions that I believe school leaders will find useful as they endeavor to understand the normative order of the schools and school districts they are leading. I offer similar practical questions in Chapters Three through Nine.

In Chapter Three I describe the relationship between systemic change and the patterns of adult compliance that are required to implement this type of change. My goal is to shed some light on reasons that efforts at systemic change so often fail, as well as to describe some of the ways systems interact to make successful implementation possible.

Part Two (Chapters Four through Nine) addresses in detail the six critical systems that must change. In Chapter Four I describe the recruitment and induction system. The framework I present is drawn largely from insights gained from my study of the sociology of occupations, especially studies of the way physicians, nurses, lawyers, and other knowledge work professionals learn their crafts. In this chapter I am concerned with the way existing organizational members are recruited and inducted into systems that are being transformed, as well as with the way persons new to the organization are recruited and inducted into its systems.

Chapter Five describes the knowledge transmission system. I discuss how variation in the way knowledge is created, disseminated, and distributed in an organization affects the way people behave and what they learn. I also show how changes in the knowledge transmission system require supportive changes in other systems and how failure to bring about these changes will almost certainly result in failure to successfully alter the way teachers teach and what students learn.

Chapter Six deals with the way power and authority are distributed in schools and the effects alterations in the power and authority system can have on the performance of teachers and students. Considerable attention is given to the role of central office personnel in facilitating and inhibiting change efforts. I also try to untangle some of the issues that emerge when schools undertake efforts to redistribute power through decentralization. Again, I present readers with questions they might pose as they try to understand the power and authority system of the schools they lead and are trying to change.

Chapter Seven concerns evaluation systems, for both personnel and programs. Though this is sometimes overlooked, authority often finds its most meaningful expressions in evaluation. Therefore changes in the way power and authority are exercised often bring about changes in the evaluation system. Conversely, when one tries to change the existing evaluation system, power and authority are almost always involved. My intent in this chapter is to help readers see more clearly how evaluation systems operate and how these operations are related to the other critical systems that shape behavior in schools. So rather than laying out an agenda for designing new means of evaluating people or programs, I alert readers to matters they will need to consider if they undertake such a difficult task.

One of the most difficult tasks confronting leaders is the task of establishing and maintaining direction, especially when the intent is to change direction or to establish a new agenda for the organization. Chapter Eight addresses these matters. Here I discuss such matters as goal displacement, competing loyalties, goal clarity, and goal consensus. I show how the way goals are set often has to do with the way evaluations are conducted and the way power and authority are distributed.

Chapter Nine deals with the boundary system. In this chapter I discuss the problems school leaders confront in establishing and maintaining the social boundaries that define who is inside and who is outside the schools' organizational framework. Among other things I discuss the difference between the boundary definitions used by elementary schools and by high schools and show how these differences make high schools more difficult to change than elementary schools. I also discuss strategies that are sometimes used to maintain boundaries, even when these strategies may be harmful to the long-term interests of schools and the effectiveness of school programs.

Part Three (Chapters Ten and Eleven) addresses moving forward with disruptive innovations. Chapter Ten presents a framework for analyzing the degree to which people are complying with the official norms that guide behavior in a system. Particular attention is given to the issues that arise from efforts to introduce new norms and to support new values and direction.

In Chapter Eleven I present the reader with a personal view of the future of public education in America.

Appendix A provides a framework that teachers have found useful in their efforts to design engaging schoolwork for students. My intent is to provide readers with a tool that might be useful as they go about designing more effective induction systems. Readers who are familiar with my earlier work will find much that is familiar here, but the essay this appendix contains is unique to the present work.

Appendix B provides a set of guidelines for creating learning communities that will support the transformation of schools from organizations in which compliance and attendance are the focus of operations to organizations in which attention and commitment are the focus of all that goes on in the school.

Acknowledgments

This book had its origins in a graduate seminar in organizational theory, which now seems, as the *Star Wars* phrase goes, "long ago, in a galaxy far, far away." It was in the autumn of 1964 at The Ohio State University, and Professor Ronald Corwin, who was at the time working on a book chapter that would define the organizational properties of schools, was conducting the seminar. In his chapter Corwin outlined some of the critical systems that define the operation of schools.[3] Though a great deal has been learned about life in schools since 1964, much that Corwin wrote is as current today as at the time he wrote it, and I have relied heavily on some of Corwin's framework for the basic architecture for this book. I want to acknowledge my debt to him.

I also owe a great intellectual debt to Robin M. Williams Jr., whom I have never met but whose work has influenced me throughout my career, as has the work of Robert K. Merton, Amitai Etzioni, C. Wright Mills, Émile Durkheim, and Willard Waller. It was in studying the works of authors such as these that the sociological lens I use to understand schools began to be formed.

At a more personal level, there are many other people I want to thank.

Three sets of reviewers took the time to read and react to an early version of this book. The advice they gave me led to major revisions. I know the book is much improved. If the reader still finds

---

[3]See R. G. Corwin, "Education and the Sociology of Complex Organizations," in D. Hansen and J. Gerstl (eds.), *On Education: Sociological Perspectives* (New York: Wiley, 1967), pp. 156–223. Corwin's chapter never received the attention I thought, and continue to think, it deserved. The writing is dense, but the subject was and is important. (*On Education* is now out of print and available only in libraries.)

the book lacking, I am to blame. The advice I was given—some of which I took and some of which I did not—was good advice.

Among those who advised me were Randy Bridges, superintendent, Rock Hill Schools in South Carolina; Bruce Hawkins, superintendent, ESD 123 in Washington state; Carlos Hicks, superintendent, Gulfport Schools in Mississippi; Mark Keen, superintendent, Westfield Washington Schools in Indiana; Rodney Lafon, superintendent, St. Charles Parish Schools in Louisiana; Steve McCammon, superintendent, Fife Schools in Washington; and Pam Saylor, superintendent, Lake County Schools in Florida. Not only did they take time out of their busy schedules to read and react to an early version of this book, they spent two days with me in a seminar, helping me to think of ways to make what I am trying to say more clear and more compelling.

I also had the advantage of spending a day at the University of Southern Maine, where Betty Lou Whitford, who is dean of the School of Education and who always gives me good advice, gathered together a group of faculty members who shared their views of my effort. I thank each of them—Ken Jones, Flynn Ross, Debora Smith, and Diane Wood.

And I owe a great deal to three anonymous reviewers who, as they will see, caused me to radically revise some of my initial chapters.

I have had the privilege of publishing four books with Jossey-Bass. Each time Lesley Iura, executive editor for Jossey-Bass, has been there to encourage me and guide me. I have also had the opportunity to work with an outstanding copy editor, Elspeth MacHattie, who has done much to help me say what I mean. Finally, Michele Quiroga, as the production editor for Jossey-Bass, has done much to make the difficult task of final production as easy as possible. Thanks to each of them.

As is always the case with my work I am indebted to the staff at the Schlechty Center for Leadership in School Reform and to the teachers, principals, and superintendents who are affiliated with this center. I learn from reading and research, but I learn even more from conversations and interactions with these kindred spirits.

There are also several individuals to whom I want to give special thanks:

Tena Lutz is my assistant and good friend. We have worked together for over twenty years. As she always has, Tena has made sure that the details of writing a book are taken care of, and she has pushed me to stay at it when I was down.

My two grandchildren, Daniel and Lily, give this senior citizen the motive force to keep on trying.

My wife, Shelia, keeps me alert to the little things that make a difference to children. She taught me much when our children were young, and now that we have grandchildren she is teaching me even more.

And my daughter Jennifer, who grew up in a house where her father was always writing and talking about schools, has recently assumed the role of my local editor. Thanks, Jenny.

The Author

Phillip C. Schlechty is founder and CEO of the Schlechty Center for Leadership in School Reform and the author of such books as *Working on the Work: An Action Plan for Teachers, Principals, and Superintendents* (2002), *Shaking Up the Schoolhouse: How to Support and Sustain Educational Innovation* (2001), *Inventing Better Schools: An Action Plan for Educational Reform* (1997), and *Schools for the 21st Century: Leadership Imperatives for Educational Reform* (1990), as well as numerous other publications. He serves as an adviser to many school districts in the United States and Canada and conducts seminars and training sessions for superintendents, school board members, union leaders, principals, teachers, and parent groups.

Schlechty is one of the nation's most sought after speakers on topics related to school reform. Business groups as well as educators find his perspective useful and understandable. Born near Rossburg, Ohio, he has two daughters and two grandchildren, and he and his wife reside in Louisville, Kentucky.

Creating Great Schools

Part One

The Need for Change

Rather than simply asking, How does the way schools are organized affect the behavior of teachers and students in classrooms? I have come to ask, How do the structure of schools (by which I mean rules, roles, and relationships) and the culture of schools (by which I mean the beliefs, commitments, myths, physical artifacts, and lore that are transmitted to members of the school community) affect the behavior of teachers and students in classrooms, and how is this behavior related to what and how students learn in schools?

This section (Chapters One through Three) explains why systemic change is desperately needed in our schools. It also offers an overview of the norms and values that gain expression in rules, roles, and relationships in schools.

Chapter One

From Compliance to Engagement

As late as the 1970s it was common for academics to argue that differences in schools make little difference in the life chances of children. Some went so far as to suggest that because schools themselves make so little difference, educators might be better advised to worry about the quality of life students experienced in schools than to worry about long-term results. Christopher Jencks put it this way:

> Instead of evaluating schools in terms of long term effects on their alumni, which appear to be relatively uniform, we think it is wiser to evaluate schools in terms of their immediate effects on teachers and students, which appear to be more variable. Some schools are dull, depressing, even terrifying places, while others are lively, comfortable and reassuring. If we think of school life as an end in itself rather than a means to some other end, such differences are enormously important. Eliminating these differences would not do much to make adults more equal, but it would do a great deal to make the quality of children's (and teachers') lives more equal. Since children are in school for a fifth of their lives, this would be a significant accomplishment.[1]

Today schools are expected to guarantee that all students will learn at high levels. Furthermore, it is assumed that those who work in schools should be held accountable if the students fail to

---

[1] C. Jencks, *Inequality: A Reassessment of the Effect of Family and Schooling in America* (New York: Harper Colophon Books, 1972), p. 256.

perform at the level required. The public schools of America are being asked to do things they have never done and things they were not designed to do.

It may well be that schools can independently overcome the conditions of poverty and produce equivalent results for culturally diverse populations—indeed, I believe this is possible—but schools designed to ensure that all students take advantage of the opportunities provided must surely look and feel different from schools designed with the notion that *all* that is required is that they provide equal opportunities to learn.

The Great Mutation

Not only are the expectations currently imposed on schools without precedent but schools are expected to meet these expectations in a social context vastly different from the context that existed at the time the public schools were being created. The changes that have occurred since the period in which America's basic system of public education was invented (about 1830 to 1910) have been so great that Carl Bridenbaugh, in his 1962 presidential address to the American Historical Association, referred to them as a *great mutation*. He said:

> The Great Mutation, or historical change, has taken place so rapidly, and life has sustained such sudden and radical alterations (in the long course of time) that we are now suffering something like historical amnesia. In the present century, first Western civilization and now the entire globe have witnessed the inexorable substitution of an artificial environment and a materialistic outlook on life for the old natural environment and spiritual world view that linked us so irrevocably to the Recent and Distant Pasts. So pervading and complete has been this change, and so complex has life become—I almost said overwhelming—that it now appears probable that mid-nineteenth-century America or Western Europe had more in common with fifth-century Greece (physically, economically, socially, mentally, spiritually) than with their own projections into the middle of the twentieth century. Is it possible that so short a time can alter the condition of man?[2]

---

[2] C. Bridenbaugh, "The Great Mutation," *American Historical Review*, 1963, *68*(2), 315–331.

Too many policymakers overlook the fact that America's system of elementary education emerged at a time when America was a nation of small towns, villages, and farms, with only a few urban centers of note. In this era the idea that schools were community centers much more clearly squared with empirical reality than is now the case. Today, in fact, one of the greatest concerns in America is the decline of the American community.[3] How, one might ask, can the schools serve the community when there is no community to serve? Or better, one might ask, as David Matthews does, Is there a public for public education?[4]

The American high school emerged later than the elementary school. Though the public high school was an American response to the needs of the industrial society, it too has its roots in the *common school* movement that gave rise to the elementary schools.[5] Critical to the common school movement was the idea of community and the belief in a common culture worthy of being transmitted to the young. Indeed, the high school was viewed as a means of dealing with diversity by "Americanizing" the young born to immigrant parents. *E pluribus unum*—"out of many one"—was the motto, and the high school was viewed as one of the great cauldrons that made America a "melting pot."

Today educators are being challenged to promote a common culture without dishonoring the diverse traditions that command the loyalties of the citizens of this nation. Inventing an educational system that can deal with the many paradoxes embedded in this challenge is a daunting task indeed.

---

[3] See, for example, R. D. Putnam, *Bowling Alone: The Collapse and Revival of American Community* (New York: Simon & Schuster, 2000).

[4] D. Matthews, *Is There a Public for Public Schools?* (Dayton, Ohio: Kettering Foundation Press, 1996).

[5] One of the concerns of the educational reformers of the nineteenth century, including Horace Mann, was that the combined impact of frontier living and immigration would lead to cultural disintegration. They thus sought to create a system of public education that ensured the promulgation of what they viewed as the *common culture*. This culture included a preference for Protestant morality and those forms of civic virtue and literacy essential to the preservation of a republic. The *common school* was intended to promote the maintenance of this common culture and to ensure an essential level of literacy.

The Ends of Schooling

By 1920, the system of education that shapes our schools today was in place. Unfortunately for our current needs, this system was designed for a world in which it was assumed that *higher learning*, by which was meant academic learning, was reserved for the elite. Furthermore, it was designed on the assumption that most students would be better served by a nonacademic curriculum. And indeed, as late as 1960, fewer than 10 percent of Americans above the age of twenty-five had graduated from college and fewer than 50 percent had graduated from high school. As Diane Ravitch has observed:

> Thinking they could bridge the gap between school and society and make the schools socially useful, pedagogical theorists sought alternatives to the academic curriculum for non-college bound students. Curricular differentiation meant an academic education for some, a nonacademic education for others; this approach affected those children—mainly the poor, immigrants, and racial minorities—who were pushed into undemanding vocational, industrial, or general programs by bureaucrats and guidance counselors who thought they were incapable of learning much more. Such policies, packaged in rhetoric about democracy and "meeting the needs of the individual child," encouraged racial and social stratification in American schools. . . . this stratification not only was profoundly undemocratic but [it] was harmful, both to the children involved and to American society.[6]

So long as there was no need for a large number of well-educated citizens, and so long as Americans in general assumed that higher learning was largely the purview of the rich, the wellborn, and the most able of the lower classes, this system based (theoretically, at least) on meritocratic principles was generally accepted. As the last half of the twentieth century unfolded, however, it became clear that more and more Americans were becoming dissatisfied with their schools, and the source of that dissatisfaction had to do primarily with the fact that the schools were perceived to be failing to ensure

---

[6] D. Ravitch, *Left Back: A Century of Failed School Reforms* (New York: Simon & Schuster, 2000), p. 15. Reprinted with permission per copyright page.

that *all* students learned at high levels. A recent publication sponsored by a subunit of the National Academies of Science and Engineering and the Institute of Medicine puts the matter this way: "[Though] there has been some wavering . . . the dominant policy emphasis that has emerged at the start of the 21st century has been to hold all students accountable for achieving high educational standards . . ., focusing especially on reading and math. For this to occur, a much broader range of students must become *engaged* in learning the kind of curricula that, until recently, only students bound for four year colleges were expected to master" [emphasis added].[7]

The Meaning of Engagement

Though different authors define the word *engagement* differently, there is a widespread tendency among educators, especially those of a constructivist bent, to imply that engagement is present only when students are involved in tasks that call on them to solve problems or in other activities intended to develop what Bloom and others describe as higher-order thinking skills.[8] Unfortunately, linking engagement directly to any particular level of learning detracts attention from the fact that learning and engagement are two distinct concepts, each with its own attributes, potentials, and limitations. More than

---

[7] National Research Council and Institute of Medicine of the National Academies, *Engaging Schools: Fostering High School Students' Motivation to Learn* (Washington, D.C.: National Academies Press, 2004), p. 16.

[8] For one example of the way educators typically define engagement, see P. B. Mosenthal, "Understanding Engagement: Historical and Political Contexts," in J. T. Guthrie and D. E. Alvermar (eds.), *Engaged Reading: Processes, Practices and Policy Implications* (New York: Teachers College Press, 1999), pp. 1–16. What is commonly known as Bloom's taxonomy was actually developed by a large committee of psychologists and involves three domains: the cognitive, the affective, and the psychomotor. The cognitive domain has received much more attention than have the other two. The taxonomy is available in a wide range of publications by various authors and on the Internet. See, for example, B. S. Bloom and D. R. Krathwohl, *Taxonomy of Behavioral Objectives: The Classification of Educational Goals by a Committee of College and University Examiners: Handbook I. The Cognitive Domain* (White Plains, N.Y.: Longman, 1956).

that, it detracts attention from the fact that although learning does result from engagement, students who are engaged are not engaged in learning. Rather they are engaged in tasks, activities, and experiences that it is assumed will *lead* to learning. Similarly, the centrality of learning to schools sometimes leads to the mistaken notion that the business of schools is learning, just as the centrality of profit in business sometimes leads to the mistaken notion that the business of business is to make a profit. As some business leaders are beginning to learn, their business is to create goods and services that customers will buy at a price that makes a profit possible. Profit happens when businesses do their business. Similarly, educators must learn that their business is to design tasks and activities with attributes that encourage students to invest their most precious resources, that is, their time, energy and attention. Learning in schools happens when schools do their business.

Some of these tasks and activities may result in students' learning how to evaluate and synthesize (Bloom's two highest cognitive levels) and solve problems, and some may result in learning at lower levels: for example, learning to count, to label, and to identify (illustrative of Bloom's lower levels of learning). Rather than being defined by its result (that is, by a particular type or level of learning), engagement should be defined in terms of the meaning students give to the tasks and activities their teachers encourage them to undertake.

To say that a student is engaged means, first, that the task in which the student is involved commands the student's attention. Because the task commands attention, the student focuses his or her energy on completing the task at a level that will satisfy the requirements specified in the task. Second, it means that the student is committed to the task or activity to the point that he or she is willing to allocate scarce resources (for example, time and psychic energy) to completing the task or participating in the activity *and* that he or she is willing to persist with the task even when difficulties are confronted and even when no promise of extrinsic reward is attached to continuing with the task or activity. To measure engagement, then, it is necessary first to measure attention and commitment. Students who are high in attention and high in commitment are engaged. Students who are high in attention but low in commitment are simply compliant.

When students are engaged, it is because the tasks and activities they are being encouraged to become involved with have inherent meaning and value for them. That is, they perceive that the values they bring to the task or activity are likely to be satisfied if they participate in the activities associated with completing the task. The values they want satisfied are values associated with doing the task rather than values that might be gained as a result of having completed the task.

Engagement does not result from students' desire to learn. Engagement results from students' desire to do things they cannot do *unless* they learn. Thus the only means that teachers have to increase engagement is to design school tasks in ways that take into account the values and motives that students bring to the classroom. *The art and science of teaching is designing schoolwork that the students want to do and that results in students' learning what their teachers, their parents, and the larger community want them to learn, and then leading students in ways that ensure successful completion of the tasks and activities contained in that work.*

Engagement Versus Compliance

Engagement is best understood as the interaction between attention and commitment. Students who are engaged pay attention and are committed because they find value in doing what the task or activity calls upon them to do. They may or may not place value on learning the things they must learn to successfully complete the task or participate in the activity. In other words, engaged students may learn things on which they place no particular personal value because they *do* value doing the tasks or participating in the activities that result in their learning these things.

Whereas engagement results in a clear focus on the task or activity and persistence with the task in spite of difficulties—even in the absence of extrinsic rewards—compliance requires only attention to the task. Furthermore, a compliant student's level of attention may vary from high to low. For example, the promise of a highly valued extrinsic reward (a good grade, teacher approval, parent approval, college entry, an opportunity to play on an athletic team, and so forth) may bring about a clear focus and a high investment of energy. When the work students are provided is not engaging, such rewards are the only means of gaining attention and ensuring the investment of the energy necessary to complete the task. However, if the extrinsic rewards are removed, attention will diminish or disappear, and energy will dissipate because there is nothing attractive in the work. This is so precisely because the task or activity, in itself, has no inherent meaning or value for the student. Attention can be gained with rewards. Commitment can be earned only through meaning and values.

Two types of compliance can be distinguished. Compliance based on the promise of extrinsic rewards is *strategic compliance.* In making the decision to do a task, the student attends to the reward received for doing the task and to a calculation of the worth of that reward. He or she does not attend to the nature of the task itself. So far as the task or activity is concerned, the student may find it meaningless or totally without merit. Strategic compliance, if the stakes are sufficiently high, can produce high attention, so high that students will learn at relatively high levels. Students who are compliant for calculative, or strategic, reasons may even learn at Bloom's middle levels (analysis and application), but what they learn is not as likely to be retained or transferred as it would be if they had learned it in a context that had meaning and value for them—that is, a context that produced engagement.[9]

It is important to understand, however, that the promise of extrinsic rewards is not the only means by which compliance is induced. The threat of punishment or unpleasant and unwanted consequences can also produce some attention, though it cannot induce commitment. The student will focus on the task only to the extent that he or she must to avoid unpleasant consequences. The student will invest only as much time and energy in the task or activity as is

---

[9] I believe a case could be made that one of the reasons many schools with predominantly middle-class children have more high-performing students than do schools with more poor children is that students in the former are more likely to be calculative in their involvement in both the school and the work the school assigns. Though I know of no research that bears directly on this matter, indirect support can be found; see, for example, D. C. Pope, *Doing School: How We Are Creating a Generation of Stressed Out, Materialistic and Miseducated Students* (New Haven, Conn.: Yale University Press, 2003); E. Burkett, *Another Planet: A Year in the Life of a Suburban School* (New York: HarperCollins, 2002); E. Humes, *School of Dreams: Making the Grade at a Top American High School* (Orlando, Fla.: Harcourt, 2003).

minimally required to avoid whatever it is he or she wants to avoid—for example, parental disapproval. This type of compliance is *ritual compliance*.[10]

In summary, *engagement* comes into existence in response to students' desire for meaning and for relevance to their own values. *Strategic compliance* is motivated by the desire to get something or to get ahead. *Ritual compliance* is motivated by the desire to get by and to get along.

Engagement, Compliance, and Learning

As I indicated earlier, I disagree with the notion that it is only when students are involved in tasks that require them to develop higher-order thinking skills that they can be said to be engaged. I do, however, agree that unless the student is engaged in the work, he or she is not likely to develop higher-order skills (evaluation and synthesis) and complex understandings. In addition I would argue that even in the development of lower-level skills and less sophisticated and less complex understanding, students who are engaged learn differently from those who are only compliant. I believe this for several reasons:[11]

- First, the development of higher-order understandings and skills requires considerable self-direction, discipline, and persistence, elements likely to be lacking when inducements external to the task or activity (and not engagement) are the primary means of gaining attention and action.
- Second, the likelihood that what is learned will be transferable to contexts other than the specific context in which the learning has occurred is increased when the tasks that result

---

[10] In some of my early books I referred to what I now call *strategic compliance* as *ritual engagement*. I also referred to what I now call *ritual compliance* as *passive compliance*. The new labels more closely reflect my present understanding of the importance of distinguishing between engagement on the one hand and both forms of compliance on the other.

[11] To explore the research underlying these reasons, see C. Brewster and J. Fager, *Increasing Student Engagement and Motivation: From Time-on-Task to Homework* (Portland, Oreg.: Northwest Regional Laboratory, Oct. 2000).

in the learning have meaning and value to the student. Engagement increases the likelihood that such meaning will be present.

* Third, considerable evidence exists that retention is also increased when new learning occurs in contexts that have meaning and value to the student.

What those who insist on equating engagement with higher-order thinking and the creation of profound knowledge sometimes overlook is that engaged students are also willing to undertake tasks that call for rote memorization, especially when the task is associated with some performance, product, exhibition, or problem that the student values and sees as important. Anyone who has watched an adolescent boy memorize football plays knows that this is so. Anyone who has watched choral music groups rehearse knows that this is so. Rote learning can be meaningful learning when the rote tasks are associated in the student's mind with an exhibition, performance, or problem that has inherent value to the student. Learning by rote can be learning produced through engagement just as certainly as it can be learning produced through compliance. The difference is that rote learning produced through engagement has meaning to the student; rote learning that results from compliance lacks meaning. When the learning has no meaning, what is learned is soon forgotten and has little transfer value.

Disengagement and Noncompliance

Of course some tasks and activities are not engaging to students, and at times the rewards and punishments available to support such tasks and activities are not sufficient to induce students to comply either. In such cases students have two options. The first is to withdraw or retreat from the task (*retreatism*). The second is to overtly reject the task or activity and replace it with some preferred task or activity (*rebellion*).[12]

---

[12] As I have noted in many of my earlier books, I am indebted to Robert K. Merton and Amitai Etzioni for some of the language I use here, but only I am responsible for the way I have employed their words.

Sometimes retreatism goes undetected, especially in classes where the teacher is the focus of activity and where students who are engaged are more engaged in the teacher than they are in the tasks and activities the teacher designs for them or encourages them to design for themselves (I discuss the difference between engaging teachers and engaging schoolwork later in this book). Because the student is not "acting out," and may even have learned, as Bill Cosby has said, "to sleep with his or her eyes wide open," retreatism is not a problem for teachers who value compliance over engagement. Rebellion is another matter. Whether concerned with gaining engagement or simply compliance, most teachers are highly attuned to signs of rebellion and are quick to address it when it occurs.

Intrinsic Versus Extrinsic Motivation

The concept of engagement is often associated with the concept of motivation, and in discussions of motivation it is common to distinguish between intrinsic and extrinsic motivation. Properly framed, the ideas of intrinsic and extrinsic motivation can be useful in understanding engagement. Poorly framed, these ideas can be distracting and misleading. For example, it is sometimes suggested that extrinsic motivation depends on the presence of rewards, whereas intrinsic motivation requires no rewards; students engage the task for the pure delight of the task or the challenge they find in the task. This view is illustrated by Brewster and Fager in their definitions of extrinsic and intrinsic motivation:

- *Extrinsic motivation*: A student can be described as extrinsically motivated when he or she engages in learning "purely for the sake of attaining a reward or for avoiding some punishment" (Dev, 1997). School practices that seek to motivate students extrinsically include publicly recognizing students for academic achievements; giving out stickers, candy, and other rewards; and taking away privileges, such as recess, on the basis of students' academic performance (Brooks et al., 1998).

- *Intrinsic motivation*: A student can be described as intrinsically motivated when he or she is motivated from within: Intrinsically motivated students actively engage themselves in learning out of curiosity, interest, or enjoyment, or in order to achieve their own intellectual and personal goals. According to Dev, 1997, "A

> student who is intrinsically motivated . . . will not need any
> type of reward or incentive to initiate or complete a task.
> This type of student is more likely to complete the chosen task
> and be excited by the challenging nature of an activity."[13]

The distinction made by Brewster and Fager, and by many others, misses the fundamental point that in both cases the student is gaining a reward. In the case of extrinsic motivation the reward is extrinsic to the task (for example a grade). In the case of intrinsic motivation the reward is intrinsic to the task: for example, the task might be designed so that the significance of the student's contribution is made apparent and the student gains affirmation of personal worth.

Rewards may be extrinsic or intrinsic, but motives are always intrinsic in that they have to do with values and meanings the student brings to the task. Motives may result from values that have been learned and internalized, or they may derive from basic needs that are "wired" into the human organism,[14] but in either case they are internal and they have to do with the attitudes, dispositions, and values individuals bring to the task. These attitudes, dispositions, and values determine whether those things offered in exchange for doing the task or those things one gains as an integral part of doing the task or participating in the activity are in fact rewards.

Tasks that are in themselves without meaning or value to the student require rewards extrinsic to the task to induce compliance, whereas tasks that have meaning to the student earn both the attention and the commitment of the student. Schoolwork that is designed in ways that gain the attention and commitment of students needs no extrinsic reward to ensure compliance. Students comply because compliance is a condition of participating in an activity or task in which they see value and to which they attach meaning and personal significance.

---

[13] Brewster and Fager, *Increasing Student Engagement and Motivation*, p. 13. Brewster and Fager are citing S. R. Brooks et al., "Improving Elementary Student Engagement in the Learning Process Through Integrated Thematic Instruction" (Master's thesis, Saint Xavier University, 1998); and P. C. Dev, "Intrinsic Motivation and Academic Achievement," *Remedial and Special Education*, 1997, *18*(1), 12–19.

[14] See W. Glasser, *Schools Without Failure* (New York: HarperCollins, 1969), for a discussion of basic needs.

Engagement and Equity

School tasks as typically designed are likely to have qualities built into them that appeal to some categories of students more than to others. For example, students who have learned to enjoy problem-solving activities are likely to become engaged in schoolwork that gets them involved in problems, whereas students who have not learned to enjoy problem solving will not find problems a source of motivation. There seems little doubt that students who have learned in nonschool settings to enjoy verbal exchanges and the manipulation of abstract symbols (including words) are more likely to be engaged in academic work than are children who come from environments where the development of verbal skills and manipulation of symbols is less highly valued. Moreover, there is little else built into most intellectually demanding schoolwork to make it engaging to the student who does not enjoy academic work. *This is one of the reasons children from less educated, working-class families do less well in academic studies than do children from better educated, upper-middle-class families.*

Too many educators overlook the fact that there are many ways through which students might become fully engaged in academic work even when they do not bring academic values to that work. For example, in a school environment in which full participation in the peer-group culture required one to be able to engage in intellectual discourse, students would be more likely to be engaged in academic pursuits than they would if the peer culture made few such demands on them. Moreover, students do not need to do academic work, or even to work in the style of the academy, to learn those things the academy requires. The way academics go about doing their work is not the only way that intellectual work gets done, and it is not always the best or only way to learn.

Nonacademics often develop abstract understandings because they must do so to achieve other ends they value. One vivid example of this appears in the autobiographical book *Rocket Boys*,[15] which tells of the effort of some adolescent boys in a West Virginia coal-mining town to launch a rocket. Only one of the boys was

---

[15] H. H. Hickam, *Rocket Boys: A Memoir* (New York: Delacorte Press, 1998). A movie, *October Sky*, was made from this book in 1999.

interested in the study of science and mathematics, but all learned much that was academic during this activity. They got involved because they saw their involvement as a means of maintaining a sense of camaraderie, of gaining affirmation of their significance as leaders, and so on. They learned, but the values they were pursuing that led them to learn what they did had in many instances little to do with the love of learning. Furthermore, a personal conversation with some of the participants in this enterprise forty years afterward has persuaded me that the learning gained was lasting, transferable, and life altering. And more than that, it was not simply academic, though academic learning was clearly involved. To insist that the learning most valued in schools is that which is "learned for the sake of learning" is an elitist claim that is almost certain to exclude from "real learning" many students who come from non-intellectual and anti-intellectual environments where academic chattering is not held in high regard and where academic work is looked down on as less worthy than is "real work." Just as there is an anti-intellectual strain among many Americans,[16] there is an antiwork strain among many intellectuals and academics. *I suspect this is one of the reasons that some academics and intellectuals are uncomfortable with the idea of the student as worker and the use of work language to describe learning environments.* Some may fear that if what academics do is viewed as work—even if it is knowledge work—the coin of the realm will have been debased and the status of the life of the mind somehow compromised.

A Needed Paradigm Shift

America's schools have been designed to produce compliance and harvest engagement. If our schools are to succeed in the twenty-first century, they must be organized to nurture and develop engagement, just as they are now designed to produce compliance. Such changes will require dramatic alterations in the way teachers do their work as well as in the nature of the work students are expected to do.

---

[16] See R. Hofstadter, *Anti-Intellectualism in American Life* (New York: Knopf, 1963).

This is not to say that compliance will be unimportant in the future. Indeed, students who are engaged are also compliant, in that they do what they are expected to do. But engaged students comply because they believe in what they are doing, see meaning in the tasks they are assigned, and are willing to voluntarily commit personal resources (time, energy, attention) to these tasks and activities. Students who are compliant without being engaged have a much more calculative view of their work in school and seldom attach personal meaning to that work. They do it solely to gain access to some reward extrinsic to the work or to avoid some unpleasant consequence for failing to comply.

Unfortunately, the present system is designed to produce compliance and attendance. What we need are schools that ensure that most students learn at high levels and that much of what they learn is *academic:* that is, it involves study of the academic disciplines and development of the skills and attitudes needed to think and reason well and in a disciplined way. To achieve this, schools must be redesigned to nurture commitment and attention. This will indeed constitute a paradigm shift, and such shifts will involve major changes in schools' social systems.

Chapter Two

Understanding the Normative System

If public schools are to meet the needs of American society in the twenty-first century, they will need to transform themselves from organizations in which the core business is producing compliance and attendance to organizations in which the core business is nurturing commitment and attention. (An organization's *core business* consists of those things on which the organization's attention is fastened and toward which most of the organization's energy is directed.) This transformation will necessarily disrupt the way schools define critical roles, and this in turn will disrupt critical social systems. For example, if engagement becomes a central focus of schooling, teachers will need to view themselves and be viewed by others as leaders and designers of engaging work for students rather than, as is the case for many now, seeing themselves and being seen as performers or diagnosticians and clinicians. The role of the principal will need to be recast to support this new definition of the role of the teacher. Teachers' decision-making autonomy will no longer be an option; it will be a mandate. Similarly, the role of the superintendent will need to be recast as will the relationship between the superintendent and the board of education.[1] In addition, the relationships among students, teachers, and schools will need to be altered in fundamental ways.

---

[1] I have discussed these matters in considerable detail in earlier publications: see, for example, P. C. Schlechty, *Schools for the 21st Century: Leadership Imperatives for Educational Reform* (San Francisco: Jossey-Bass, 1990); *Working on the Work: An Action Plan for Teachers, Principals, and Superintendents* (San Francisco: Jossey-Bass, 2002).

Given the emphasis most schools now place on compliance and attendance this transition will not be easy. The present tendency in schools is to define students as *conscripts,* as persons whose attendance can be commanded and whose compliance can be demanded. If engagement, rather than simple compliance, is the goal, then students will need to be defined as *volunteers.* This means many of the teaching strategies now in vogue will need to be changed because they are aimed at compliance rather than commitment, attendance more than attention. Neither commandments nor coercion will gain commitment and attention. Commitment and attention must be earned; they cannot be commanded or even demanded.

The needed transformation will, of course, require considerable change in the means by which schools do the job they are expected to do. In other words, it will require innovations in the *technology* of schooling, that is, in "the means of doing the job, whatever the means and the job may be."[2] Furthermore, the kinds of innovations required will likely exceed the present social systems' capacity to sustain them. These changes will necessarily be disruptive and will require changes in systems as well as changes in the technical skills and understanding of individual men and women.

If schools' existing systems are not altered to accommodate the disruptive innovations required, one of two things will happen:

- The innovations will be expelled, or
- The innovations will be domesticated.

If the disruptive innovations are expelled, it is likely that new organizations will be created to take advantage of these innovations, and eventually these new organizations will take over the business of the schools.[3] If the innovations are domesticated (transformed

---

[2] P. C. Schlechty, *Inventing Better Schools: An Action Plan for Educational Reform* (San Francisco: Jossey-Bass, 1997). This definition is paraphrased from R. S. Dreeben, *The Nature of Teaching and Schools: Schools and the Work of Teachers* (Glenview, Ill.: Scott, Foresman, 1970), p. 83.

[3] For a more detailed, relatively stark appraisal of what I think will happen if those who lead public schools cannot muster the skill and moral energy to install the disruptive innovations required to make the schools truly focused on nurturing student engagement, see the epilogue to P. C. Schlechty, *Shaking Up the Schoolhouse: How to Support and Sustain Educational Innovation* (San Francisco: Jossey-Bass, 2001).

into innovations that do not require much in the way of systemic change), it is again likely that new organizations will be created to take advantage of these innovations in their undomesticated forms. In addition, *it is likely that the process of domestication will drain energy from the schools and make them even less productive than they were prior to beginning that process.*[4]

Perhaps this is why teachers say they have had too much change. Perhaps they would be more accurate if they said they have had too much innovation and too little systemic change. Perhaps it is time to recognize that the reason so many innovative efforts have failed has to do with the way present systems operate and to recognize further that the only way the dramatic innovations needed to truly "break the mold"[5] will succeed is to change the systems that define public education in America.

The Normative Order

As indicated in Chapter One the structure and the culture of schools, like those of other organizations, are defined by social norms. These are the norms that prescribe and proscribe behavior. These norms define the rules, roles, and relationships that govern behavior, and they also contain the beliefs, values, myths, lore, patterns of preference, and tradition that make up the culture of the schools. It is through understanding this normative order that leaders can hope to gain power over the systems they are trying to change, and it is only when leaders have such power that they can begin to move these systems in purposeful ways.

Among the most basic things one needs to understand about norms is that norms are not static and unidimensional. Norms vary

---

[4] See, for example, R. E. Herriot and N. Gross (eds.), *The Dynamics of Planned Educational Change* (Berkeley, Calif.: McCutchan, 1979), especially chapter 14.

[5] The phrase "break the mold schools" was quite popular in the years immediately following the issuance of the now famous report by the National Commission on Excellence in Education, *A Nation at Risk* (Washington, D.C.: National Commission on Excellence in Education, 1983). It is certainly clear by now that many of these efforts scarcely cracked the plaster. They accepted the mold as a given and tried to work within it.

in many ways.[6] For example, some norms are enforced only episodically or on special occasions. This can be seen in the day-to-day life of schools, where it is commonplace for teachers to be more forgiving of boisterous behavior immediately after a pep rally than they are during a schoolwide testing period. Anyone who has observed school life even casually knows that teachers routinely make situational adjustments in their expectations for students' behavior. However, other norms are expected to be regularly and rigidly enforced, no matter what the situation. Indeed, *zero tolerance* policies are efforts to reduce variance in the enforcement of those norms that school leaders find especially critical. Whether or not a given norm or set of norms will be enforced often has to do not only with the strength of the norm itself but also with the relationship of the norm enforcer to the norm violator and with the personal commitment the enforcer has to the norm. A zero tolerance policy (which itself is a norm) attempts to forestall these personal variations. A rigorously applied norm is less likely to be challenged when the only violators are students whose parents accept the legitimacy of the norm in question and do not challenge its application to their child. When, however, parents question the applicability of this norm to their child, especially if these parents are socially powerful or have access to such power, school leaders will be pressed to make the enforcement of even this strict norm more flexible.

It is essential that those who would lead systemic change understand how norms function and how they vary, for when leaders seek to change systems they are seeking as well to change the norms that define these systems.

Four Types of Norms

An important way in which norms vary has to do with their content. Robin Williams describes four sets of norms that are distinguished by their content:[7]

---

[6] Many of the ideas in this section were suggested to me by R. M. Williams Jr., *American Society: A Sociological Interpretation*, 3rd ed. (New York: Knopf, 1972).

[7] Williams, *American Society.*

- Moral norms
- Aesthetic norms
- Technical Norms
- Conventions

Moral norms have to do with a shared understanding of what is right and what is wrong, good and bad, appropriate and inappropriate. Moral norms are sometimes based on religious traditions and sometimes on long-standing customs that have been bestowed with nearly sacred value. Moral norms provide a primary basis for evaluating the merit and worth of other norms in all areas of social life. Sometimes the principles underlying moral norms become so codified that they are enshrined in sacred and semisacred documents and texts. The Ten Commandments are illustrative of such codified moral norms, as are professional codes of ethics.

Aesthetic norms have to do with matters of taste and refinement, with style as well as substance. Aesthetic norms define the beautiful, the ugly, the eloquent, and the crass. Aesthetic norms, like moral norms, provide a base against which new norms are evaluated while they serve as a vital part of the normative structure itself. Matters such as how a teacher should be addressed (Mr., Ms., Mrs., or by given name) are largely aesthetic choices. Such choices clearly affect—as well as reflect—status systems and relationships between and among teachers and students.

Technical norms define the ways the business of a group is to be conducted: for example, they affect how one prepares a lesson plan, uses a computer, and so on. Unlike moral norms and aesthetic norms, which are usually based on or derived from larger systems of thought and tradition, technical norms are generally based on concrete experience and empirical studies. Technical norms are evaluated by their consequences in action. Moral norms and aesthetic norms are more likely to be evaluated in terms of their consistency with traditions and sacred or semisacred beliefs. Much that is taught in the curriculum of teacher education institutions has to do with technical norms. Research that bears on teaching and learning is illustrative of the type of knowledge base from which technical norms derive. *Technical norms have to do primarily with an organization's instrumental functions. Moral and aesthetic norms have to do primarily with its expressive functions.*

Finally, some sets of norms describe the "way things are done around here." Such norms make no particular moral claims, no aesthetic claims, and no technical claims. These norms, which Williams refers to as *conventions,* simply express local preferences and habits. For example, some teachers' workrooms are quiet and somber places; others are filled with a great deal of joking and backstage behavior. The expected and acceptable behaviors are defined by conventions that have simply grown up in the organization. Failure to understand such conventions and comply with them, however, has been known to do major harm to the reputation and potential effectiveness of newcomers, including new principals and superintendents.

As will be shown throughout this book, the nature of norms and the ways norms interact go far to explain why social systems operate as they do and why some systems produce positive and productive relationships whereas other systems become almost pathological in their effects. Furthermore, a detailed understanding of the ways norms interact can provide powerful clues as to the kinds of reforms that are needed and the likelihood of the success of a given innovation in a given situation.

For example, one of the reasons that teacher educators have difficulty in getting what they teach to directly affect practice is that the technical norms they are trying to transmit are sometimes out of harmony with the moral norms, the aesthetic norms, and the conventions of the workplace.[8] This observation lends considerable support to the idea that power and authority systems must be modified so that those who officially transmit technical norms and those who transmit and uphold the moral order of schools can coordinate and unify their work.

The Complexity of Norms: Preachments, Practices, and Pretenses

Those who would lead systemic reform must understand that norms vary not only in their content but also in the ways they relate to human action in groups. All groups have cultural norms that

---

[8] See, for example, D. F. Larabee, "The Peculiar Problems of Preparing Educational Researchers," *Educational Researcher,* May 2003, pp. 13–21.

contain the *preachments*[9] regarding the way things are supposed to be (these may also be called the *ought* norms). For example, it is a commonly held preachment in education that parents should take an active interest in the education of their children and that schools should solicit and encourage that interest.

Other social norms define *practices,* prescribing how things are "really done around here" and proscribing certain things. Frequently, preachments and practices get out of synchronization. Indeed, it is variance between preachments and practices that gives rise to some school change efforts. So-called gap analysis, which some researchers use to discover areas where change is needed, is nothing more nor less than an effort to reveal discrepancies between the way things are supposed to be (the preachments) and the way they are (the practices). Returning to the example given in the previous paragraph, school leaders typically hold that parent involvement is a moral imperative. Parents ought to be involved in the education of their children, and schools ought to encourage that involvement. Yet a gap analysis would typically reveal that many parents are not actively involved in the education of their children and that many schools tacitly discourage too much "uncontrolled" interaction from parents.

It would seem that the revelation of such discrepancies would be a powerful motivator for change. Sometimes it is. Sometimes it is not. When discrepancies can be addressed with sustaining innovations, introduced through programs and projects, it is likely that the revelation of these gaps between preachment and practice will encourage innovation. However, when the innovations needed are disruptive, when rules, roles, and relationships must be changed and when moral norms, aesthetic norms, and local conventions are threatened, it is likely that another, more hidden normative structure will come into play—that is, the *pretense* structure.

Pretenses are cultural fictions (shared myths, stories, and interpretations).[10] They serve to explain away discrepancies between

---

[9] The preachment, practice, pretense framework was first suggested to me by Professor John F. Cuber, in a graduate course I took from him many years ago.

[10] The notion of pretenses is similar to the idea of cultural fictions, which was initially developed by Robin M. Williams Jr. in his book *American Society.*

preachments and practices and to make otherwise intolerable conditions tolerable. For example, one of the causes of the home schooling movement in America seems to be that at least some parents who are highly committed to being involved in their children's education do not feel that the public schools provide them with avenues to participate at a level they find satisfying. Furthermore, few educators are willing to reject the idea that parents should be involved in the education of their children. Yet many believe that as *professionals* they are better qualified than most parents to make decisions regarding the way children should be educated. As Willard Waller observed many years ago:

> From the ideal point of view, parents and teachers have much in common in that both supposedly wish things to occur for the best interest of the child; but in fact, parents and teachers usually live in a condition of mutual distrust and enmity. Both wish the child well, but it is such a different kind of well that conflict must inevitably arise over it. The facts seem to be that parents and teachers are natural enemies predestined each for the discomfiture of the other. The chasm is frequently covered over, for neither parents nor teachers wish to admit to themselves the uncomfortable implications of the animosity, but on occasion it can make itself clear enough.[11]

The ways such uncomfortable contradictions are "covered over" take on a normative quality as well. These norms include shared understandings about how discrepancies between preachments and practices are to be handled. The fairy tale about the emperor whose new clothes were no clothes is a morality tale that points up this tendency. And as this morality tale shows, individuals can get in just as much difficulty by violating the pretense norms as they can by violating the preachment and practice norms.

All three of these normative systems relating to group actions are involved in bringing about change. Because sustaining innovations

---

[11] W. Waller, *The Sociology of Teaching* (New York: Wiley, 1967), p. 68 (Originally published 1932).

does not require systemic changes, those who lead such innovative efforts need to be only marginally concerned with the pretense structure. When the innovation is disruptive, however, it is likely that little change will occur unless the pretense structure is addressed. Otherwise the pretense structure will ensure that the disruptive innovation is expelled or domesticated. To understand why this is so, consider how pretenses are established and maintained.

Maintaining Fictions and Preventing Systemic Change

As indicated earlier, two conditions give rise to the need for systemic changes in schools:

- *The moral values and commitments expressed in the school culture are demonstrably at odds with manifest reality.* For example, nearly every school's vision and mission statements contain an assertion to the effect that all children will be expected to learn at high levels and that there will be no race-based or social class–based discrepancies in student performance. Yet in nearly every school any reasonable examination of the data will demonstrate that this preachment is regularly violated in practice.
- *Fundamental shifts in the larger culture require that schools serve ends or meet expectations not formerly required.* For example, in the not too distant past, society in general assumed that one of the proper functions of schools was the selecting and sorting of students based on the students' demonstrated ability to master a rigorous and standardized curriculum. Nowadays it is generally argued that it is not acceptable for students to fail to meet this standard, dropping out of school is not to be tolerated, and success for each student is a requirement. The schools and those who work in them are accountable for ensuring student success, even for those students who in the past would have been destined for failure. Change outside the schools requires change inside the schools if the schools are to survive.

Organizations use a number of strategies to cope with such discrepancies between preachments and practices. The most obvious is to bring about changes that bring reality and aspiration closer together. To assume that this will happen once the facts are clear is, however, naive. Sometimes facts are enough to drive change, but often facts are not enough.

Systems are inherently conservative, and they encourage the use of strategies designed to maintain the status quo. One of the ways the status quo is defended is through strategies that explain the facts away or that make these facts less obvious and bothersome. Among the more critical of these strategies are

- The use of euphemisms
- The suppression of realists
- The indoctrination of the naive
- The denial of manifest reality

Schools are fraught with *euphemisms* and misleading statements. Who has not gone into a school and found a lounge where teachers go to relax and talk with each other labeled a teacher *workroom*? The term *study hall* is another illustration of the use of a euphemism to mask over uncomfortable facts. This term translates an organizational arrangement that is often nothing more than a managerially convenient way of warehousing large numbers of students in order to ease scheduling problems into a culturally accepted form. Study, after all, is a legitimate school activity. Except for a few students, however, about as much studying goes on in most study halls as resting goes on in rest rooms.

The many labels used to describe special education students may at times serve euphemistic functions as well. For example, the most recent diagnostic fad in education concerns the condition called *attention deficit hyperactivity disorder* (ADHD). I have no doubt that some students suffer from this disorder and need and deserve special treatment. I am also convinced, however, that many students are labeled attention deficit hyperactivity disordered simply because they do not find much in school worth attending to. Some ADHD-labeled students seem to have little difficulty with attention span or with attending when they find something that interests them (by today's standards, Thomas Edison would probably have been considered ADHD in many schools).[12]

The *suppression of realists* takes many forms, the most common of which is the practice of insisting that only insiders are in a position to know what is going on. People who disagree with the insiders' views of things often have their views dismissed as irrelevant because, as outsiders, they have not been there and done that.

School administrators often find their views increasingly suspect in others' eyes as they move further and further from the classroom. This suspicion becomes even greater when the administrator begins to show that he or she is very serious about the need for systemic changes, changes that will dramatically affect a school's social arrangements. Indeed, one of the easiest ways to discount a person who says that existing realities are different from the present cultural fictions is to charge this source of discomfort with not being in touch with reality, when in fact what the person is not in touch with are the pretenses that mask over the discrepancies between preachments and practices.

Suppression of realists occurs in all groups and at all levels. Sometimes, especially in high schools, a teacher becomes known as a person who "tells it like it is," and sometimes what he or she tells makes others (including the principal and some colleagues) very uncomfortable. One way such persons are managed is by defining their position in the group in such a way that their obser-

---

[12] I know of no empirical studies that directly relate to my assertions about ADHD diagnoses, but I am a trained observer who has for over forty years and in many schools and school districts observed fads in the labeling of children. In the 1950s, labeling children as *brain damaged* was a common practice, especially in upper-middle-class schools where most students were high performing. The parents of the low-performing student in effect got a "parenting pass" if they could be satisfied that the reason for their child's poor performance was physiological. I always found it curious that brain damage was more likely to be diagnosed among children of the affluent, even though the affluent were more likely than the less well-to-do to receive sound prenatal care. Some of this statistical difference probably reflects affluent parents' greater willingness to seek clinical explanations for their children's behavior. Moreover, some explanations may be more satisfying than others. It would, for example, be interesting to see how the ratio of students labeled *behaviorally disordered* (BD) has changed since the more socially acceptable ADHD has come into existence.

vations become irrelevant to discussions. Recognizing that deviant (that is, nonnormative) responses are going to be offered by a certain person, the group begins to discount these responses through trivialization: commenting, for example, "Well, there goes old Charlie again. Just wait him out. He always has something crazy or critical to say." This strategy is so common and powerful that it probably should be treated as a separate subject, under the heading "institutionalizing deviancy." In effect the group deals with the person who brings discomfort but continues to be valued by creating a *specialty norm* that defines the person's role in the group as an idiosyncratic one, tolerated in this person but not in others.

It has also been my observation that when persons in authority present data or arguments that reveal discrepancies between preachments and practices, a preferred way of suppressing the person's impact is to label him or her *out of touch* or *unrealistic*. When the person bringing the bad news has little authority or when he or she is challenging the official view promulgated by those in authority, words like *crank, gadfly,* or *advocate* are more likely to be employed.

Indoctrination of the naïve is another strategy employed to support cultural fictions and bolster the pretense structure. Every organization and every social group has some preferred images and preferred definitions of situations that group members try to maintain, even in light of considerable evidence to the contrary. One of the ways these preferred definitions are maintained is by systematically exposing new members of the group to cultural guides (sometimes in the form of mentors or faculty friends) who convey not only the way things are but also the way things are supposed to be. (It is for this reason that those who develop mentoring programs should be sure that their selection criteria for mentors lead them to choose individuals enlightened by experience, rather than those blinded by experience.)

The official role of induction is to help new members learn what they are to do and how to do it in the context of their new organization. It is also intended that they will learn to *talk about* what they are doing in a socially approved way. For example, the new teacher may learn that the teacher who is caustic and disrespectful to students, yet beloved by colleagues for past services rendered (such as leading a movement that resulted in the dismissal of a particularly incompetent principal), is "really not caustic and disrespectful." This behavior is simply his or her way, and it is a way students accept and understand—yet another example of institutionalizing deviancy. One means of maintaining such fictions is to make it taboo (unprofessional) for one teacher to inquire into the perceptions students have of the performance of other teachers.

The *denial of manifest reality* involves shared distortions of fact. The use of euphemisms, suppression of realists and realism, and indoctrination of the naïve invite participants to look past events and data and to interpret reality in terms of preferences rather than facts. Denying reality requires the invention of shared distortions and the transformation of the facts themselves.

I recall, for example, working in a large urban school district that had located its staff development center near the geographical center of the school district. Although the center was widely used by teachers elsewhere in the district, teachers from an affluent set of schools in the northernmost part of the district were seldom in attendance. When asked why this was the case, they most frequently answered that it took too long to get to the center. When asked how long it took, respondents said, on average, about forty-five minutes and sometimes an hour. Having driven to all the schools on numerous occasions, I personally knew that this trip never took more than twenty-five minutes and sometimes could be made in fifteen. When I reported this fact to respondents who estimated forty-five minutes or more, the typical response was, "You just didn't drive at the right time of day," or, "You must drive a lot faster than I do."

The fundamental problem of course was that these teachers had other reasons for not wanting to attend functions at the staff development center. The center was located in a place that had a very different ambiance from the ambiance of their quasi-suburban schools. It was not inner city, but it was not suburban either. Housing in the neighborhood was generally integrated and reflected a nonsuburban motif. ChemLawn had few customers in the vicinity of the staff development center. Rather than rolling lawns, one was more likely to see raised porches with several dogs lying beneath them, and barred windows to protect against break-ins.

Teachers accustomed to suburban living, where the diversity of the district's population was less apparent, were made uncomfortable by this urban setting. (This was affirmed in later interviews with these teachers.) Though they believed they should embrace diversity, many of these teachers (though certainly not all) found it convenient to distort manifest reality so that they could uphold the preachment without engaging in practices with which they were uncomfortable.

No Iconoclasts Needed

As a young man I taught an introductory sociology course to college freshmen. Much of my emphasis was on what was then called the *normative order* and the ways that order is established, maintained, and changed,[13] and one of the frameworks I presented was the preachment, practice, pretense framework. For my students, who like most young people enjoyed the role of iconoclast, thinking about the world by identifying the disparities between aspirations and performances seemed a great deal of fun. What was not so much fun, and what was more difficult to convey to them, was the fact that myths are not always lies and that fictions contain many truths.

To set out to debunk myths and to do away with fictions without first understanding why the myths exist and what functions they serve is to be an iconoclast rather than a leader of change. Aspirations and visions are in many ways nothing more nor less than myths. They are stories and descriptions of how we want to be. Such myths become harmful only when they are taken as descriptions of how things are in spite of evidence to the contrary.

For example, the idea that faculties ought to be united has clear support in the preachments of school reform. Indeed the

---

[13] I generally refrain from using terms like *normative order* because they make what I say sound a bit archaic. However, those who would lead systemic change would learn much if they would read some of the classic literature in sociology, such as Durkheim's *Rules of Sociological Method* (New York: Free Press, 1966) or Robert K. Merton's *Social Theory and Social Structure* (New York: Free Press, 1968). As Dan Lortie has shown in *Schoolteacher: A Sociological Study* (Chicago: University of Chicago Press, 1975), and as I hope I have shown, Willard Waller's *The Sociology of Teaching* (Hoboken, N.J.: Wiley, 1967) remains in many ways the most cogent analysis of life in schools ever published and should be read by anyone who wants to understand what goes on in schools.

literature on effective schools almost enshrines the idea of faculty cohesion, seeing it as a basic underpinning of improved school performance. However, faculty cohesion can also do harm to children, as it does, for example, where the maintenance of cohesion imposes on teachers the expectation that teachers should back each other even when the person needing the backing is demonstrably wrong, or the equally pernicious expectation that a good principal always supports the teacher.

Creating and communicating ennobling and inspiring myths is a critical part of what leaders do. Leaders must be careful, however, about the way they frame the myths they want to perpetuate. Some ways of framing myths inspire action whereas other ways support the maintenance of the status quo.

For instance, the principal or teacher who asserts, "In our schools, all children are expected to learn, and when they do not, we try to figure out why this is so and do something about it," is in a very different position from the teacher or principal who asserts only that "all students can learn." In the former case the myth that all children can learn serves as an inspiring guide to action. In the latter the same myth begs for the creation of pretenses designed to explain why what is supposed to be is at odds with what is observed to be.

To tear down the myth structure of schools without replacing it with equally compelling myths is irresponsible. Myths contain hopes and aspirations as well as descriptions of some realities. Though they can be used to maintain the status quo, they can also serve to inspire action. Abraham Lincoln's Gettysburg Address is a monument to positive myth making. Standing in the midst of a battlefield of the civil war that was tearing this nation asunder, Lincoln developed an idealized (mythical) vision of an America "conceived in liberty" (the only recently emancipated slaves would not have said so) "and dedicated to the proposition that all men are created equal" (many women nowadays would object to this phraseology). Certainly, a case can be made that the ideas of liberty and equality upon which our nation was founded did not, and do not, square with the facts. Yet the fact is that because we think we ought to believe in liberty and equality, women have received the right to vote, the Civil Rights Act of 1964 has been passed, and the public schools are now integrated. Sometimes powerful myths are more likely to produce change than is too heavy a reliance on reality.

Myths are not all bad. They are not necessarily even lies. Some of the great truths and principles by which our society aspires to live are conveyed in the myths we choose to perpetuate. One of the tasks of leaders is to ensure that myths are used not to conceal reality but to illuminate it.

Normative Coherence

Without careful attention, the norms that define behavior in one area of school life may develop in ways that are inconsistent with the way behavior is defined in another area of school life. For example, if it is decided that a primary function of a principal is to develop leadership capacity in teachers, then the norms that define how principals are recruited and inducted must be attuned to this expectation. Otherwise, principals may be recruited who are more oriented to command-and-control functions than to teacher development.

Similarly, changes in the technical norms that typify school operation may or may not require changes in the moral and aesthetic norms and in the workplace conventions. So long as the changes in technical norms are simply additive—doing more of or doing better what is already being done—there is little or no need for systemic change. Roles can stay essentially the same. For example, Direct Instruction is a highly touted program of instruction that has been shown to produce relatively dramatic gains in student performance in low-performing schools. Although very scripted and didactic, it simply makes it possible for teachers to do more systematically what many teachers already do. It does not alter the role of the teacher.

Other technological innovations may, however, require changes in moral norms, aesthetic norms, and conventions. For example, to properly use the power of distance learning and the Internet, it is essential to redefine the role of teachers and reassess the value of the individual classroom teacher as the prime source of information. Rather than being an information source, the classroom teacher becomes a guide to sources of information and a source of inspiration in the pursuit of information. Indeed, properly used, new information technology would transform the role of teacher from that of answer giver to question asker and from supervisor of tasks to the leader of learners.

Such changes threaten the existing moral order and aesthetic order, and they require the acquisition of new technical skills. Teachers must learn to derive satisfaction from the performances of their students rather than from the quality of their own performances. They must learn to spend more of their time designing experiences for students and less of their time delivering information to those students. They must learn to see the creation of engaging work for students as being at the core of what they do and renounce the idea that their core business is to perform for students or for those who evaluate them in terms of their performance.

For such changes to occur, the way teachers are evaluated must change, and the way teachers are inducted must change as well. And all of these changes will have an impact on what is defined as good and bad, appropriate and inappropriate, tasteful and in bad taste. Such changes are by definition systemic, and systematic change is, as Adam Urbanski, president of the Rochester Teachers' Association has said, "real hard."

The failure to bring about these changes has, among other things, caused many schools and many educators to view distance learning as a less than desirable alternative to having a real teacher in a real classroom working with real students in real time or, worse, has led to the domestication of distance learning in a way that ensures that once a week—at a given time—all students will be able to watch a professor deliver a lecture on a topic in which he or she is expert and even less engaging than was the case in his or her real classroom.

There is of course no way to ensure that even the most competent leaders will be always be able to bring about the systemic changes needed to accommodate disruptive innovations, but two things are clear:

• Unless educational leaders are prepared to implement— with fidelity—disruptive innovations, our schools will fail to respond to the dramatic shifts that have occurred in our society since the American school system was invented, and these social changes will almost certainly overwhelm that system. When this happens, the public school system will be replaced.

- Disruptive innovations can be introduced only by leaders who have a detailed understanding of the systems they must change and a grasp of the kinds of questions they need to ask about these systems if they are to understand them and give them direction.

I, like many others, believe that a vital public school system is essential to the quality of life in American democracy. Indeed, I believe the public schools are the last, best hope we have for ensuring the continuation of our grand experiment with democracy. I have written this book as an aid to those educators who are committed to the survival of public schooling and who believe as I do that the only way schools can survive is to undergo disruptive changes in the systems that define how schools and those who work in them go about their tasks.

Much of the remainder of this book is given over to considering the nature of those systems as they are reflected in the life of schools.

Key Questions

The questions a leader must be prepared to answer about the school or school district (or any other organization) he or she is trying to change include the following questions about norms and related issues:

- *What are the preachments of this organization with regard to moral, aesthetic, and technical norms? More specifically, what do those who have status and power in the organization hold up as the great "oughts" and the official proclamations? How, for example, do they define the core business of schools?* "Ought" norms describe aspirations. They indicate what the group believes ought to be the case. Such norms shape the way group members envision themselves and the group more generally.
- *To what extent are the "ought" norms of the organization upheld in practice, and what happens when deviations occur?* The tolerance the group has for behavior that is at odds with the vision

suggested by the group's preachments defines the level of commitment to the vision and the degree to which the beliefs on which the vision is based are compelling. The first act of leadership is getting beliefs straight: for without beliefs there is no vision, and without vision there is no direction.

- *What are the prevailing fictions and pretenses in the organization?* Newcomers are more likely than old-timers to detect fictions and pretenses, simply because they have not yet learned "the way it's supposed to be." Learning to adopt the posture of a naïf is a critical leadership skill.

- *Are some types of norms more apt to be routinely violated than are others? For example, are teachers allowed considerable latitude in applying technical norms but narrowly restricted in applying the organization's moral norms, or is the reverse the case?* It is one of the peculiarities of schools that although much more official attention is given to the transmission of technical norms than to the transmission of aesthetic norms and moral norms, it is the moral norms and aesthetic norms that are most resistant to change. Indeed, one of the reasons that many desirable technical changes fail in schools is that few school districts have developed the capacity to deal with moral and aesthetic concerns as well as they deal with technical issues, so their new technical norms lack the necessary moral and aesthetic support.

- *What differences, if any, do observed differences in the normative order make in terms of what students and teachers do in classrooms and what students learn in school?* (This question will be explored again and again throughout the remaining chapters of this book.) Seeking explanations for behavior within systems requires one to look beyond individuals and to locate causal mechanisms in the structure of relationships. Such explanations are sought too seldom when educators confront difficult problems. Rather than fixing the problem, the tendency is to fix the blame.

- *How coherent is the normative structure? More specifically, are the norms that define operations in one area of school life (such as evaluations) and the norms that define operations in any another area (such as goal setting and establishing direction) based in the same beliefs and values?* One of the greatest problems confronting school leaders is ensuring coherence and maintaining structural integrity. This is especially the case when the school is introducing major innovations, which is to say disruptive innovations. Such innovations are almost always introduced as a means of solving a problem in one area of school, but for these innovations to be successful it may be necessary to bring about changes in other, seemingly unrelated areas. For example, asking teachers to behave as leaders and designers will have a major impact not only on the way knowledge is created and transmitted in the school but also on the way teachers are evaluated and the way curriculum materials are evaluated. It will also likely affect the way induction occurs and may even affect the way power and authority are assigned and distributed.

Chapter Three

Patterns of Commitment, Engagement, and Compliance

Conformity to norms is essential to life in schools, just as it is in other organizations. Norms provide a basis on which members of the school community can judge what is expected of them and what others can be counted on to do. Without such conformity, discourse becomes impossible and life in schools degenerates into anarchy or aimless wandering. Without such conformity, there can be no psychological or physical safety, and without safety, creativity diminishes and the quality of learning deteriorates.

This does not mean that maintaining a good school depends solely on ensuring conformity and the maintenance of the status quo. Groups that are incapable of change and cannot adapt to emerging realities are as dysfunctional as are those that fall into anarchy and confusion because they cannot gain sufficient conformity to function as a purposeful unit. In healthy organizations, including healthy schools, the ideas of change, progress, and improvement are built into the normative system.

Given that innovations, whatever their origins, have leader support, the expectation that teachers, principals, and other school personnel will embrace these innovations assumes that norms of continuous improvement and progress are firmly embedded in the life of the school. It assumes as well that the new practices required by the innovations are either consistent with participants' values or that leaders are capable of bringing about changes in these values. When these assumptions are met, commitment to an innovation is likely to be present. When these assumptions are not met or are somehow violated, commitment will be lacking and resistance is likely to increase.

Norms of Continuous Improvement

Only organizations that have embraced the idea of continuous improvement are likely to successfully implement disruptive change. *Indeed, I would argue that the first steps any leader who is anticipating installing a disruptive innovation must take are those designed to ensure the presence of a cadre of leaders who understand and embrace the idea of continuous improvement, for without such a cadre the difficulties certain to be confronted in the change process simply cannot be surmounted.* In addition leaders should understand that continuous improvement is not to be confused with mastery.

Mastery, as the term is commonly used, assumes an end point. *Continuous improvement* assumes a constantly expanding universe, with new things to know and new skills to be mastered, only to be abandoned and replaced again. Mastery is a limiting notion. Continuous improvement is expansive. Mastery encourages "yes, but . . ." questions. Continuous improvement encourages "what if . . . ?" questions.

Continuous improvement, unlike mastery, assumes that no matter how bad *or* how good things are, the goal is to make them better. People are valued in terms of their demonstrated ability to improve and to help others improve, as opposed to being valued in terms of how well they have mastered a particular technique or set of performance skills.[1] In an organization where value is placed on continuous improvement, roles are flexible, and power and authority tend to be assigned on an ad hoc basis, rather than becoming the permanent possession of individuals who occupy preferred positions in the hierarchy. In organizations where continuous improvement is the

---

[1] See, for example, L. B. Resnick and M. W. Hall, "Learning Organizations for Sustainable Education Reform," *Daedalus,* 1998, *127*(4), 89–118.

norm, participants use shared beliefs and common values as guides for evaluating the merit and worth of decisions. In contrast, where mastery is the norm, standards derived from values are too often transformed into bureaucratic rules that make standardization, rather than the pursuit of high standards, the goal.

Modes of Adaptation to Norms

For the most part the way rules, roles, and relationships are defined is determined more by the moral and aesthetic norms than by the technical norms. Sustaining innovations usually require little or no change in rules, roles, and relationships. Therefore sustaining innovations present relatively little threat to the moral order of the organization and are thus much easier to implement.

Disruptive innovations, however, usually require changes in rules, roles, and relationships and thus constitute a major threat to moral norms as well as to local customs and technical norms. Unlike sustaining innovations, disruptive innovations pose threats to the norms that define such things as how power and authority are to be distributed, how one gains status and privilege in the group, and so on. It is for this reason that disruptive innovations are likely to be resisted, repressed, or domesticated. For example, it seems likely that one of the reasons efforts to install merit pay and other pay-for-performance systems in schools have usually failed is that the installation requires the disruption of norms that support the idea that teaching is a calling rather than an occupation in which one is calculatively engaged. As one teacher said to me, "Paying me a bonus for test scores is something like paying an evangelist on the basis of the number of sinners he brings to the altar."

Regardless of the type of innovation introduced, it is essential that present organizational members invest the time and energy needed to learn what they must learn to support the norms suggested by the innovation. Given this fact, if leaders are to proceed with the introduction of an innovation, it is essential that they develop a reasonable assessment of the level of commitment to that innovation. The following framework can facilitate such an assessment. It posits five ways individuals might respond to a request for their support for an innovation:[2]

- *Moral involvement.* The innovation is associated with an end or value that the participant (teacher, principal, and so on) finds compelling, or it would allow some value she holds dear to be more fully realized.
- *Calculative support.* The participant has limited confidence in the innovation and does not see it serving any end he values, but feels he might gain some ancillary rewards through participation—for example stipends, in-service credit, opportunities to travel to conferences, or systemwide visibility that enhances opportunities for promotion.
- *Grudging compliance.* The participant is willing to expend whatever effort is needed to avoid negative consequences, though she sees little meaning in the tasks assigned or in the consequences of doing those tasks. Grudging compliance is often accompanied by the expectation that "this too shall pass."
- *Benign neglect.* The participant covertly refuses to comply with the expectations of the innovation but shows no external signs of disapproval. Indeed, he may even feign support. It has been my experience that benign neglect is more widespread in schools where the norms of the closed classroom door and limited peer interaction prevail, so these norms may do much to encourage innovation-resistant teachers to adopt this retreatist stance.

---

[2] In a now classic discussion in his *Social Theory and Social Structure* (New York: Free Press, 1968), Robert K. Merton provides a framework for analyzing the way persons adapt to norms, positing five modes of adaptation: conformity, ritualism, retreatism, rebellion, and innovation. Amitai Etzioni, in his *A Comparative Analysis of Complex Organizations: On Power, Involvement and Their Correlates* (New York: Free Press, 1961), describes three ways persons might be involved in the life of an organization: moral involvement, calculative involvement, and alienation. The framework presented here derives from these two now classic formulations, whose ideas inspired me. At the same time, the reader should be aware that the way I am using the concepts suggested by Merton and Etzioni differs considerably from the original intent of those authors.

- *Rejection and sabotage.* The participant summarily refuses to embrace the innovation and acts in ways intended to discourage others from giving their support. On the one hand there are those who reject an innovation because they sincerely think the changes required are technically or morally unsound or are not in the best interests of children. These *informed resisters* are likely to openly confront the advocates of the change and engage in sustained and often enlightening and useful debate. Saboteurs, on the other hand, often engage in covert coalition building, often with groups and persons outside the organization who have an interest in gaining control of the school's internal operations: for example, school board members given to micromanagement, union leaders needing to shore up a power base, or central office staff seeking to enhance their influence in the school district through the exchange of support. Whereas those who engage in benign neglect and those who comply grudgingly are prone to simply wait it out, and whereas informed resisters will be proactive in voicing their concerns, saboteurs are usually covert in their actions. They may, for example, be prone to parking-lot meetings and may manifest many of the behaviors psychologists attribute to passive-aggressive personalities. The important point to keep in mind when leading a change effort is that there is a difference between informed resistance and sabotage. Informed resistance should be encouraged, for among other things it can prevent the introduction of dumb ideas.[3]

Leaders will find it is a mistake to assume that the way persons respond to an innovation is strictly a function of personality, and also a mistake to use the framework outlined here to label individuals once and for all or to simplify the process of understanding others' thinking. Though personal inclinations certainly affect the way individuals will respond, so does the way individuals view

---

[3] In an unpublished paper I wrote in 1987, I developed the idea of creating a change team within the school undergoing reform, and one of the team roles I defined was the *informed resister.* Michael Fullan, among others, makes a similar point about the importance of intelligent resistance to the health of the change process; see M. Fullan, *Leading in a Culture of Change* (San Francisco: Jossey-Bass, 2001).

themselves in relation to the norms of the schools. Persons who have not embraced the norm of continuous improvement are more likely to engage in resistance and sabotage than are those who have embraced this norm. Even those who believe in the idea of continuous improvement may be engaged in different ways with different innovations. Sometimes an individual may resist an innovation precisely because he is *not* persuaded that the innovation will result in improvement. Sometimes an individual may provide only grudging support because she is already involved in other innovative efforts that are consuming most of her time and energy.

The absence of voluntary support and even the presence of resistance should not be taken as prima facie evidence that an individual is a change resister. What these responses do indicate is that the leader attempting to implement a major sustaining innovation should pay considerable attention to attaching high-quality extrinsic rewards to support the initiative and quickly embedding the expectation of compliance with the demands of the innovation into the existing evaluation system. Without these steps it is doubtful that the leader can successfully introduce the innovation. More important, for those intent on installing a disruptive innovation that calls for considerable systemic change, the absence of a high degree of voluntary support indicates that the level of commitment needed to launch the innovation is almost certainly absent. To understand why this is so, one must first understand that sustaining innovations and disruptive innovations place different demands on social systems and that these demands change as the innovations go through their stages of development.

Stages of Innovation Development

In the initial stages of implementation, disruptive innovations require a substantial number of persons to voluntarily take on new roles and assume new responsibilities, in spite of the fact that reward systems, evaluation systems, and power and authority systems have not (yet) been changed in ways supportive of these persons' efforts. Furthermore, these persons must be committed to bringing about the required systemic changes at the same time that they are working to master and help others to master the requirements of the innovation itself.

Sustaining innovations, in contrast, can benefit from the fact that the existing systems of power, authority, rewards, and sanctions are usually adequate to command enough calculative support and grudging compliance to sustain early efforts at implementation. In sustaining innovations, voluntary support is useful, but it is usually not necessary—at least in the initial stages. This is why sustaining innovations can sometimes be successfully initiated through mandates, directives, programs, and projects, whereas disruptive innovations can be successfully introduced only through the exercise of leadership, that is, persuasion, inspiration, and teaching.

Leaders who would introduce a disruptive innovation and the systemic changes needed to support it must depend on a cadre of persons who have sufficient commitment to the innovation to volunteer to put their effort into it even when there is no immediate promise of reward and threats to status are real. Kotter calls such a group, or cadre, a *guiding coalition*,[4] by which is meant (among other things) a group of persons who assume the responsibility of ensuring that the change effort maintains direction and momentum even when the formal system to support and maintain it has yet to be established.

As innovations move into the middle stages of development the compliance requirements shift as well. For example, for those who are installing a sustaining innovation, the task involves such things as modifying the content of induction programs so that newcomers perceive the innovation as simply "the way business is done around here." The middle stages of installing a disruptive innovation are quite different. Whereas the early stages of implementation require volunteerism, the middle stages require that existing systems be transformed in ways that are supportive of the innovation, which means that the way power and authority are assigned, the way status is earned, and even the way people learn within the organization are subject to change. It is at this point that the implications of Rosabeth Moss Kanter's observation that all change feels like a failure in the middle stages[5] become apparent; it is in the middle

---

[4] J. P. Kotter, *Leading Change* (Boston: Harvard Business School Press, 1996).

[5] R. M. Kanter, *Rosabeth Moss Kanter on the Frontiers of Management* (Boston: Harvard Business School Press, 1997), p. 129.

stages of implementing disruptive innovations that system transformation begins to occur. Furthermore, it is at this point that leaders, even good ones, seem to lose their nerve or their enthusiasm,
thereby committing the innovative effort to the long line of failures
to bring about real change in schools. There are several reasons for
these failures. Among the more critical are the following:

- Leaders of efforts to install disruptive change often attend
  more to reducing the number of resisters and combating
  saboteurs than to expanding the circle of volunteers and
  increasing the visibility of the ancillary rewards available for
  those who support the innovation (thereby increasing the
  number of persons who are calculatively supportive). The
  result is that in the transitional middle stages, where systemic
  changes are required, there is sometimes not enough widespread support to sustain the effort.
- In their enthusiasm for an innovation (often encouraged by
  support from early volunteers), leaders sometimes overlook
  the fact that some persons may be less than enthusiastic about
  the innovation because existing systems do serve their interests and those interests are well established. If systemic change
  is to occur, leaders must either work to help participants redefine their interests (for example, by creating a new and
  more compelling vision of the future), or they must find ways
  to link the requirements of the change to the interests of the
  persons who believe they stand to be losers as the change goes
  forward. Some theorists believe that systemic reform cannot be
  implemented without firing a substantial number of employees
  or waiting until some retire. However, most organizational
  members who resist change do so because they are committed
  to an existing system. Thus, the preferred strategy of the leader
  is not to fire them but to persuade them they would be better
  served by placing their loyalties with a reformed system. Nevertheless, if this strategy fails, the unpersuaded must be
  removed—for as some wise person has observed, losers may
  not be able to do anything else but they can sabotage.
- Those who introduce disruptive innovations often fail to
  understand or fail to appreciate the nature of the systemic
  changes needed to support the innovation. It is only when the

time comes to introduce these systemic changes that these leaders begin to realize that they have failed to develop the same enthusiasm for the systemic changes as they have developed for the innovation itself, but by this time it may be too late for a remedy.[6] For example, one of the major sources of innovation failure in schools is the prior failure to provide adequate time and resources for the necessary levels of training and renewal opportunities. Furthermore, when things begin to go awry and time and resources become strained, leaders often abandon training and increasingly rely on improved "supervision" to do the job.

Sources of Variance in Compliance with Norms

Individuals will vary in the degree to which they comply with the norms officially upheld by their group, and this variance has a number of sources. Among the more obvious are

- The extent to which an individual is aware of and knowledgeable about the norm in question
- The extent to which an individual has the skills, attitudes, and habits of mind that make compliance possible
- The individual's idiosyncratic choices
- The extent to which the knowledge transmission system, evaluation system, and recruitment and induction system are coordinated and properly aligned with the norms in question

In Chapter Five I will discuss the knowledge transmission system. As that discussion unfolds it will become clear that the way the knowledge transmission system operates has much to do with the patterns of engagement, commitment, and compliance that are followed. The evaluation system, the induction system, and the other systems discussed in later chapters also affect these patterns. In addition, idiosyncratic choices and individual differences make

---

[6] Robert E. Herriot and Neal Gross present a brilliant essay, "Theoretical and Practical Implications," dealing with issues such as these in their book *The Dynamics of Planned Educational Change* (Berkeley, Calif.: McCutchan, 1979), pp. 353–379. Although published nearly a quarter of a century ago, it is highly applicable to today's problems.

a difference, though perhaps not as much as some educators would have us all believe.

I am persuaded that many things that educators attribute to the structure of the intellect or the structure of personalities may in fact have their origins in the structure of systems. Systems are real and they have real consequences, consequences that transcend the consciousness of individuals, though individuals respond to them nonetheless. Indeed, as C. Wright Mills helps us to understand, many things that are felt as private troubles are really located in public issues. Private troubles are properly located in the biographies of individual men and women. Public issues are located in the history of groups and the way that history has shaped the social systems in which individuals live out their lives.[7]

For example, as I will show in Chapter Six when discussing power and authority, the tendency of central office personnel to become gatekeepers in the change process is built into the system, yet it is common to treat the problems this gatekeeping function presents as a personnel issue. Similarly, the way school boards are elected and selected goes far to explain why many board members see themselves as representatives of special interest groups and political factions rather than as a part of the leadership structure of a complex social system. Unfortunately, too many of us assume that when a school board becomes dysfunctional, and many do so, all that is wrong is that the wrong people were elected or that board members need more training.[8]

Manifest and Latent Consequences

Anyone who has seriously studied social systems quickly comes to understand that not only do systems have consequences but many of the consequences they have are unintended and often unrecognized. Robert Merton refers to the intended ones as *manifest* functions and the unintended ones as *latent* functions.[9] Others refer to the latter as

---

[7] C. W. Mills, *The Sociological Imagination* (New York: Oxford University Press, 1959).

[8] I have written elsewhere on this subject; see, for example, P. C. Schlechty, *Inventing Better Schools: An Action Plan for Educational Reform* (San Francisco: Jossey-Bass, 1997).

[9] Merton, *Social Theory and Social Structure.*

simply *unintended consequences.* Unintended consequences are not necessarily bad or dysfunctional. Indeed, sometimes they are more valued by group members than are the intended consequences. For example, the official function of public schooling is to provide a common education for children. One of the unintended consequences is that school provides a relatively reliable form of child care for families that would otherwise not have access to such services.

Understanding the nature and effects of unintended consequences is important for those who would lead a serious school reform effort. For example, anyone who has tried to alter school schedules in order to provide teachers with time to engage in activity that promises to improve the overall quality of instruction (team building, functioning as *critical friends,* and so on) has certainly had to come to grips with the fact that for many parents the custodial function of schools is at least as important as the educative function and that any effort to improve schools must take this fact into account.

There is of course more to unintended consequences—much more. One of the reasons teachers, principals, and school boards resist abandoning programs and projects even in the face of evidence that these programs and projects are not producing the intended results is that sometimes the programs are producing other valued results. For example, programs that employ large numbers of paraprofessionals become valued sources of employment for persons who otherwise would not be employed. To abandon such programs may have consequences well beyond the money saved by the effort. School board members are often quite sensitive to these facts, as are persons who have been employed to supervise these efforts and to train the paraprofessionals.

It is equally true that an innovation can be seen as so threatening to latent consequences valued by powerful outside interests that implementation will be resisted even though the official logic supporting the need for change is generally agreed to by all or nearly all inside the organization. For example, it has long been understood that one of the major impediments to substantial change in the American high school is the Carnegie unit. Many panels have called for it to be abandoned, yet the Carnegie unit remains one of the most enduring aspects of the architecture of the American high school. Why is this so? Well, much of the motivation behind the creation of the Carnegie unit was the need of colleges and universities for a uniform accounting mechanism to facilitate communication about student qualifications between institutions of higher education and public schools. Given the nature of the Carnegie unit, few would argue that these units signify equivalent amounts of learning. What such units do signify is equivalent amounts of "seat time." In spite of its limitations, both past and recent experience clearly demonstrate that university admissions officers find this accounting mechanism preferable to less easily quantifiable data, such as the performance data that might be contained in a portfolio. Thus resistance to abandoning the Carnegie unit has more to do with the manifest functions of this unit in institutions of higher education than with either its latent or manifest functions in the schools themselves.

Who Complies, How Much, and Why?

Understanding the normative order requires leaders to ask and answer five questions about each norm.

- How much compliance is required?
- Is the norm prescriptive or proscriptive?
- Is the norm narrowly defined or broad in scope?
- Who complies, or is expected to comply?
- Do participants comply with the norm voluntarily (self-control), only when observed by others (informal control), or only when there is an official policy of negative sanctions and positive rewards (formal control)?

Norms vary from being universal and applying to everyone in the group to being specialized and applying to only a few persons in the group.[10] For example, in American society, monogamy is a universal norm; everyone knows or should know about it and everyone is expected to comply. Monogamy is also perhaps the best example of the complexity of norms and the way even universal norms

---

[10] Much of what I say about the normative order in organizations can be found in any good introductory sociology text. In addition my discussion in this chapter, especially as it deals with the dimensions of norms, owes much to the work of Robin M. Williams Jr., especially his *American Society: A Sociological Interpretation*, 3rd ed. (New York: Knopf, 1972). Williams's work continues to serve as a source of inspiration for me.

change. Up through World War II, monogamy had a relatively clear meaning: one spouse over the course of a lifetime and no remarriage if divorced (and divorce was generally difficult and carried a social stigma), though widows and widowers could remarry. Though the Catholic Church continues to struggle to uphold this meaning of monogamy, the fact is that in America over the past fifty years, divorce has become less stigmatized, and the idea that one will have only one mate in a lifetime is increasingly being replaced by the idea that having serial mates is acceptable. So although monogamy is still a universal norm, its meaning is changing and thus the general compliance with it looks different today from the way it looked fifty years ago. In contrast, priestly celibacy is a specialty norm. Everyone knows about it, but it applies only to priests.

Understanding the nature and impact of specialty norms is critical to understanding how schools and school districts work. For instance, special education almost by definition is intended to create a whole set of specialty norms that apply only to group members labeled as somehow *special*. These norms may apply to both special education students and special education teachers. Sometimes the consequences of these norms are obvious, and sometimes they are not. I recall, for example, being a consultant to a young principal who was concerned because, in spite of his best efforts to be responsive to faculty members, a recent survey had revealed that the vast majority of faculty found him to be inaccessible. Yet a review of his activity log revealed that he spent much of each day (50 percent or more) in conversations and meetings with teachers. On further examination it became clear that the problem was a system problem rather than a principal performance problem. He was spending a great deal of time with teachers—but only with teachers whose schedules had enough flexibility that they could just pop in to see him without getting a substitute. Those teachers turned out to be the special education teachers who had relatively small classes and one or more aides to cover for them when they were absent. Because this was a school with a high incidence of special education students, the proportion of special education faculty was relatively high as well. Conversely, teachers in regular classrooms with regular students seldom saw the principal except when there was a problem. In this case the principal could not change the system, but he could adjust to it once he recognized its effects. Among other things he began to schedule routine visits to the classrooms of regular teachers, and he limited the number of instances in which spontaneous meetings with special education teachers and counselors would occur.

There are other ways that specialty norms may manifest. For example, it is not unusual to find that even though a norm or a set of norms is officially universal, some categories of persons are given tacit permission to deviate from it whereas others are given little or no latitude. In effect, deviation from a universal norm is redefined for some persons so that they operate under specialty norms. One of the first field research projects I ever took on addressed such an issue. As a beginning teacher in a small rural high school, I was struck by the fact that some teachers on the faculty were expected to lead a narrowly prescribed social life, whereas others were given much more latitude. For example, the expectation that male teachers would wear ties was rigorously enforced with the exception of two male teachers who never wore ties. Similarly, the use of profanity, tobacco, and alcohol was proscribed, and attendance at all school functions was prescribed—but all faculty were not held to these norms. For example, although for most teachers local bars were off limits, a few could go to these bars with impunity. What accounted for the variance? From interviews and observations in the school and in the community, I came to the following conclusions:

- The teachers fell into two broad categories. The first and largest group comprised those whose only identity in the community was the identity they had as teachers. Paraphrasing Willard Waller, their interactions with adults in the community were always strained through the needs and perceptions of students, and they were identified in the community through the students.[11]
- The second category of teachers comprised individuals who had some basis for meaningful, sustained, and ongoing interaction with adults in the community outside the context of school and outside the context of students. For example, two

---

[11] W. Waller, *The Sociology of Teaching* (New York: Wiley, 1967) (Originally published 1932).

owned farms and regularly went to the grain elevator and
visited with local farmers on Saturdays, one moonlighted as
a shoe salesman, and one was a minister's wife.

- Those who had outside identities were provided much more
flexibility in conforming to some of the universal norms than
were teachers whose only identity was as a teacher.

As evidence to support my conclusions, I offered the following:

- So far as I could determine, the categories were mutually
exclusive. No one in the larger category—those whose only
identity was that of teacher—occupied any position in the
community that provided him or her with a widespread non-
teacher identity. Teachers in this category were of course
known by their neighbors and a few belonged to civic and
social clubs, but when they belonged to social clubs, they were
more likely to be elected secretary than president.
- No one in the second category—which I referred to as the *not
teachers*—was exempt from all the universal norms at issue, but
all were exempt from at least one of them. For example, on
the one hand, the minister's wife did not drink alcoholic bev-
erages (at least not publicly), but she seldom attended school
athletic functions. She was not sanctioned for her deviation,
whereas others received notes from the principal on Monday
morning if they missed a Friday night football game. On the
other hand, both of the farmers were expected to be at school
functions and were subject to sanction if they did not attend,
but they were the only faculty members who could be seen in
local bars without being called to account.

This unpublished study was certainly of limited scope and less
than rigorous design—and in the context of the modern urbanized
and unionized high school the situation described may seem a bit
quaint—nevertheless it makes some useful points. Most important,
it clearly illustrates how specialty norms can develop and operate
in schools. It also reveals that the normative order of schools is affected not only by what goes on in the schools but also by what goes
on between those who work in schools and those who are members
of the larger community. And it reminds us that not too long ago

the expressive functions of schools were held by many to be as critical as the instrumental functions (as discussed in Chapter Ten)—and that this was not always liberating for teachers.

Norms of Evasion

Robin Williams long ago made me aware of the presence and significance of what he refers to as norms of *evasion,* by which he means approved and patterned ways to violate some norms officially supported by the group.[12] Sometimes these norms come into play only under special circumstances. For example, government officials are more likely to be permitted to violate civil rights under the cover of "national security" than for any other reason. Therefore, in times of clear threats to national security, one is likely to see more aggressive breaches of the rights of individuals.

Sometimes norms of evasion become routine prescriptions for performance, with the official norm coming into play only episodically. When the official norm (the preachment) is enforced, the enforcement is likely to be of a ritual nature. For example, it is common practice in some urban schools to encourage teachers or principals whose performance is unsatisfactory to transfer out of the school so the administration does not have to go through the difficult task of dismissal. Similarly, it is common practice in some school districts to write job descriptions in such a way that the only person who could qualify for the job is the person whom those in authority have already decided they want to hire. When elected boards of education have strong input into hiring decisions, such norms of evasion often emerge. Furthermore, when the evasive efforts become so blatant that they begin to offend the moral sensibilities of significant members of the group, it is likely that those who are engaging in the practice upheld by the evasive norm will be somehow sanctioned or corrected. An observation I have made regarding the implementation of the Kentucky Education Reform Act reinforces this point.

Historically, Kentucky schools, like most schools in this nation, operated on the assumption that school boards should play a key role in the selection of personnel. Usually this meant that the

---

[12] Williams, *American Society.*

superintendent had only recommending authority and the school board had final hiring authority. In 1990, the Kentucky state legislature changed this situation and mandated that boards should not be involved in the employment of any person other than the superintendent, the school board attorney, and the treasurer. Furthermore, the law specified specific sanctions for board members who violated this new mandate. On the basis of personal observation and private testimony from superintendents in Kentucky, I am confident that this new preachment is regularly violated in practice. The norm of evasion is usually framed as the "need to seek advice" from the board. As one superintendent told me, "Any superintendent who does not seek and act on advice from his or her board regarding important personnel assignments won't last." And as other testimony made clear, in some school districts at least, *important* personnel assignments include the appointment of custodians and bus drivers as well as teachers and principals. Furthermore, it is clear that for some superintendents and board members, *advice* includes recommending a particular person for a position. Thus *advice* has in many cases become a euphemistic term that permits boards to continue the practice of approving the superintendent's recommendations while seeming to uphold the preachment that they should not. Such is the nature of norms of evasion. In this case, state law does make it possible for a superintendent to report such tampering and seek to have the offending school board member removed from office, but I am not aware of any instance where this has happened, and I believe it would take an extreme deviation from the evasion norm to make it likely. The fact is that long-embedded norms that define the rules, roles, and relationships related to hiring in schools have long ago accommodated the fact that schools are often the largest single source of employment in the community and that there are many community values, in addition to those suggested by the technical competence of employees, that are satisfied by employment decisions.

How Much Compliance Is Required?

Norms also vary with regard to the amount of compliance required. Sometimes norms are prescriptive and narrow, and all people are expected to comply all of the time. At other times though, they are prescriptive but broad and allow a great deal of variability around the norm. Sometimes they are proscriptive, indicating what cannot be done but silent on what should be done. Here are two illustrations of these variances:

- In some schools, principals require lesson plans, and the format of the plans is carefully prescribed. The principal routinely reviews the lesson plans and makes his or her appraisal of these plans a part of each teacher's formal evaluation report. In other schools, principals require only that teachers be prepared to explain what they intend to do and why they did what they did. The manner and format of the presentation—if and when a presentation is called for—is left up to the teacher. Both norms are prescriptive—teachers are expected to consciously develop plans. However, one prescription is much narrower than the other.
- In many states, corporal punishment is prohibited; and even in those states where it is permitted, many local boards of education have prohibited the practice. Such a norm is proscriptive. It informs teachers and school leaders what cannot be done to establish order in the schools, but it does not indicate what must or should be done. In school districts where corporal punishment is permitted, the norm is often very prescriptive, some going so far as to specify the exact number of blows that may be struck.

Some of the most difficult issues confronting those who would reform schools have to do with changing definitions of norms' flexibility and with the nature of the prohibitions suggested by norms. Moreover, the more closely norms are linked to the moral order of the schools and to the way school roles, especially authority roles, are defined, the more likely it is that difficulties will arise.

For example, the principal who decides to adopt a policy of requiring detailed lesson plans and routinely monitoring and evaluating these plans, in an environment where a lesson plan requirement did not exist before, is making more than a claim that he or she is technically qualified to render a judgment regarding the teachers' plans. That principal is making a moral claim as well. He or she is asserting that the bureaucratic authority of the principal supercedes the professional authority of the teacher, that even if the principal is no more technically qualified than the teachers are, he or she still has the right to exercise authority over them. This is almost certain to create negative reactions among teachers who see themselves as semiautonomous professionals.

Conversely, in those situations where the authority of the teacher is expanded—in what is sometimes called *teacher empowerment*— many of those teachers who have long accepted a moral order in which the principal is assumed to be the ultimate authority on all matters of importance in the school may experience considerable discomfort. And the discomfort will not be limited to their relationship with the principal. One of the classic complaints of teachers when first invited to participate in making decisions that were once the sole responsibility of the principal is that they do not have the time to be involved in these decisions or that it is not their business to be involved.

It is my view that until the moral norms that define the role of the teacher are changed and until the systems that emerge from these norms are altered (so that, for example, teachers see themselves as part of the leadership team and have the time to operate as leaders need to operate), it is unlikely that teacher empowerment efforts will succeed, just as it is unlikely that any other disruptive innovation will succeed without systemic reform. Indeed, I have observed that after an initial flurry of activity in the 1980s and early 1990s, in many if not most schools the innovations that require teacher empowerment are well on their way to being domesticated.

The issue of corporal punishment illustrates how changes in rules, roles, and relationships without corresponding changes in the moral norms from which they derive lead to divisiveness and potential disaffection among participants in the life of the school. The idea of "spare the rod and spoil the child" is deeply embedded in American culture. We even have songs that celebrate the virtues of corporal punishment, including one titled "School Days" that recalls "readin' and writin' and 'rithmetic, taught to the tune of a hickory stick." There are many inside schools and many more outside schools who continue to believe that children would be better off if teachers were more generous in their use of the paddle and other coercive measures (expulsion, for example). This belief is one of the reasons that Joe Clark, the New Jersey principal of bullhorn fame, became a cultural icon and the subject of a movie during the 1980s. It is especially widespread among older Americans, those inclined to uphold traditional values (such as religious conservatives), and parents belonging to cultural subgroups that value authoritarian relationships between children and adults. Though these individuals might prefer a less realistic and more euphemism-laden description of the matter, the schools they envision come very close to the vision set forth by Waller when he wrote:

> American communities have chosen to use the schools as repositories for certain ideals. The ideals which are supposed to have their stronghold in the schools are of several different sorts. The belief is abroad that young people ought to be trained to think the world a little more beautiful and much more just than it is, as they ought to think men more honest and women more virtuous than they are. A high-school student must learn that honesty is always the best policy; perhaps his father secretly believes that he knows better; perhaps the boy himself may be learning something quite different in the world of business, but it does the boy no harm to start with that assumption. We can teach him enough honesty to keep him out of jail all his life; later he can make such amendments to our principles as seem necessary to him. All must learn that the United States is the greatest and best of all the nations of history, unequalled in wealth or virtue since time began. Perhaps it does no harm for students to think that the world is getting better and better, though this is a very dangerous doctrine if one thinks about it very long.
>
> Among these ideals are those moral principles which the majority of adults more or less frankly disavow for themselves but want others to practice; they are ideals for the helpless, ideals for children and for teachers. There are other ideals which are nearly out of print, because people do not believe in them any more. Though most adults have left such ideals behind, they are not willing to discard them finally. The school must keep them alive. The school must serve as a museum of virtue.[13]

Those who oppose corporal punishment often do so on technical grounds based on research. They argue that corporal punishment

---

[13] Waller, *The Sociology of Teaching*, pp. 33–34.

is abuse and that children who are abused become prone to violence, pathological behavioral disorders, and the like. Those who approach their opposition to corporal punishment as a moral issue are likely to be labeled by their critics as "too permissive." This label is of course embedded in moral norms that define the relationship between adults and children as necessarily and properly a despotic one.

Though it seems clear that over the years schools have become less despotic than was the case in Waller's day, this change has not been without costs. Though courts have sanctioned teachers and schools that use corporal punishment, and parents are more prone to sue when they perceive their child as abused, the fact remains that in the larger community there is a great deal of sentiment behind the idea that the traditional moral order of the schools is the preferred moral order—research and progressive arguments notwithstanding. Until members of the community—both parents and nonparents—develop shared beliefs regarding the moral norms of schooling, moral issues (as the arguments over corporal punishment show) will be among the most divisive issues to confront the communities whose support is required for the schools to thrive. Until school faculties can agree about such matters among themselves and until a vast majority in the community share this agreement, the ability of schools to fulfill the expressive functions parents expect the schools to fulfill will be compromised.

Compliance Through Self-Control, Informal Control, and Formal Control

Most sociologists would agree that there are at least three forms of social control available in any human situation. First, there is formal control, accompanied by formal sanctions and law. Second, there is informal control, supported in large part by well-understood though seldom discussed sanctions like derision, shunning, and humor. Finally, there is self-control, where the beliefs and values that guide the group are so internalized that individuals serve as their own censors and their own critics.

It is much easier for leaders to maintain uniform compliance in schools and other organizations when self-control and informal control can be counted on as the primary control mechanisms. For self-control and informal control to thrive, however, school members must be clear about the norms, committed to the norms, and have the skills, attitudes, and habits of mind required to support the norms. The development of such understanding and commitment requires a heavy investment in the creation of *social capital*.[14] Social capital consists of norms of reciprocity, trust, and a feeling of common identity. It is, for example, essential that leaders carefully attend to the induction of new members and the nurturing of more established members. The personal and human needs of members must be responded to along with their professional and technical needs. And chief among the former are the needs for positive recognition, a sense of involvement, feelings of support, and opportunities for collegiality.

Absent substantial self-control and absent substantial informal controls, organizations—and whole societies—must fall back on formal controls. (Evidence that informal controls and self-control are insufficient or breaking down includes an increasing need for policing actions.) Though formal controls are not as effective in maintaining norms as are informal controls and self-control, they are easier to manage and more highly visible. Formal controls have the additional advantage of allowing leaders to show they are "doing something." For example, the creation of a formal evaluation system coupled with merit pay is often advanced as a means of getting teachers to do "what they ought to do." There is very little evidence that merit pay works, and considerable evidence that it often does harm. We would likely be better off focusing on incentives intended to induce people to do as well as they know how the things that need to be done, rather than offering merit pay that assumes only those capable of heroic performance should be recognized. Nevertheless merit pay programs continue to have strong advocates, especially among some members of the business community, who are prone to see economic rewards as a solution to the problems of schools.

What advocates of the increased use of formal controls sometimes overlook is that they are assuming that teachers and administrators already possess the technical knowledge they need to produce the results desired. What is lacking, critics seem to be saying, are the moral

---

[14] See R. D. Putnam, *Bowling Alone: The Collapse and Revival of American Community* (New York: Simon & Schuster, 2000).

commitments that would encourage teachers and school leaders to act on what they know. Absent these moral commitments, the alternative is to create a formal system of punishments and rewards that is not dependent on self-control or even on informal control.

Experience and some limited research suggest that a different strategy might be more effective. Perhaps those who would improve teacher performance would do better to examine the way recruitment and induction systems are presently organized and the way the knowledge transmission systems are structured. I am certainly prepared to argue that this is so. I am also prepared to argue that without the moral commitments generated by careful induction, without a heavy reliance on routine, informal evaluations by individuals who are close to and socially significant to the teacher or administrator being evaluated, and without careful attention to the means by which knowledge is transmitted in the school, a heavy reliance on formal sanctions is more likely to generate patterned deviation from the norms and the emergence of elaborate norms of evasion than it is to generate improved performance.[15]

Key Questions

Leaders who intend to introduce innovations, especially disruptive innovations, need to ask and answer questions like the following:

- *In order to initiate the innovation, whose voluntary support is needed and whose resistance cannot be tolerated?* Sustaining innovations can often be introduced to all concerned parties at the same time, or nearly the same time, and communication to the various participants about the nature of the innovation can often be fairly uniform. For disruptive innovations, however, it is usually impossible to develop an implementation strategy that brings everyone on board at the same time or even fully informs everyone at the same time. It is critical, therefore to identify the persons whose voluntary support will be required to launch the effort, and to work to gain that support. This is

---

[15] See J. W. Little and M. W. McLaughlin (eds.), *Teachers' Work: Individuals, Colleagues, and Context* (New York: Teachers College Press, 1993), for discussions that bear on the issues discussed here.

true whether the innovation is initiated from the bottom up, from the top down, or from the middle of the organization. It is also important to identify those persons whose resistance would be most harmful in the early stages and to develop strategies to ensure at least their benign neglect if not their grudging support.

- *Is the school typified by a mastery or a continuous improvement orientation?* Sustaining innovations can be successfully introduced in schools where mastery is the norm. Disruptive innovations, however, are likely to fail unless a substantial cadre of key leaders and persons of influence embraces the idea of continuous improvement.
- *Who knows about, understands, and is committed to the innovation, and what is the level of that commitment?* Individuals necessarily become aware of innovations at different times and under different conditions, and some persons are in a position to have a clearer understanding of the nature of an innovation. However, nowhere is the axiom that information is power more true than in the early stages of implementation. One of the most certain ways to create saboteurs is to leave persons whose support is not essential—but whose resistance cannot be tolerated—out of the information loop. For example, it is often the case that active support from union leaders—or even from the superintendent and the board of education—may not be necessary to initiate a potentially disruptive innovation, and it may be tempting for middle-level change leaders to deemphasize the disruptive qualities of the innovation until "sometime later." Unfortunately, when later becomes sooner, those who only passively approved of the action may well become resisters and saboteurs.
- *What systemic changes are likely to be needed to support the innovation, and at what point in the implementation process will these changes be needed?* Quite often the presence of early voluntary support distracts leaders' attention from the fact that the implementation of a disruptive innovation means that at some point systems will need to be transformed to accommodate the demands of the innovation. For example, it will typically be necessary to realign the evaluation system to support the innovation, and to redesign the induction system so that it can

accommodate the new demands placed on it by the transformation. One of the most difficult tasks in bringing about systemic change is the induction of present school members into the demands of the new system and into the new norms that these new demands create.

- *To what extent do the school and the school district reflect those qualities and attributes most commonly associated with change adeptness, and where are these qualities and attributes lacking or deficient?*[16] One of the primary reasons innovations fail in schools is that schools are notoriously deficient in the attributes commonly associated with change adeptness. When leaders are intent on introducing disruptive change, the first thing they must do is determine the extent to which these attributes are present in the schools, and where the attributes are lacking, they must identify or develop leaders who are capable of creating the systems needed to support innovative efforts.

- *What new skills and knowledge will be required to install the innovation, and to what extent are these available within the existing staff?* Failures in implementation often occur because present staff have neither the skills nor the knowledge needed to implement the innovation and little or no attention has been given to the provision of these skills through training and development, the employment of new staff, or the employment of outside consultants.

- *Has attention been paid to the latent functions of existing systems so that important functions can be preserved and unintentional harm avoided?* For example, one of the unintended consequences of creating the comprehensive high school was an increase of depersonalization in these schools. Nowadays it is argued that high schools must be made smaller so they can be more personalized. However, care must be taken to ensure that what is gained in personalization is not lost in terms of the schools' ability to offer a rich and varied academic curriculum. Less may be more, but smaller is not always better.

---

[16] I present a detailed discussion of these qualities and attributes in P. C. Schlechty, *Shaking Up the Schoolhouse: How to Support and Sustain Educational Innovation* (San Francisco: Jossey-Bass, 2001).

- *Of the official norms that guide the school or district, which are the most likely to be violated with impunity or violated in patterned ways?* Sometimes the need for innovation arises only because official norms are being violated, and if they were reinstated and upheld, the problem the innovation is intended to resolve would be eradicated. For example, if systems were in place that supported and encouraged teachers to personalize instruction (after all, there are few schools that place a high value on depersonalized instruction), it is likely that some of the need we now have for new and strengthened guidance programs would disappear.

Part Two

Six Critical Systems

The successful employment of disruptive innovations requires dramatic alteration in both the structure and the culture of a school or school system. Most important, such innovations require changes in the ways vital functions are carried out: the way new members are recruited and inducted, the way knowledge is transmitted, the way power and authority are distributed, the way people and programs are evaluated, the way directions and goals are set, and the way boundaries that determine who is inside and who is outside the school are defined. Understanding these six critical systems is key to dramatically changing the way schools do their business.

Chapter Four

The Recruitment and Induction System

Recruitment has to do with those processes by which schools (or any other organizations) identify new members and gain from those who are identified an agreement to participate in the life of the school. Induction has to do with those processes employed in the effort to ensure that recruits are aware of and become committed to the norms that guide behavior in the school. Induction also has to do with the way existing members are retrained and resocialized when systems are undergoing changes that redefine rules, roles, and relationships and when changes modify the normative order in substantial ways.

My intent in the present chapter is to describe the nature of the recruitment and induction system (or induction system, as I sometimes refer to it because, properly understood, recruitment is a part of the induction system). Creating an effective induction system is, in my view, one of the most important and highest-leverage activities a leader can engage in.

Induction as High-Leverage Activity

Great leaders understand and use the concept of leverage. They know that they cannot attend to everything, so they try to attend to those things that are likely to have the most impact on all the systems they are trying to affect. Creating an induction system is one such high-leverage activity, and any leader who is serious about changing systems needs to give considerable personal attention to the design of this system and should also be prepared to play a central role in the processes that are developed. The reason for this is that the creation of an effective induction system brings into play all the other systems that are critical to the operation of the school and school system. It touches on the moral order of the schools as well as the technical competence of individual men and women. It requires attention to power and authority as well as evaluation. It moves outsiders into the position of insiders and serves to define the good, the bad, and the ugly. More particularly, effective induction systems endeavor to ensure that:

- Knowledge about the school's moral, aesthetic, technical norms and local conventions is widespread throughout the group.
- Most members of the group have the skills needed to comply with the norms and have internalized the norms to the point that the primary means of control is self-control. Consequently, the need for formal control is limited, and when notable deviations do appear, informal sanctions will be sufficient to restore conformity.
- Commitment to the organization is high, and turnover is low.
- Peer support is high and sustained.
- Patterned deviation is limited.

These results are most likely to be forthcoming when:

- The critical systems that shape life in the organization derive from a set of clearly stated beliefs, and the norms that define these systems are based on and consistent with these beliefs.
- Those who lead the school act on the assumption that recruitment and selection are a part of the induction process rather than separate from it.
- The recruitment and induction system requires evidence of commitment as a condition of admission and provides for staged entry.
- The processes involved in this system encourage cohort identity and shared ordeals.
- The processes involved in this system require vocabulary building and an understanding of the myths, lore, rituals, and traditions that bind the group.

- Leaders define clear points of mutual commitment (for example, the granting of a permanent employment contract) and treat each point as a significant organizational event.
- Leaders provide intensive coaching, feedback, demonstration, and supervision in the earliest stages of entry and intentionally place new members under considerable stress while providing great support and encouragement.
- The evaluation system (discussed in Chapter Seven) is designed to ensure that responsibility for evaluation is diffused throughout the group rather than limited to a few designated officials.
- The evaluation system is designed to ensure that evaluators are believable and are positioned to demonstrate as well as to criticize.
- The evaluation system is designed to ensure that all members are evaluated continuously, not just episodically or periodically.

The remainder of this chapter is intended to present the base from which the conclusions just listed derive.

A Sociological and Anthropological Lens

Sociologists and anthropologists have long been interested in how groups maintain themselves. Owing to this interest, they also have an abiding concern with describing and analyzing the characteristics of effective induction systems. Much of what I know about the subject of recruitment and induction comes from some of the classic studies in these fields.[1]

The reason I have opted to look at recruitment and induction through a sociological lens is that I believe such a lens adds much to our understanding of the way policies and practices associated with these phenomena affect the potential of schools to change. Systemic change almost always involves changes in the normative

---

[1] Two books have been particularly influential in shaping my thinking on these matters: H. Becker, B. Geer, E. C. Hughes, and A. Straus, *Boys in White: Student Culture in Medical School* (Chicago: University of Chicago Press, 1961); D. C. Lortie, *Schoolteacher: A Sociological Study* (Chicago: University of Chicago Press, 1975).

order. Systemic change usually requires changes in rules, roles, and relationships as well as changes in beliefs, values, commitments, meanings, lore, and tradition. Such changes clearly are affected by, and affect, the means by which persons are recruited to the school, inducted into the normative order of the school, and brought to internalize the values that guide behavior in the school. Concern with such matters is one of the things that distinguishes the effective leaders of systemic change from those who are less effective.

Two Types of Recruitment and Induction

Recruitment and induction most certainly are involved in any group effort to gain and socialize new members. Recruitment and induction also have to do with the way people inside the organization are identified and prepared for promotions and job changes. Recruitment and induction are clearly related to the process of change (for example, bringing in new members with new skills and new ideas is a change strategy). What is sometimes overlooked, however, is that prevailing patterns of recruitment can also affect the capacity of the schools to support some types of change initiatives.

For example, prior to the divestiture and deregulation in the U.S. telephone industry, marketing and market development played only a small role in the work of the Bell system's operating companies. Most of the important work was legal and financial. As a consequence, people with backgrounds in law or accounting were highly sought after and were more likely to be promoted than were those with less technical backgrounds. For instance, one of the Bell operating units discovered that 148 out of its 150 top-level executives came either from law or from accounting. With deregulation, marketing skills and customer service skills became extremely important, but they were in short supply in many of the new "Baby Bells." The result was that some of these companies "encouraged" early retirement among those with legal and financial backgrounds and at the same time sought to employ from the outside persons with marketing backgrounds. This in turn created morale problems, especially among those who were forced into retirement and those who feared they would soon be forced to retire. These morale problems had measurable effects on productivity.

What this example illustrates is that changes in the external environment can reshape internal needs, especially needs associated with recruitment, induction, leadership development, and career paths. In the context of school life one might ask whether the skills and understandings needed to lead a school that is centered on compliance and attendance are the same as the skills required to focus on attention and commitment. *If, as I believe, they are not, then the implications for the way prospective principals are identified and developed are huge.*

The efficient move, of course, would be to select new people from the outside who possess the necessary skills and replace those on the inside whose skills are less valued in the new environment. The more difficult, less efficient, but in the long run probably more effective way to deal with this problem is to first offer insiders the opportunity to develop the skills needed.

In considering such matters, change leaders who are bent on systemic change (that is, change in both structure and culture) need to understand that existing members of the school need to be recruited to and inducted into the new system just as certainly as do the rawest recruits from the outside. One of the reasons school reform efforts fail is that leaders have often not given this task the attention it deserves.

The Focus of Induction

The effectiveness of an induction system—regardless of how it is designed—is in large measure determined by the clarity of the beliefs that guide the organization into which recruits are to be inducted and by the understanding leaders have of the nature of the enterprise they are leading. Induction has to do with moral and aesthetic norms as well as with technical norms and with conventions. An effective induction program for teachers ensures that new recruits possess not only the technical skills they need to teach well but also the sentiments and attitudes that bring shared meaning to the act of teaching in a particular school and school district. Too often, however, induction programs in education are narrow in scope and truncated in time. If they involve an internship at all, it is short, and the primary concern is with the development of technical skills. Little if any attention is given to the moral and aesthetic norms and values that should guide what is done.

The Jesuits' religious order has a powerful system of induction, at least in part because its members know with certainty what they believe and what they want to do about what they believe. The Disney Corporation, reputed to have one of the most effective induction systems in American business, is also very clear about its vision and beliefs and about the nature of the business it is in. This is especially true in the Disney theme parks. The U.S. Marine Corps, the U.S. military academies, the top-flight law schools and medical schools, and some top-flight business schools also have effective induction systems, at least in part because they have clearly articulated the values they intend to promote among new entrants as well as the skills they intend to develop.

One of the greatest barriers to the creation of effective induction systems in schools is leaders' lack of clarity about the beliefs that should guide their organizations and even uncertainty about the purpose of the schooling enterprise. This too often results in induction programs that are little more than suggested strategies for adjusting to current realities, practical tips from old hands, and a mishmash of workshops intended to develop technical skills overlooked in teacher education programs. It would seem, therefore, that *the beginning as well as the end of an effective system of induction is the creation of a clearly articulated system of beliefs to guide action and a well-understood sense of purpose and direction among those employed in the school.* Without such beliefs and understandings, induction systems become meaningless activities focused primarily on the development of technical skills and some understanding of local conventions, for example which forms to fill out and which to ignore.

If the intent is to transform schools from organizations that focus on compliance and attendance to organizations that focus on commitment and attention and thereby nurture engagement, then engagement must become a core value. Engagement and activities that produce engagement must enjoy a special place in the aesthetic structure of the school and in the preachments in which the moral norms of the school are expressed. Those who are new to the school must be brought to understand that engagement is a primary value of the school, and they must be provided technical training that enables them to purposefully create engaging work for students. The language used to discuss teaching and learning must be a language that focuses on engagement and the creation of engaging work for students. (To get a notion of what such a language might look like, see Appendix A, which presents the basic ideas underlying my concept of "working on the work.") And the standards used to evaluate teachers must reflect a commitment to engagement.

Because designing induction systems brings such issues to the fore, the design of a powerful system of induction can be a catalyst for change in other systems as well. This can only happen, however, when the top leaders are clear in their own minds about the nature of the enterprise they lead and the core values on which that enterprise is based.

The Linkage Between Recruitment and Induction

As I observed earlier, properly understood, recruitment is a part of the induction system. The way people are attracted, identified, and selected by an organization sends clear signals to prospective employees about what the organization is likely to expect of them and what they can expect of the organization. Rushed interviews, sloppy communications, and poorly designed information packets all communicate that school leaders are more concerned with filling positions than they are with the quality of the persons who fill those positions. Clear statements of the standards to be used in selecting teachers and other employees and indications of the degree of selectivity involved serve to communicate that leaders are concerned about the quality of those employed. Statements like, "Our school district employs fewer than 10 percent of the teachers who apply" (assuming the statement is true), can go far to communicate that a new teacher is being invited to join a special group where expectations are likely to be special as well.

It is because of such considerations that I would argue that the induction process actually begins at the point when a prospective employee begins to seek information regarding the possibilities and conditions of employment. This being the case, those who would design effective induction systems must be concerned with recruitment as well.

Effective Recruitment Systems

In a time of teacher shortages such as those now confronting our schools, it is easy to confuse an effective recruiting system with a recruiting system able to attract enough people to fill the existing vacancies. It is not uncommon to hear educators ask, often plaintively, "Where are we going to get people who want to be superintendents, principals, and teachers? They're just not out there, and we don't see them on the horizon either."

The supply-and-demand issue is important. Indeed, when demand exceeds supply, it puts pressure on an otherwise effective recruitment system to change or lower its admission standards. These changes in turn put additional pressure on the system of induction, because the assumptions on which the present system is based will be violated by the introduction of changed or lowered standards. At the same time that changes in admission standards affect the induction system, they also have the potential to affect the perceptions that outsiders (including potential recruits) have of the relative merits of those who are recruited. They are also likely to have an adverse impact on attrition. Ease of entry facilitates ease of exit as well.[2] Nevertheless, regardless of the supply-and-demand issue, it is still useful to define an effective recruitment program as a program that produces an adequate supply of applicants for school jobs (including jobs that involve promotions from within) who meet clear standards related to and derived from the core values on which the school is based. This means of course that it is impossible to design an effective induction system until one is clear about the moral, aesthetic, and technical norms that are held to be central to school operation.

What, then, do we know about the characteristics of effective recruitment systems in schools?

- They tend to have very clear standards for admission that are well known within the school and outside as well. For example, the academic standards a prospect must meet to be considered for initial employment are clear to veteran employees and applicants alike. They also have and are per-

---

[2] For a helpful discussion of staged entry into occupations, see Lortie, *Schoolteacher.*

ceived to have some degree of selectivity. Those who get in are perceived to be somehow special and set apart (just as the U.S. Marines want "the few and the proud"). Furthermore, the basis of this selectivity communicates the nature of the school's core values to those who are selected.

- The nature of the incentives they offer is clear and designed to appeal to the kind of persons the school wants to attract. Just as a high-powered law firm that wants bright, energetic, and somewhat driven persons who have graduated from prestigious law schools will find it necessary to give a great deal of attention to monetary incentives, and just as most religious leaders would be at least uncomfortable with the idea of "signing bonuses" for missionaries, a school will have to find incentives that single out the prospects it most desires.

- Where large-scale monetary incentives are not available or are considered inappropriate, as is the case not only for many schools but also for religious orders and most nonprofit agencies, effective recruitment systems make a considerable effort to demonstrate the psychic rewards associated with membership, appealing to individuals' need for self-satisfaction and idealism (the Teacher Corps and Teach for America come to mind here). They systematically employ ancillary rewards as well. For example, they recognize that some persons enter teaching in part because the school calendar means they can uphold traditional family values more easily than they might in other careers.

Recruiting New Teachers

If one were to take this nation's present discussion of teacher quality literally, one might conclude that the present teacher shortage is a new phenomenon and that issues of teacher quality have emerged only recently. This is nonsense. There has never been a time in the history of education when most American schools have been able to attract and retain an adequate supply of those whom both school and society considered to be highly qualified teachers. For example, I entered teaching in the late 1950s, when it was beginning to be asserted that at a minimum, a highly qualified teacher would have a college degree. Though I did not have a degree at the time, the school that employed me was happy to have my services, simply because no better alternative was available. And my case was not unique. Many of my colleagues were normal school graduates who had never been to college.

One of the reasons the teaching occupation has difficulty attracting highly qualified teachers involves salary and lifetime-earning prospects. Teaching in America has never been a well-paid profession. Furthermore, the problem is more fundamental than schools can address by ensuring that beginning teacher salaries are competitive. The fact is that as a highly qualified, competent, and committed individual progresses in the teaching career, he or she must give up more money to remain in teaching.[3]

Unfortunately, given the problems low teacher salaries introduce into the equations associated with teacher recruitment, the tendency is to use the word *incentives* in a way that suggests that salary is, or should be, the primary method to attract and retain teachers. This is wrongheaded. Certainly, teachers need to be well paid; and just as certainly, many are underpaid. This problem cannot, however, be adequately addressed with merit pay, signing bonuses, or "combat pay" for agreeing to teach in troubled schools.

So long as the basic salary structure remains inadequate, the only consequence of merit pay is to ensure that a few outstanding teachers receive pay at a level that more closely approximates what their peers in other occupations might be receiving, while ensuring at the same time that the vast majority of teachers who are doing a difficult job well continue to receive a wage that they find discouraging. In addition, the difficulties associated with identifying those deserving of merit pay often cost more in terms of morale and productivity than schools gain by the little incentive that merit pay programs might provide for a few.

Signing bonuses, if they are large enough, have the potential to encourage a few science and mathematics majors who otherwise might go to work for private industry to enter teaching instead. But signing bonuses are onetime events that do little to help retain the

---

[3] Though it is now dated, I know of no better discussion of these issues than that provided by Dan Lortie in his now classic book, *Schoolteacher*, especially chapters 2 and 3.

new teacher. Career options and opportunities, rather than beginning salaries, are what is required here.

Differentiated pay schemes (such as those that are designed to increase the pay of physics teachers or teachers in difficult schools) based on an otherwise inadequate salary schedule suffer from the same difficulties as signing bonuses and merit pay. So long as the base pay for teachers is inadequate, paying a chemistry major more than an inadequately compensated kindergarten teacher only ensures that the chemistry teacher loses a bit less than he or she would otherwise lose. The salary will still not be competitive with the salary paid by a large chemical firm.

To serve as a positive incentive, teachers' salaries need to exceed what individuals might receive in occupations like engineering— an unlikely prospect. If salaries are only "competitive," they will not serve as incentives. Competitive salaries will simply decrease the prospect that candidates will reject teaching because of salaries.

Though it is critical that teachers' salaries are sufficiently high so that salary prospects do not discourage those who have the requisite qualities to be good teachers, procuring the services of highly qualified teachers requires more than providing good salaries.[4] Indeed, salaries alone will not attract the teachers we need to teaching.

There is, in fact, some danger that viewing salary as an incentive, as some do, can distract attention from the fact that, in the end, schools must purposefully seek to recruit persons who place less value on monetary rewards than they place on other values (feelings of personal efficacy, the opportunity to make a contribution to the common good, high regard and high status, personal respect, and so on). Furthermore, one of the tasks of school leaders is to ensure that these other incentives are in place. Those who

---

[4] I once led an effort to create a career development program in Charlotte, North Carolina, that was intended to address this issue as well as to provide other career incentives to teachers; for example, the plan provided ways for teachers to gain promotions and increases in status as well as salary, without abandoning the classroom. Unfortunately, this program was domesticated over time, and it, along with many other programs that were influenced by it (for example, the Tennessee Career Ladder program), the Charlotte program became nothing more nor less than a cumbersome merit pay program. (For a more detailed discussion, see P. C. Schlechty, "Career Ladders: A Good Idea Going Awry," in T. J. Sergiovanni (ed.), *Schooling for Tomorrow*, (Needham Heights, Mass.: Allyn & Bacon, 1989).

design incentive systems to recruit highly qualified teachers need to keep in mind that for teachers to be morally involved, the tasks they undertake must have inherent meaning for them. They must feel that their moral commitments are recognized and honored and that they are trusted to make decisions that are consistent with the values of the school to which they are morally committed. Moral involvement requires a great deal of collegial support as well as the support and respect of leaders. Moral involvement is more likely to occur when teachers know they can depend on getting positive recognition for a job well done and that the cumulative effect of doing the job well is increased status among their peers. For teaching to attract and retain persons who are prepared to make the moral commitments the role of teacher demands, the conditions under which teachers work must be made more ennobling, the equipment they use more adequate, and the support they receive more generous (for example, more and better leadership development opportunities provided under better circumstances). It is well to tend to hygiene factors like salary and limited financial incentives, but the truly powerful incentives that can attract talented persons to teaching are embedded in the way the role of teacher is defined and the work of teachers is designed.

Unfortunately, some of the changes being advocated by reformers are as apt to threaten these job-related incentives as to enhance them. For example, in the effort to promote accountability, some schools are adopting strategies that make teachers feel more like clerks and scorekeepers than like leaders, designers, and inventors of work for students. *Some schools have gone so far as to provide scripted lessons for teachers and have increased supervision to ensure that the script is followed, thus taking away both feelings of trust and opportunities for personal expression.*

Equally important is the fact that the conditions of entry into teaching require many potential teachers to go through rituals that they find without meaning if not inherently demeaning. For example, many critics of teacher education programs are convinced that in too many instances the intellectual quality of the experiences to which some teacher education institutions submit teacher candidates is so vacuous as to discourage all but the most committed or the most compliant and unimaginative. Although I do not totally agree with some of the more shrill critics, I do recognize that as things now stand, the supply of entrants into teaching and into leadership positions in schools is more controlled by colleges, universities, and state departments of education than by the schools.

If this condition is ever to be remedied, reform leaders will need to consider joining the decertification movement (at least for school administrators). In place of certificates, reformers might want to install leadership development programs for both teachers and administrators, programs that have substance and that make a demonstrated ability to master academic subjects and to think well about schools and schooling a condition of entry.[5]

Effective Induction Systems

The most effective induction systems tend to admit *classes* of persons (sometimes referred to as *cohorts*) rather than isolated individuals. These classes take on a shared identity and undergo common and sometimes grueling initial experiences (anthropologists call these *shared ordeals*). Entry into the group is typically *staged* in that at different points in the entry process an individual occupies different statuses, ranging from applicant or supplicant to full member or person of senior status and an exemplar. The presence of such staging is clear, as are the rights and privileges associated with each stage. (Even weak induction systems usually provide some trial period before full benefits are bestowed.)

The effective induction process usually involves moral and aesthetic teachings as well as teachings that bear on the technical and

---

[5] I know this assertion is controversial and opens up a wide range of issues not dealt with here. For more about my thinking on matters such as these, see P. C. Schlechty, *Reform in Teacher Education: A Sociological View* (Washington, D.C.: American Association of Colleges for Teacher Education, 1990). The point I would stress here is that for schools to become more change adept they must assume much more responsibility for the development of their own leaders and the induction of new employees than they do now. Change-adept businesses build leadership development into their systems. Too many schools depend on colleges and universities to do this work for them. Colleges and universities have a role to play in the development of both teachers and administrators as leaders, but only those inside schools are in a position to design the kind of leadership development needed to ensure direction to those schools, especially when a school or school district is undergoing systemic change.

on local conventions. Usually, considerable ritual and celebration is associated with these entry processes, and important symbols emphasize the importance attached to the processes. For example, the superintendent might serve as an instructor for each class of prospective leaders. Business leaders might be encouraged to serve as mentors to prospective school leaders. Late in the induction process, those approaching full membership (or promotion) might be offered opportunities to make presentations at state and national conferences. The effective induction process also takes place over a considerable period of time—it is more than an orientation or a two-day or even a two-week summer program for new teachers.

Most effective induction systems also make extensive use of mentors. These mentors are almost always persons highly skilled in doing whatever the recruit is being prepared for (teaching second grade, for example, or leading a high school faculty). Furthermore, they are usually held in especially high regard by their colleagues and are taken by colleagues to exemplify the values and beliefs most important in the school.

New recruits are positioned so that their performances are highly visible to established members of their organization. Furthermore, their performances, especially in the initial stages, are carefully scrutinized and commented on by a wide range of persons, including but not limited to their mentors(s) and immediate supervisors. Finally, there is a pattern of extensive communication between and among new recruits as well as between new recruits and senior members of the school.

Improving Induction Systems

Reform-minded educators are obviously aware of the importance of recruitment and induction. Along with evaluation and standards, recruitment and induction is one of the most frequently discussed topics on the reform agenda. The professional development school movement is evidence of this interest. The emergence of the National Board for Professional Standards in Teaching is another illustration. The rise of interest in the concept of mentoring and the creation of beginning teacher programs and school district–

based leadership development academies are still other examples. However, a problem remains in that each of these initiatives is too often thought of as a distinct program or activity, each operating more or less separately from the others. Thus in a large urban school district one might find that some of the people in the staff development unit have developed a strong tie with university teacher educators and have created professional development schools within some schools, one purpose of which is to induct new teachers into the school district. Unfortunately, those who hire and place new teachers may not have been involved in the creation of these professional development schools, so these schools emerge in precisely the venues where new teachers are least likely to teach—that is, schools that serve high-performing students. Similarly, a university department that prepares school administrators may have worked out some type of internship with a school district, but the internships have little real connection with the district's promotion system. The consequence is that the university uses the internships to certify new principals, but the actual supply of principals for the district comes from some other source (such as a university that offers internships in some other district).

Leaders need to pursue a coherent body of thought so they see the connections among such activities and also see the connections between outside systems and the various parts of the school system with which they are working. The sociological framework that has informed the preceding discussion can, if properly used, provide such a framework.

Key Questions

The framework outlined in this chapter suggests that leaders deploying a recruitment and induction system should ask these questions:

- *Given the way current leaders define the business of schools and the values and beliefs that guide that business, what personal qualities and characteristics should our school or school district be looking for in individuals being recruited or considered for promotion?* A recent study finds that educators and reformers are much more narrowly focused in their concerns about schools than are parents

and other citizens.[6] More specifically, noneducators are concerned with social and personal dimensions of schooling (the
expressive values) and also with standards and technical competence, whereas educators and reformers are likely to narrow
their concerns to such observable matters as technical competence and performances that can be measured by tests. This
presents reformers with a problem: if all they attend to are
the instrumental concerns, then they are almost certain to
fail to address many of the matters of interest to the community. If, however, they take these community concerns into
account—especially when designing recruitment and promotion systems—they are likely to move directly into the
center of many of the controversies that divide communities.
Affirmative action is but a minor illustration of these controversies. How to deal with the issue of employing openly gay
teachers is another, even more divisive matter. What to do in
the case of an applicant who is technically well qualified but
who displays attitudes inconsistent with the stated beliefs that
guide the school is yet another concern. For example, in a
time of teacher shortages, should a school committed to the
proposition that all students can learn at high levels employ a
chemistry teacher who believes that chemistry is a subject that
should be reserved for the academically talented?

One way of dealing with issues such as these is to look past
them until and unless a confrontation occurs. Another way,
and a way I prefer, is to recognize that these issues are real in
the community and that the school is obliged to encourage
community leaders to confront them, and to provide direction
on the values that are at stake and the values that must be preserved. For example, there should be public discussion of
whether it is better to have an academically talented teacher
who is oblivious to the personal and social needs of students
or to have a teacher who is sensitive to student needs but has
only a limited understanding of the subject to be taught. If

---

[6] B. Goodwin, *Digging Deeper: Where Does the Public Stand on Standards-Based Education?* Issues Brief (Aurora, Colo.: Mid-continent Research for Education and Learning, 2003).

neither is acceptable, what is the community prepared to do to make it possible to avoid such a choice?

- *How do we communicate our expectations to those inside the organization? to outside providers such as colleges and universities? to individual applicants?* School leaders often complain that teachers' colleges are not sending them graduates who are prepared to teach. Perhaps this is so, or perhaps it is simply a claim that permits school districts to avoid assuming responsibility for developing and sustaining an appropriate induction system. In any case, few school leaders seem to be prepared to establish clear standards for employment, to communicate these standards to universities, and then to give preference to employing new teachers from those institutions of higher education that develop programs that meet those standards. Rather, most public schools seem content to allow state education agencies and institutions of higher education to set employment standards for them. It is my view that the only way real reform in teacher education is likely to occur is when schools—as employers—begin to use the power they have to refuse employment to graduates of nonsupportive universities to get leverage over this important resource. If IBM let it be known that it would no longer employ MBAs from Harvard Business School, my guess is that Harvard Business School would try to figure out why and do something about it. Likewise, if a large urban school district let it be known that it would no longer employ teachers from institutions that did not have programs that met the district's standards (not merely state certification standards), my guess is that schools of education would be more reform minded than many now are.

- *Do those who are selected believe that their selection has special meaning inside the school as well as to them?* Great organizations shape their recruitment and selection processes so as to clearly communicate a sense of selectivity and privilege. Those who are employed perceive that they have indeed been chosen from among other attractive options. For example, a selective school's letter of acceptance to a new candidate might be truthfully able to state how many persons were considered for the position and how few were selected.

- *When systemic changes are made, is the potential impact of these changes on the feelings of personal satisfaction that the present system brings to employees assessed and taken into account?* Systemic change necessarily disrupts lives and creates uncertainty. Existing employees sometimes receive the message that change is needed because they have somehow failed or are not adequate to the task. In addition to resocializing existing employees to embrace the new norms that will need to be embraced if the disruptive innovation is to be successfully installed, it is essential that existing employees be given special support and encouragement during this difficult period.
- *Will the changes diminish the extent to which people now in place are able to pursue their own ideals, or reduce the extent to which they feel a sense of personal efficacy in their jobs? If so, what should be done about these losses?* Systemic change brings about changes in roles as well as in rules. For example, changing the role of the teacher from performer to leader, designer, and inventor of school work for students is particularly threatening to teachers who have previously based their success on an engaging personality, a quick wit, and a good sense of humor combined with an acceptable level of academic accomplishment. Such teachers usually prepare their lessons more in terms of what they themselves are going to do than in terms of what they want the students to do. These teachers assume that students learn from the performance of the teacher. The idea that most students learn more from their own performances is almost certain to be upsetting to many of these teachers.
- *Where impending change threatens the status of individuals, departments, and positions or introduces uncertainty about future employment, control over resources, and so on, what has been done to minimize or offset these threats and uncertainties?* Fear and uncertainty create negative responses. At no time is the character of leaders more important than when change has advanced to the point that substantial numbers of persons recognize that the roles they will fulfill in the future will place very different requirements on them than do the roles they presently occupy and that the status the present system provides is no longer secure. It is at this point that there is absolutely no substitute for honesty, and it is at this point that the integrity of leaders is

the most important asset available to support the change effort. Leaders who are trusted and who have a reputation for integrity can navigate these dangerous waters. Leaders who are not trusted or who are seen as self-serving and duplicitous will almost certainly meet resistance and sabotage.

- *What is and also what is perceived to be the means by which persons are given tasks and assignments critical to the change effort?* The way persons are recruited and selected to provide leadership to a systemic change effort is a critical determinant of the likely success of the effort. This is especially true when persons from the outside are brought into the school leadership. There are a number of reasons for this.
  - Systemic change is almost always preceded by the creation of a new, modified, or expanded vision of the organization undergoing the change. If those selected to lead are not committed to this vision or if they are unclear about it, they are as likely to sow confusion and to inspire dissent as they are to provide strong and clear direction.
  - When an outsider is brought in to lead systemic change, it is likely that the vision that will drive the change is already clearly established in the minds of those who have initiated the change. When this is the case, what is needed is a person who is capable of leading by vision rather than a person who "has a vision," unless of course the vision the prospective leader has corresponds closely to the vision intended to give direction to the change effort.
  - If it is perceived that persons are assigned to lead a change effort simply because they are available, have nothing better to do, or have the support of clear and powerful sponsors with a vested interest in the change, it is likely that the importance of the effort will be discounted or that it will be defined as a Machiavellian scheme intended to advance some special interest.
- *How strong is the commitment of those who are being recruited to pursuing the tasks assigned, and what is the likelihood they will stick with the school district if they are accepted?* One of the most commonly expressed fears of those who are prone to resist or sabotage a change is that leaders will not stay the course or that they are using the effort to build their résumés so they can move on to

the next initiative. Until it is believed that leaders have serious and long-term intentions, it is unlikely a change effort will get the support needed to sustain it over time.

- *Are those who are being introduced to the school district and those who are being required to participate in change being given ample opportunities to network with each other, share experiences, and generally support each other as they undergo recruitment and induction stresses and ordeals?* The opportunity to identify and interact with colleagues who are similarly positioned can transform what might otherwise be a traumatic personal experience into what anthropologists call a *shared ordeal.* Traumatic personal experiences often serve only to debilitate. Shared ordeals, in contrast, can inspire exceptional performance and increase commitment beyond that commonly generated through individualized approaches.

- *Are the benchmarks for entry and success sufficiently clear that individuals and groups know when they have passed milestones?* Staged entry and clear career paths, perhaps more than any other features of a school's structure, communicate expectations and values. Clear standards for entry and promotion can be powerful tools for communicating expectations and for enforcing them as well.

- *Is the passage of milestones accompanied by celebrations and other symbolic acts that amplify the significance of the accomplishments?* Meaningless rituals and shallow celebrations can do as much harm as good. Powerful rituals and celebrations build and sustain culture. Such rituals and celebrations do not need to be elaborate or formal to be effective. For example, a superintendent or principal might have a special luncheon honoring first-year teachers who are offered a continuing contract. The superintendent might send each person that is promoted a professional book with a personal note attached. Such activities, properly presented, can do much to ensure that meaning and significance are attached to continuing employment.

- *Are exemplars of desired practices clearly available? If not, is it acknowledged that such exemplars are needed, and are early participants assisted in becoming exemplars?* Nowhere is the power of what are now called *learning communities* more clear than in the induction of new employees into organizations that are in the process of installing disruptive innovations.[7] Such innovations often have the effect of making past practices obsolete, thereby rendering those who were once models of excellence almost as incompetent as those who are totally new to the organization. The competence all need now is the competence of the *learner*, and what needs to be modeled is how one goes about living the life of the continuing learner. The beginning teachers who are participants in a learning community with senior teachers are more likely to have the experiences they need than are teachers who have only the example of a single mentor.

- *Are those new to the school or new to the change program provided opportunities in which they can test out their skills without the threat of public humiliation and failure and at the same time receive continuous and intensive corrective feedback and instruction?* Again, the creation of learning communities can be a useful tool. (Appendix B describes characteristics of a learning community aimed at transforming schools into organizations that are focused on engagement.)

Answering these questions about the recruiting and induction system, like answering the key questions related to the other systems, will not solve the problems of developing an effective system, but will suggest the direction in which solutions might lie. Great leaders are known more by the questions they ask than by the answers they give—at least I have found it so.

---

[7] Learning communities and critical friends groups are becoming increasingly popular among teachers. Though these groups and processes take many forms, the basic idea is to provide teachers with structured opportunities to share ideas, identify issues, and support each other in solving problems. Usually such groups find it beneficial, at least in the beginning stages, to employ a protocol to discipline their conversations.

Chapter Five

The Knowledge Transmission System

Knowledge and information have always been central to the life of schools. Increasingly, knowledge and information are becoming key determinants of the success of other organizations as well, so much so that Peter Drucker[1] refers to *knowledge work* organizations as a special class of organization, and Peter Senge[2] and others write of *learning organizations*. As a result of the discussion of knowledge work organizations and learning organizations, it is becoming clear that the way an organization deals with change is determined in large part by the systems devised to support the creation, importation, and diffusion of knowledge within the organization, as well as by the way knowledge is shared between the organization and the larger environment. It is for this reason that I believe that school leaders can learn much by studying other organizations that are becoming what the schools have always been, knowledge work organizations. Much can also be learned by studying how some of these new organizations are becoming what schools should be but often are not, learning organizations. This chapter reflects the current state of my thinking on this important matter.

---

[1] P. Drucker, *Management: Tasks, Practices, Responsibilities* (New York: HarperCollins, 1974).

[2] P. Senge, *The Fifth Discipline: The Art and Practice of the Learning Organization* (New York: Doubleday, Currency, 1990).

Convincing and Persuading

In a book titled *Evaluating with Validity*,[3] Ernest House distinguishes between *convincing* evaluation and *persuasive* evaluation. Convincing evaluations must appeal to a universal audience (usually a scientific audience) and be based on or directed toward generalization. Persuasive evaluations on the other hand are concerned with particular situations and are addressed to the specific audience that will be called to act on the evaluation. Typically, this audience is neither researchers nor scientists. I have found House's distinctions extremely useful in understanding the role and function of knowledge in the change process in schools.

For example, one of the assumptions underlying the federal No Child Left Behind legislation (NCLB) is that there is a body of research about teaching and learning that has sufficient warrant to justify its universal application. Furthermore, the preferred warrant is knowledge that has been experimentally derived and verified, the same warrant that is valued in the physical sciences. It is not surprising that the experimental method is once again becoming the sine qua non of education evaluation. Up through the 1960s, experimental design was the preferred way of knowing in most graduate schools of education. It was not until the mid-1970s that nonexperimental designs and research techniques employed by sociologists and anthropologists began to find some favor among evaluators. If NCLB has the impact it could have, the agenda of the American Educational Research Association is likely to look more and more as it looked in the 1950s rather than as it has looked in recent years. If this should happen, educational researchers will become less and less interested in studies of systems and the effects that alternative systems might have on student learning and more and more interested in child studies and experiments that are, or appear to be, easily controlled. This will bring joy to some but will cause distress among others.

For those who believe that individuals, rather than systems, are the only proper unit of analysis for education study, the assumptions underlying NCLB are common sense. Indeed, it appears that

---

[3] E. House, *Evaluating with Validity* (Thousand Oaks, Calif.: Sage, 1980).

in the view of those who designed NCLB, system effects, to the extent that they are acknowledged to exist, are control variables. The experimental variables consist of the programs and practices being evaluated. Program or method A is to be compared to program or method B under circumstances where students are randomly assigned, apparently on the assumption that whatever system effects exist are effects the students bring with them. Little thought has been given to the possibility that the same program might have very different effects in different types of systems, and it is extremely difficult, if not impossible, to randomize systems.

As might be expected, many practitioners and many researchers with a more sociological and anthropological bent are not persuaded that the pursuit of experimentally derived knowledge to the exclusion of other forms of publicly verifiable knowledge is either justified or warranted. These persons, following the classical sociological reasoning of sociologists like Émile Durkheim,[4] believe that social facts, though sometimes transcending the consciousness of individuals, are nonetheless real in their consequences. Context is not simply a potentially contaminating variable to be controlled for; context is a causal mechanism to be understood. Indeed, context is sometimes a more powerful explanatory variable than is any action or set of actions within the context.

What happens or works in one context, system, or set of systems may not happen or work in another context, system, or set of systems. For example, it seems unlikely that monetary incentives would have the same effects on monks who have taken vows of poverty as they would have on trial lawyers in a law firm where billable hours are the primary measures of merit and worth. Similarly, it seems unlikely that instructional strategies that work well for students whose parents place a high value on academic achievement would work equally well for children whose parents place less value on academic achievement. Although these observations are almost truisms, they need to be clearly stated today, because the NCLB legislation's implicit quest for programs that work with random audiences suggests that some in the policy and educational research

---

[4] É. Durkheim, *The Rules of Sociological Method* (New York: Free Press, 1966) (Originally published 1895).

communities have overlooked—or are now willing to look past—system effects when seeking solutions to the problems that beset America's schools.

What those who would lead systemic change in schools must understand is that technical norms are supported by local customs as well as by a system of moral and aesthetic norms. Unless those who work in schools can persuade specific persons in specific contexts to alter what they believe—and what they hold to be sacred and true, what they believe to be beautiful, and what they find comfortable and convenient—evaluations of what works and doesn't work, no matter how convincing to the universal audience, are not likely to persuade local parties to act. Programs and projects do not persuade. Persuasion is a leadership act, and unless leaders are themselves persuaded, they are unlikely to persuade others. Without persuasive leaders, many will not even bother to try. The consequence is that only those innovations that call for little persuasion—that require little systemic change—are likely to work in schools.

Consider the following example. Direct Instruction has been found to be a useful and successful technical innovation in many schools and especially in schools with large numbers of low-performing students. Furthermore, Direct Instruction, which is highly structured, is also relatively easy to observe and supervise and generally consistent with traditional views of the role of the teacher. Thus Direct Instruction is generally quite congruent with the present systems that guide behavior in schools—especially systems in bureaucratically structured, inner-city schools.[5] And thus the implementation of Direct Instruction places only limited demands on leaders to change the system. What leaders are required to do is to communicate the technical norms clearly and to support them consistently through positive rewards and negative sanctions.

When these things happen, there are some relatively quick and easily measured consequences, not the least of which is that children who have historically done poorly on standardized tests do better—so much better that the mean scores for an entire group

---

[5] Direct Instruction is based on associationist assumptions, assumptions quite congruent with the systems that presently shape behavior in most schools; see, for example, L. B. Resnick and M. W. Hall, "Learning Organizations for Sustainable Education Reform," *Daedalus*, 1998, *127*(4), 89–118.

are sometimes raised dramatically. This has led some to argue that it is such "proven programs" that should be given preference in funding and in adoption.

There is, however, another possibility. It seems to me more than coincidental that Direct Instruction and Success for All, two of the three programs that were recently judged to have sufficient support from rigorously conducted research and evaluation studies, were among the most structured programs in the group of programs being evaluated.[6] Not only are these programs highly scripted; they also assume that student compliance, as contrasted with student engagement, is the most important determinant of learning results.[7] Furthermore, the assumptions on which such programs are based are congruent with traditional views of schools and teachers and thus are much less likely to require disruptive changes than are programs based on less traditional assumptions— for example, assumptions made by constructivists.

I have long held that the introduction of nontraditional teaching methods into schools without an accommodating change in supporting evaluation systems, induction systems, coordination systems, and power and authority systems, will compromise the effectiveness of the nontraditional approach to the point that it may appear that the approach not only does not work but is also harmful in its consequences.[8] *One of the reasons many of the ideas advanced*

---

[6] See American Institutes for Research, *An Educators' Guide to Schoolwide Reform* (Arlington, Va.: Educational Research Service, 1999).

[7] I know the authors of Success for All and Direct Instruction as well as many who use these programs will disagree with me. My response is that the way they understand the terms *engagement* and *compliance* is different from the way I understand these words. Compliance requires only that one does the task specified, in the way that is specified. Compliance requires no commitment to the task itself. Indeed, the task can be meaningless. The things that have meaning to the person who is complying are the rewards gained by compliance and the fear of negative consequences if he or she does not comply. Engagement requires commitment, and commitment requires that the task have, in itself, meaning and significance. See Chapter One for an elaboration of these points.

[8] See P. C. Schlechty, *Teaching and Social Behavior: Toward an Organizational Theory of Instruction* (Needham Heights, Mass.: Allyn & Bacon, 1976).

by constructivists often fare so badly may be that those who introduce these ideas introduce them as though they were sustaining innovations when they are in fact disruptive innovations. As a result, those introducing these ideas sometimes place too much reliance on programs and projects and give too little attention to the development of leaders and the systemic changes that only leaders can introduce.

If disruptive innovations are truly to be tested, they must be accompanied by supportive structural and cultural changes. Such changes take time—more time than it takes to install a sustaining innovation into existing systems. For disruptive innovations to be appropriately appraised, evaluators must reconsider the present penchant for insisting that only programs based on convincing (as contrasted with persuasive) data are worthy of support. They must make provision for the fact that disruptive changes require systemic change and that systemic change takes time. If they do not, the result will be that in the long run only organizations other than the public schools will be in a position to produce the dramatic improvements in learning (especially learning that requires synthesis, evaluation, reflection, and critical analysis) being demanded by today's knowledge work society. Should this happen, we may find ourselves entrusting the education of our children to the same class of entrepreneurs that gave us Enron. Such an unhappy outcome would not be good for children or for American democracy.

Four Types of Knowledge

To more fully understand social systems, it is important to recognize that these systems employ various types of knowledge. Furthermore, differences in knowledge types primarily reflect the types of norms and values addressed by those who generate, codify, and transmit knowledge in the organization. (See Chapter Two for a discussion of norms.)

Technical knowledge is the type of knowledge commonly of concern to those who want to improve schools. Technical knowledge has to do with the way the job is done. Technical knowledge is based on experience and evaluated in terms of consequences in action. Technical knowledge is oriented toward the future. The validity of technical knowledge is determined by "what works best." If what works best today is replaced in the future by something proven to work better, the existing form of technical knowledge will be relatively easy to abandon and the new form will be substituted in its place. When new technical knowledge is to be transformed into new means of doing the job (new technologies), it is essential that the knowledge be persuasive in the context where it is to be employed. For technical knowledge to be made persuasive, three additional knowledge bases must be taken into account: the moral knowledge base, the aesthetic knowledge base, and the uncritically held conventions of the group.

Moral knowledge and *aesthetic knowledge,* unlike technical knowledge, are anchored in the past and tend to be settled rather than problematic. Sometimes moral knowledge is expressed in sacred and semisacred documents, and confirmed through rituals and ceremonies. Both moral and aesthetic knowledge are justified more in terms of the wisdom and experience of the group and the image group leaders have of the group than in terms of any immediate result that might be forthcoming from acting on the belief. Indeed, when acting on beliefs suggested by the moral and aesthetic norms of the group does not produce the desired result, it is likely that group leaders will explain the failure as a failure to act in a way that was really consistent with the belief.

The consequence is that moral knowledge and aesthetic knowledge are less subject to change than is technical knowledge. Furthermore, when technical knowledge suggests technologies that would require a shift in the group's moral knowledge and aesthetic knowledge (changes in beliefs about the proper role of the teacher, for example, or in beliefs about the best relationship between schools and communities), it is up to leaders to persuade local audiences that such changes are needed. Without such persuasion the innovation suggested by the technical knowledge will either be abandoned or domesticated (see Chapter Two).

Finally, there is *conventional knowledge,* which, like technical knowledge, has to do with the "way things are done around here." But unlike technical knowledge (which also informs us of the way things are done), conventional knowledge is the received wisdom of the group and is not justified through research or critical examination. An interesting aspect of conventional knowledge, however, is that it may reflect the technical knowledge of a bygone era, which has now become enshrined in local custom and is therefore more difficult to change than is knowledge that is only technical. For example, there was a time when textbooks on paper were the only means of ensuring that all students had easy access to the wide range of materials that go into conveying broad understandings of school subjects. Although this is no longer so, the textbook will be hard to replace as the preferred means of communicating information in schools because many parents believe that textbooks on paper are the way things should be done in school and many teachers agree with them. It is going to take more than research and impeccable logic to root out textbooks on paper as preferred sources and focus primarily on other types of information-transmitting technologies.

Conventional knowledge or, better, knowledge of local conventions, functions more like moral and aesthetic knowledge than like technical knowledge. Indeed, in many instances, local conventions take on a semisacred quality and sometimes are transformed into moral knowledge. Conventions, while they are still conventions, are more amenable to change than are moral knowledge and aesthetic knowledge. Sometimes all that is needed to change local conventions is a visit to another organization where other ways of doing things can be observed. Moral and aesthetic norms are not so easily modified, and the more local conventions take on a sacred quality, the less malleable they become.

Knowledge Transmission Systems

Moral knowledge, aesthetic knowledge, and conventions tend to be transmitted in the form of stories, metaphors, morality tales, and social dramas. In recent years school leaders (and leaders in other organizations) have adopted the habit of codifying moral and aesthetic knowledge in vision statements, mission statements, and belief statements. Policy manuals also contain a certain amount of moral and aesthetic knowledge, along with considerable commentary on conventions. Though moral knowledge and aesthetic knowledge are sometimes codified and formally transmitted, more often such understandings remain tacit, more *caught* than *taught*. Indeed, much of the moral and aesthetic knowledge that is transmitted in a school is transmitted when a naïf unwittingly or unintentionally violates norms based on that knowledge or when a senior teacher informs new teachers about "the way it really is around here." Thus models and exemplars, including mentors and admired veterans, are among the more important conveyers of moral, aesthetic, and conventional knowledge, for it is through direct observation and efforts at imitation that the tacit understandings that make up these forms of knowledge are acquired. For example, senior colleagues in a school where there is no specified dress code for teachers but where informality is the norm may refer with derision to the tie worn by the new male teacher or ask the well-dressed female teacher if she is "going somewhere." Politically incorrect language may be sanctioned in some schools and not attended to at all in others.

Technical knowledge is more likely to be codified, justified, and verified than are moral knowledge, aesthetic knowledge, and conventions. Furthermore, technical knowledge is more likely to find its way into formal training programs and developmental activities than are moral knowledge and aesthetic knowledge. The reason this is so is probably obvious. Much of the technical knowledge in education is embodied in books, articles, and lectures that address issues related to teaching, learning, and school management. It is commonplace for schools to depend on colleges and universities to transmit technical knowledge, because it is in these institutions, rather than in the schools, that most of the technical knowledge in education is created. Moral knowledge, aesthetic knowledge, and knowledge of conventions are more likely to be locally developed and defined. It is for this reason if for no other that the emergence of school-based teacher study groups is so important. My fear, however, is that such groups will attend too much to complaints about local conventions and examination of technical issues and attend too little to the moral dilemmas they must confront and the aesthetic choices they must make if public education is to thrive in the present environment. It is my impression that today's teachers are much less patient than my generation was with moral arguments and much more attuned to technical discussions. They are less concerned, for example, with why something should be taught and more concerned with how to teach what someone else has determined should be taught.

The Creation and Importation of Knowledge

Many years ago I was associate dean for field services in the School of Education at the University of North Carolina at Chapel Hill. The idea behind the office was to strengthen and improve the way the university, especially the School of Education, related to the public schools in the state. In an effort to develop a strategy to achieve this end, I spent a great deal of time interviewing superintendents, principals, staff development specialists, and teachers. My queries began with the assumption that the reason the School of Education was having trouble getting its message into the schools was that the university lacked an adequate delivery system. The response of one superintendent to that assumption has had a much more lasting impact on my thinking about the problems associated with the creation and importation of knowledge in schools than did all the confirming comments I received from many others. As I remember it, this superintendent said: "You can change your delivery system until hell freezes over, but until we [in the public schools] change our reception system, it won't do much good. The fact is schools are set up to keep ideas out rather than to invite them in."

Schools, unlike most major businesses, spend relatively little on training and development. Furthermore, what they do spend is often spent in ways almost guaranteed to compromise the effectiveness of the training (workshops scheduled after school, on Saturdays, or during vacations, for example). Teachers have *continuing education requirements,* and school leaders—especially in larger school districts—try to assist teachers in meeting these requirements. They provide development offerings on a variety of subjects in a variety of settings but, unfortunately, often without much attention to quality control or to consistency with district perspectives. As has been shown in numerous studies, teachers do not look favorably on such *in-service.* However, when presented with more rigorous and demanding continuing education opportunities, many teachers and administrators decline on the basis that they "do not have the time." In many instances the key questions on the minds of teachers contemplating satisfying continuing education requirements seem to be these:

- Is the presenter entertaining? (This is often phrased as, "Can the presenter keep me awake?")
- Is the site where the workshop is offered convenient, and is ample parking space available?

Many staff development specialists, along with many teachers and consultants, are seriously concerned about these matters and are struggling to address the issues that must be addressed. In spite of limited resources, some progress has been made. *Staff development today is far superior to staff development in public schools thirty years ago.* The fact remains, however, that in spite of serious efforts at improvement, staff development and continuing education offered by schools and in the context of schools is even now too often pallid and intellectually vacuous. Rather than being viewed by teachers as a learning opportunity to be embraced, staff development is a requirement to be endured. If new knowledge is to get into schools, the organization and management of continuing education requires drastic revision.

The university is another potential source of new knowledge, but the moral order of the university and the moral order of schools are very different. Among other things, university researchers are concerned with producing convincing arguments and addressing universal audiences.[9] Practitioners are concerned with persuasion and particular situations. Moreover, the new knowledge to which teachers are most likely to be exposed in their college courses is knowledge about technique rather than knowledge that might assist them in critically evaluating the moral and aesthetic knowledge base on which schools proceed. Both the history of education and the philosophy of education are subjects that can cast a needed critical light on the moral order of schools, but in many teacher preparation institutions today, prospective teachers are exposed to these subjects only in a "social foundations" course, which too often turns out to be a polemic from an impassioned professor concerned with politically correct interpretations of reality, or a series of lectures from a professor who confuses rigor with rigor mortis.

---

[9] A recent article by David F. Larabee is particularly useful on this point; see "The Peculiar Problems of Preparing Educational Researchers," *Educational Researcher,* May 2003, pp. 13–21.

The problem is that teachers' colleges are too often defined as places where teachers learn to teach. Teachers' colleges should be thought of as places where neophytes learn to study and think about teaching and then are provided with systematic opportunities to learn how to teach where they will learn to teach anyway—in the schools.[10]

Again, some efforts are being made to deal with this issue, for example, the creation of professional development schools as advocated by the Holmes Group. Bringing practitioners onto the university campus as adjunct professors is another effort, as is the increasing tendency of professors to seek ways of working in schools with students. Praiseworthy though such efforts are, most totally overlook the point that for these new arrangements to work, systems must be altered in fundamental ways. Furthermore, if these alterations are to be sustained, the knowledge base that guides them must be clearly identified, articulated, and diffused throughout the groups involved in the change. For example, the role of critical scholarship, so highly valued in the university, is not always highly valued in the schools. Critical analysis requires a long-term view. Teachers live in the short term. Critical analysis seeks generalization. Teachers live in a world of the immediate and the particular.[11]

It is fine to tell teachers that the best way to maintain discipline is to design work for students that the students find interesting—which I do on a regular basis. Unfortunately, what many teachers need—or feel they need—is one more lesson plan that will work on Monday and get test scores up next spring. The result is that when university professors "go to school," they too often tend to trivialize the profound in order to make it "relevant to the needs of teachers," or they present information in such a way that teachers gain confirmation of the widely held view that most faculty in teachers colleges have been "too long out of the classroom and do not understand teachers' reality."

---

[10] See P. C. Schlechty, *Reform in Teacher Education: A Sociological View* (Washington, D.C.: American Association of Colleges for Teacher Education, 1990).

[11] See, for example, Larabee, "The Peculiar Problems of Preparing Educational Researchers."

The action research paradigm that is gaining popularity in education circles is an effort to address this problem and to bring the places where knowledge is generated and knowledge is used into closer interaction and communication.[12] District #2 in New York City (as discussed later in this chapter) provides another model. Some of this work has produced and is producing impressive results. Unless and until the power and authority systems of both the university and the public schools are altered, however, to support and maintain these relationships, it is unlikely that such results will persist beyond the tenure of the individuals who have led their creation.

Understanding the Knowledge Base

One of the reasons past efforts at school reform have failed is that those who led the changes paid little attention to the moral, aesthetic, and conventional knowledge bases of schools and fastened attention almost entirely on the technical knowledge base. The result has been that after early efforts, sometimes with demonstrable empirical results, the new program is essentially abandoned, though it may be maintained in the fictions and pretenses used to explain away discrepancies between preachments and practices. To bring about change in schools, or in any other organization, it is essential to come to grips with the knowledge base on which the normative order rests.

The power of such thinking is shown in a brilliant essay by Lauren Resnick and Megan Hall titled "Learning Organizations for Sustainable Education Reform."[13] Resnick and Hall show how associationist theory, as developed by E. L. Thorndike, and the concept of aptitude have served as the core knowledge base from which

---

[12] See, for example, M. Cochran-Smith and S. L. Lytle, *Inside/Outside: Teacher Research and Knowledge* (New York: Teachers College Press, 1993).

[13] Resnick and Hall, "Learning Organizations for Sustainable Education Reform," p. 99. The journal issue in which Resnick and Hall's article appears contains a set of the most useful articles on change in education that I have come across in recent years. I do not agree with all that this issue contains, but it all must be taken into account; see S. Sarason (ed.), "Education Yesterday, Education Tomorrow" (Special Issue), *Daedalus*, 1998, *127*(4).

much of present pedagogy proceeds. They also demonstrate that efforts to act on contrary views, as exemplified in programs deriving from the Child Study Movement and the research and writings of such persons as Dewey, Piaget, and Bruner, have not been generally successful, observing that "Like Dewey, Piaget and Bruner are today required reading in teacher-education programs, but their ideas have only marginally penetrated the standard operating procedures of mainstream American schools."

Following their analysis, Resnick and Hall go on to develop a proposal for what they call *knowledge-based constructivism* and *effort-based education* as the new core assumptions about the way human beings learn and what accounts for variance in learning. Resnick and Hall are optimistic about the future of their ideas and the practicality of implementation, and they discuss a current example:

> Such a system currently exists in New York City Community School District #2, a district with a high proportion of poor and non-English-speaking students that, under the leadership of Superintendent Anthony Alvarado and Deputy Superintendent Elaine Fink, has organized itself to promote and sustain a continuous upgrading of teaching practice. Over the past ten years, the teaching quality in the district has improved substantially, and a variety of indicators show rising student achievement. District #2's organizational approach serves as the model for a particular form of learning organization that appears to be suited to the conditions of our large public-education systems; this concept is referred to as *nested learning communities*. District #2's success provides an existence proof that nested learning communities can produce the kind of instructional improvements called for by the proposed new pedagogical core.[14]

Resnick and Hall go on to point out that nested learning communities assume that ability can be learned through the expenditure of effort. They then explicate the implications of this and related assumptions with regard to the role of the teacher and the organization of schools. However, as they make clear and as many

---

[14] Resnick and Hall, "Learning Organizations for Sustainable Education Reform," p. 109.

others are coming to understand, changes in the technical knowledge base that guides pedagogy require changes in the systems that undergird the way knowledge is invented and transmitted in schools. The reason associationist assumptions continue to dominate the work of schools is that the assumptions made by associationists are consistent with the preachment, practice, and pretense structure embedded in the value system that currently shapes most of America's schools. Associationists' views reinforce the traditional authority of the teacher and the rational assumptions on which the division of authority in bureaucracies is based. Associationist assumptions are consistent with an emphasis on compliance. Constructivist assumptions, in contrast, assume commitment to be the primary concern.

The reason that ability, rather than effort, is currently the dominant explanation of variance in learning is that this view explains away the failure of our democratic institutions to provide equitable results as well as equal opportunities. It permits implicitly Darwinian assumptions to govern schools but without directly assaulting the myth structure that sustains the schools. For example, the myth that the provision of equal opportunities ensures equal results and that if results are not equal it is evidence that equal opportunity has not been provided fuels the perception among some that the reason minorities are not achieving at higher levels is that minority children are treated differently from children of the majority. Perhaps they are. But just as likely is the possibility that all children are treated the same when they should not be. *Differences in culture and background may call for differences in pedagogy as well.*

In the existing moral knowledge framework that guides most schools and school districts, even the *effort* argument so persuasively presented by Resnick and Hall, or the *working on the work* argument I regularly present are easily transformed into an assumption that "students should work hard because their parents and teachers want them to, and those that work hardest are best and will get better." The existing moral order does not require teachers to figure out whether or not the tasks they are assigning to students are, in the students' view, really worth doing. The traditional assumption is that students should do what their teachers say they should do because the teacher says so and, as an adult authority, has the right to say so.

Creating a Need for Change

To challenge the existing system, a system that places more value on attendance and compliance than on engagement and commitment, the fictions that surround the present system must be confronted. Such confrontations require leaders who have great persuasive power as well as deep understandings and insights. It requires crusaders and persuaders more than it requires people who are simply technically proficient. The dispassionate analysis that might lead a teacher to understand the meaning and implications of terms like *nested learning communities* and *knowledge-based constructivism* might be conveyed in seminars and dialogue. However, to move this understanding to a level of action requires more than discussion and dialogue.

The idea of the teacher as "standing in the place of the parent" and the idea that children should do what their teachers tell them to do even when what the teacher tells them to do makes no sense to them are deeply embedded in the moral order of schools. To shift this knowledge base requires exhortation as well as analysis, proselytizing as well as rational discourse. And, once again, without this shift it is unlikely that the schools envisioned by reformers like myself or like Resnick and Hall will spread far from the inspirational sources from which they are derived.

For teachers to accept the fact that they must earn the attention and commitment of students requires, first, that they understand that our schools currently operate on the assumption that students ought to provide only attendance and compliance. Such understandings do not just happen. They are taught rather than caught, and those who must teach them are those who lead. To get teachers to renounce a tradition-based view of teachers as persons who have authority because they are adults or because they have mastered a body of professional knowledge requires more than a better theory of teaching and learning. To get teachers and others who work in schools to believe that the teacher's authority is based on his or her willingness to participate in ongoing and continuous learning requires a conversion experience as much as a seminar on theories of teaching and learning. To frame the school as a learning community where children and teachers learn together and with each other requires that cherished preachments like "children owe teachers their attention" be set aside. Such changes in worldview are more than technical; they are moral as well. They also require a redefinition of aesthetic knowledge as well as a redefinition of the norms that define conventions.

The reason New York City's District #2 is having the success Resnick and Hall report has less to do with a new set of pedagogical assumptions, I suspect, than it does with a new set of assumptions about how adults and children should interact in schools. It may be that the leaders there also understand that new relationships require new rules and new roles. Given new rules, roles, and relationships, the moral order of the schools must be changed to accommodate them; otherwise the old rules and roles will reappear. It appears that Alvarado and Fink and their colleagues envisioned a system that was consistent with a moral code they held and then sought technical knowledge that they believed would support this vision and be consistent with it. In my view, this is what systems change is all about—working on systems; the rules, roles, and relationships that frame systems; and the values, beliefs, and forms of knowledge on which these systems are based.

Theory into Practice

Teachers understand that, as schools are now organized, equal opportunities do not provide equal results. But most feel helpless to do anything about this condition. This helplessness arises in part from the tacit assumptions they make based on the moral knowledge available to them. For most teachers, for example, grading is as much a matter of justice—giving students what they "deserve" and ensuring that they "deserve what they get"—as it is a matter of technically competent evaluation. Indeed, given the way the moral order of schools shapes perceptions of good and bad, right and wrong, the beautiful and the ugly, it is small wonder that teachers often place the problems they face in areas outside their own control (assigning them, for example, to bad or unsupportive parents, inadequate resources, or lack of time). *If teachers are to own these problems and not simply feel guilty for not addressing them, an entirely new moral and aesthetic framework must be installed in the schools.*

However, given the circumstances that exist in most of America's schools today, when ideas such as effort-based pedagogy are presented, it is likely that these ideas will be transformed into familiar forms and that those who present the ideas (staff developers, consultants, and trailblazing teachers and administrators) will hear the refrain, "But we are already doing that," or the equally devastating, "It's fine in theory, but it can't work in practice." When asked why it can't work in practice, people tend to be vague or to offer such statements as: "We don't have the time to do what is required"; "State testing requires that we teach to the test" (that is, follow an associationist paradigm); "Parents want to know how well their children are doing compared to other children" (in effect saying that the only way a parent knows that his or her child is successful is when some other parent's child fails). The consequence of these rationalizations is, as Willard Waller observed years ago, that the "conservatism of practice overwhelms the progressivism of theory."[15]

One of the reasons for the gap between theory and practice must surely be that many of those who develop the ideas and conduct the research on which technical changes in schools are typically based are a part of the moral and aesthetic order of the university and the research institute rather than the schools.

Those who would persuade teachers and administrators to act on their technically sound ideas must, for example, be aware that their style of discourse is not the style found in schools. The preachments of the university value disputation, open confrontation, dialogue, and theorizing. In public schools the nature of a school's relationships with the outside world makes conflict and disputes threats to the well-being of the school's order. Passivity and docility are encouraged by the norms of the public schools.[16]

In addition to understanding different styles of discourse, those from outside the schools must appreciate the kind of changes that will be required in the knowledge base that is the context within which the technical changes are to occur. For example, the effort-based paradigm apparently has considerable appeal in urban schools where children have historically not done very well in school-related

---

[15] W. Waller, *The Sociology of Teaching* (New York: Wiley, 1967) (Originally published 1932).

[16] See, for example, G. Graff, *Clueless in Academia: How Schooling Obscures the Life of the Mind* (New Haven, Conn.: Yale University Press, 2003).

endeavors. The preachments undergirding this paradigm are ennobling for many students and parents, and they provide a source of hope for teachers. Would the same preachments be as well received in communities where the majority of students are already perceived to be successful academically and where contest mobility (for example, class ranking by grades earned) is highly valued? I think not. For the effort paradigm to succeed in these high-performing environments it will take more than seminars with teachers and teacher and principal support groups. It will require a major parent and community reeducation effort. Such an effort must be clearly aimed at nothing more nor less than a moral and aesthetic transformation of the persons who have many reasons for finding their present circumstances most satisfying.[17]

The Leader as Teacher

In 1985, in summarizing the intentions of an organization I was helping to create—the Gheens Professional Development Academy, located in Louisville, Kentucky, I wrote the following:

> Every Teacher a Leader
> Every Leader a Teacher
> Every Child a Success

I continue to believe these three lines offer a fair summary of what is required if America's schools are to be transformed.

- For schools to ensure success for children, teachers must, first, think of themselves as leaders of children rather than as performers for children or diagnosticians and clinicians who treat children. The most important thing a teacher does is to lead— meaning to inform, inspire, direct, encourage, and nurture (as opposed to controlling, managing, and coercing).

---

[17] Any school reformer who has a rosy notion of the common views held by parents and school leaders would benefit from reading a controversial article on this topic by Alfie Kohn, "Only for My Kid: How Privileged Parents Undermine School Reform," *Phi Delta Kappan,* Apr. 1998, pp. 568–577.

- Leaders, especially leaders in knowledge work organizations, must understand that the most important things they do require them to teach. After all, leading in the modern world means informing, inspiring, directing, encouraging, and nurturing, that is, doing all those things we attribute (or ought to attribute) to the role of the teacher.
- When teachers view themselves as leaders and principals view themselves as teachers and when both understand that their core business is providing students with engaging school work, then every child will be successful, because every child will be engaged—at least this is something to which we can aspire.

Key Questions

The following are questions that I have found useful in understanding and redesigning the knowledge transmission system in schools.

- *When arguments are developed, how are they grounded, and do people agree on this grounding? For example, when a person advances an argument is it justified by research, by moral tradition, or by conventional ways of doing things? Which of these knowledge bases are viewed by others in the school as valid grounds, and which of these knowledge bases are rejected by others?* I have found that many of the most fundamental disagreements in schools reflect the fact that different groups and individuals are using different normative systems to justify their arguments. Revealing that this is so, and gaining discussion about norms within an appropriate context using standards appropriate to that context are steps toward consensus building. One does not evaluate moral norms by using the standards of science any more than one evaluates technical norms by applying aesthetic standards.
- *Do different groups in the school or the school district justify their arguments on the basis of different forms of knowledge, and if so, do these groups form cliques and power blocks that must be addressed? For example, do special education teachers and teachers in regular classrooms proceed on the basis of the same moral knowledge when addressing issues like inclusion? Who appeals to research, and why?* The interaction between power and knowledge is as little

understood in schools as it is in other settings. Yet it is clear that such interactions exist and that they have important consequences. For example, the No Child Left Behind legislation is putting the power of the federal government behind a preference for knowledge that derives from a narrowly defined notion of scientific knowledge.[18] Some who hold that moral norms and aesthetic norms are just as important to school life are reacting strongly to this assertion, but at the present time the relationship between the school and state and federal governments is such that the coercive power of the state can relatively easily overwhelm the normative power available to professional educators.

- *To what extent do teachers, principals, and others in the school district believe in the need for change and the possibility of change (in contrast to not perceiving a need for change or believing that the things that need to be changed are for the most part outside the control of the schools)?* Knowledge about a situation is not sufficient to bring about change, even when there is clear evidence that current conditions are unsatisfactory. In addition those who are being called on to support the change must have some feeling that the possibility of success is substantial and that the values threatened by the change are not as important as the values served by it.

- *Who are the models and exemplars pointed to, and what is the knowledge base from which these people proceed?* It has been my observation that moral knowledge and aesthetic knowledge are more powerful in developing persuasive arguments than is technical knowledge, even though technical knowledge is more likely to reveal both the need for and the possibility of change. Therefore moral leaders rather than technical leaders are especially required when the changes called for directly affect moral and aesthetic norms. Schools are likely to be more successful in implementing sustaining innovations

---

[18] The attention given to this issue by the American Educational Research Association in a recent council meeting attests that it is of widespread concern in the educational research community; see "Council Minutes from January 2003," *Educational Researcher,* June–July 2003, *32*(5), 39–45.

than disruptive innovations because technical leaders (program managers) are in greater supply than moral leaders. Technical leaders can be trained, but moral leaders must be developed over time.

- *Are the visible models and exemplars individuals who proceed from a knowledge base that is consistent with the intended change? If not, are there persons in the district who do proceed from such a knowledge base, and how might they be made more visible and significant in the life of the school?* This question is intended to shed light on the kind of leadership available to support a given change effort, and to encourage official leaders to seek ways to elevate persons with requisite knowledge, skills, and habits of mind to more visible positions so that they can emerge as leaders and as role models for others.

- *What is the level of resource commitment to staff development, and to what extent is the knowledge base from which staff development proceeds congruent with the knowledge base needed to support the desired change?* Compliance with norms requires that those who are expected to comply know what they need to know to comply and that they are oriented toward compliance. One of the greatest barriers to systemic reform is that it often calls on persons to do things that no one in the organization really knows how to do, so old forms of staff development that involve telling, feedback, and coaching must be replaced with learning teams, and norms of mastery must be replaced with norms of continuous improvement.

- *How extensive are conversations and communications about change initiative issues, and how are these issues framed (for example, as technical problems, moral issues, threats to convention)?* Dialogue is a key element of change in healthy organizations.[19] Dialogue is not efficient—it takes time—but it is effective, especially when the changes required affect moral norms, aesthetic norms, and conventional ways of doing things. Workshops and distance learning can sometimes support changes in technical norms. Changes in moral norms, aesthetic norms, and conventions are more likely to require seminars, deep conversations,

---

[19] P. Senge, *The Fifth Discipline.*

reading, and reflection in collegial groups where participants feel socially and psychologically safe.

- *Do those who have authority in the school district (including informal authority) generally agree on the nature of the problems being addressed, or do they frame the problems in different ways?* Mixed messages from recognized leaders are almost certain to lead to change effort failure. Mixed messages confuse the willing and supply ammunition to saboteurs.

Chapter Six

The Power and Authority System

For those who study life in organizations, *power, influence,* and *authority* are important concepts. There is, however, little agreement on how these terms should be defined. In the more popular literature they are often used as synonyms. In the more technical literature they are usually more distinct, but one must know the author and the intellectual tradition from which he or she proceeds to know precisely what each term means.

Over the nearly forty years I have concerned myself with the study of life in schools, I have developed some definitions and conventions that I have found useful in my quest for understanding the way schools operate and the effects of these operations on what teachers and students do and learn in classrooms. These definitions and conventions, discussed in the following sections, are used in this chapter.

Power and Influence

Both *power* and *influence* have to do with the ability to induce, encourage, or compel others to engage in activities and to support actions that the person exercising the power or influence wants them to engage in or support. The difference between power and influence is that power is related to the position one occupies in a group or organization, whereas influence is related to the personal qualities and personal relationships of individuals in the group. Power, on the one hand, derives from the fact that persons who occupy different positions in an organization have access to different types of organizational resources and are in a position to deploy their resources in support of actions they wish to have supported. Influence, on the other hand, has to do with the way individuals react and respond to each other, the social bonds and social obligations that accrue as a result of these interactions, the persuasiveness of individual men and women, and the willingness of those who are the targets of persuasion to submit to suggestions and direction without the pressure of some organizationally controlled sanction. Persons who possess power in an organization do not necessarily have influence, and influential persons do not always possess power. However, power and influence do interact. Persons of demonstrated influence tend to accrue power, and people who have power tend to generate influence by virtue of the way they exercise the power they are authorized to exercise.

Authority

Authority has to do with legitimacy. To say that a person or office has authority is to say that the person, group of people, or occupant of a designated position has the recognized right to exercise power, which is to say the right to deploy organizational resources in support of actions he or she decides to support. The way individuals exercise authority goes far to determine the amount of influence they will develop in the organization, just as the influence a person generates goes far to determine how much authority (legitimized power) he or she will eventually gain in the organization. With an understanding of the interactions among power, influence, and authority, we can gain useful insights into what is going on in classrooms, schools, school districts, and boardrooms.

A Dynamic Interaction

Systemic change almost always affects the authority system because systemic change almost always affects the way that key resources (time, people, space, knowledge, and technology) are used and deployed. When resources are affected, power is affected, and when power is affected, the authority system is inherently involved. This is one of the reasons that persons who have authority are so critical to systemic change. It is also the reason they so often resist change. *Indeed, it is usually the case that resistance to disruptive inno-*

vations (which require systemic change) is most likely to occur among those persons whose authority in the present system is least secure or most problematic and among those whose position in the authority system seems most likely to be threatened by the required changes.

Consider the case of curriculum supervisors in large urban school districts. I have often found this group to be highly resistant to systemic changes, especially when the changes are initiated by sources outside the group's control and threaten to directly affect the control of resources that these supervisors presently have the authority to assign or deploy. Typically, the authority of the curriculum supervisor derives from assumed or perceived expertise (what some sociologists call *expert authority*). This expert authority is translated into position-related power in the form of control over budgets, personnel, office space, and so on, so further authority accrues to the position occupied by the supervisor. In the day-to-day operation of schools, persons who gain power in this way often also become highly influential in the district. This influence develops for several reasons.

First, the knowledge possessed by these specialists is often in limited supply in the district, and those with access to it gain advantages. Thus there are great opportunities for social bartering, and this bartering tends to generate what some sociologists call *social exchange influence.*[1]

Second, the bulk of the resources available in schools are inflexible. School budgets tend to be categorical, highly specified, and predominantly associated with salary and wages. Furthermore, most of the flexible portions, like grant dollars, staff development funds, and so on, tend to be controlled by a person who holds his or her office because of real or perceived expertise in the area of concern to those providing the grant.[2]

---

[1] See, for example, P. Blau, *Exchange and Power in Social Life* (Piscataway, N.J.: Transaction, 1986).

[2] This observation derives primarily from my analysis of data collected between 1979 and 1984 in a large-scale field study of the organization and management of staff development in an urban school district. A cadre of graduate students conducted this study, funded by the National Institute for Education. It resulted in several dissertations and official reports, but no other publications.

Classroom teachers, for example, usually cannot be assigned to nonclassroom duties without a great deal of trouble, and when they are, someone, someplace, must come up with money to support a reasonable substitute. Staff development money is often used for this purpose, and the person who controls this more flexible budget is likely to be a curriculum director or staff development person who is administering a grant for the school district. Providing this money gives this member of the central office personnel an opportunity to generate a great deal of social exchange influence among principals.

A third, and perhaps the most important, point is that much of the flexible money available in school districts is really not flexible at all, at least from the perspective of the uninformed. Grants almost always stipulate how funds may be expended. Federal grants in particular typically operate under complex sets of regulations and guidelines. Understanding the conditions under which these funds can be expended and ensuring that expenditures meet guidelines can become nearly a full-time occupation, and the person who is so occupied is likely to hold the title of director or coordinator in a central office.

The upshot of this is that curriculum specialists and staff development specialists at the central office level, precisely because they have control over often small but flexible resources, often generate levels of influence—both upward and downward—that far exceed the authority assigned to their position. Furthermore, these resources can, within limits, be deployed at the discretion of the supervisor.

This condition presents a complex situation for school reformers. First, because the control of flexible resources is so critical to any development effort, central office supervisors are sometimes uniquely situated to determine the fate of a systemic reform effort. Not only do they typically control most of the existing flexible budgets but they are also often among the most knowledgeable about ways to access outside resources like grants and Title 1 funds and the ways these resources can be used. The axiom that "knowledge is power" has few clearer manifestations than this one.

Second, because the persons who occupy central office positions often have generated a great deal of influence, they are also in a unique position to resist efforts to redeploy the resources they control. Therefore change leaders must be concerned with ensuring that these middle-level persons are committed to the direction being set, and when they are not, the superintendent must make it clear that such commitment is a condition of the supervisor's retaining control over certain resources. This means of course that, generally speaking, systemic change cannot and will not occur unless the superintendent is prepared to give the effort the full and unqualified support of the office he or she occupies. As I have said elsewhere, superintendents can delegate every kind of authority bestowed upon the office of superintendent except for one— moral authority.[3] And without the moral authority of the office of the superintendent behind the change, it is unlikely that persons in the middle will voluntarily support systemic change initiatives, especially when the change requires them to deploy resources they control in ways at variance with what they perceive to be their own short-term power and influence concerns.

Another reason that curriculum specialists and staff development specialists in the central office present a special challenge to those who would bring about systemic change is that, because of their special knowledge and control of flexible resources, central office specialists—or those who supervise them—often become highly influential with the superintendent. Indeed, it is not uncommon for the superintendent to develop a view of what is going on in the school district that is highly distorted by the values and interests of persons whose expertise and areas of concern almost ensure that they will have a narrow rather than a broad view of the world of schools and schooling. This is one of the reasons that I argue elsewhere that the superintendent should do everything in his or her power to ensure direct, routine, and nonsupervisory interactions with building principals.[4]

Fourth, because central office supervisors or directors with flexible budgets usually gain significant expertise in all the ways their allocated funds can and cannot be expended, they effectively

---

[3] See P. C. Schlechty, *Schools for the 21st Century: Leadership Imperatives for Educational Reform* (San Francisco: Jossey-Bass, 1990).

[4] See P. C. Schlechty, *Working on the Work: An Action Plan for Teachers, Principals, and Superintendents* (San Francisco: Jossey-Bass, 2002).

become the interpreters of these rules, and teachers and administrators up and down in the organization are dependent on these supervisors to keep them out of trouble while helping them do what needs to be done.

Fifth, and finally, because the most pressing needs of the schoolhouse are not always consistent with the intentions of the funding sources, building principals are inspired to "shop around" for a person to put in charge of a funding source who will permit the principal to do what he or she believes needs to be done. For the imaginative and entrepreneurial principal who knows where he or she is going, such an arrangement has its advantages; for the central office director who enjoys the status that accrues from being associated with such principals, it is also useful. But as a device for supporting and sustaining systemic change or for supporting the introduction of disruptive innovations, this arrangement leaves much to be desired.

More often the consequences are less happy ones. Usually, if the central office person is prone to narrow and conservative interpretations of the rules, he or she will come to be viewed by those at the building level as an inflexible and nonresponsive bureaucrat. When most of the central office personnel operate in this manner, the stage is set for serious arguments about the need for decentralization (as discussed later in this chapter). If the central office person is more imaginative and gives local principals and faculties more latitude in the hope that more creative solutions will emerge, he or she is likely to develop considerable influence. Such persons can become important gatekeepers in any effort to generate support for systemwide reform efforts. More often, what happens is that whatever flexibility exists is used to divert resources intended to support developmental activity to the support of the district's maintenance needs, thus ensuring that the resources assigned to support improvement efforts will almost certainly not have their intended effects.

For example, in one of the large school districts where I conducted some of my early research on the organization and management of staff development, it was very clear that the director of staff development had a great deal of influence with high school principals. Furthermore, it was clear that many of those who had direct line authority over the high school principals (in this case, area superintendents), saw the director of staff development as a threat to their own authority, and all felt they could do a better job if the staff development budgets were assigned to their offices. Through interviews and observations it became clear that the director of staff development had generated a lot of goodwill and personal loyalty from high school principals by making it possible for them to co-opt developmental resources under her control to fund compelling maintenance activities. For example, regional accreditation required a great deal of administrative effort on the part of teachers. They needed to attend numerous meetings, fill out forms, prepare reports, and so on. The principals had no resources to support such activity. One way the director of staff development helped the principals with such problems was to make in-service credit available to teachers who worked on regional accreditation teams. Another way she helped was by providing substitute teachers so building-level teachers could be released to engage in necessary accreditation work and by assigning members of her staff—who were officially supposed to be providing training for teachers—to carry out various unscheduled functions associated with the preparations necessary to a successful regional accreditation visit.

This is but one illustration of the kind of activity that can transform limited power into increased influence. It is also an illustration of the power of unintended consequences. I am confident that the director of staff development did not provide these services with the intent of increasing her influence with principals, and I am even more certain she did not recognize the effects of what she did. In her mind she had rationalized the activities she supported as "developmental," and the loyalty she developed from principals as simply an effect of the fact that she was a likable person who understood them and cared about them. She *was* a likable person, but the fact is that *the resources she deployed for such activities had little prospect of improving the skills of teachers or the insights teachers had regarding their jobs—which was her official task.* Her willingness to permit the principals to use these resources as they did removed a burden from principals, and it did make the principals' lives a bit easier. At the same time, in the view of the area superintendents, it made her office, which had no official authority over the principals, a competitive source of direction for the principals, primarily because the influence she had developed made a simple request from her a command to some principals; a command they responded to sometimes in direct contravention to commands from their official superordinates, who had relatively few flexible resources at their disposal. Indeed, these area superintendents too were dependent on the director of staff development for such resources, which rankled even more.

There are of course many curriculum supervisors and many central office situations that do not conform to this example. However, the pattern is sufficiently common that I am prepared to argue that one of the first tasks of a leader of systemic reform, especially in a large urban school, is to get a clear picture of the way central office personnel operate, the persons and causes to which they are loyal, and the persons and interests that are loyal to them.

Successful leaders of systemic change understand that enlisting the support of those who control flexible resources is essential and that if successfully recruited these persons can become powerful allies. If they are not recruited, however, they can become equally powerful sources of resistance and sabotage. Knowing who these people are and what they value can assist in the recruitment process. It can also help change leaders to understand when the power and influence of these persons must be offset, neutralized, and in extreme cases, destroyed.

The Additive Strategy

When persons who control existing flexible budgets cannot be recruited, it is commonplace for leaders to attempt to generate additional flexible budgets (outside grants, for example) and to assign authority over these grants to a person or department that is favorably disposed toward the change. There are, however, at least three problems with this approach.

- Because the funding is new it is also likely to be seen as temporary and may not generate the commitments needed to sustain the change over time. Furthermore, the resources generated are likely to be quickly co-opted by the ongoing programs in the departments to which the funding is assigned.
- New funding is much less available in times of economic retrenchment than in more plush times, but it is in such diffi-

cult times that the needs for systemic change are most likely to become widely apparent.

- New funding accompanied by the creation of new positions inside the existing authority system often introduces even more competition among those who are already competing for authority, thereby introducing even more static into the directional system.

A case can be made that these three propositions describe the history of many federally funded programs in schools, as well as many programs mandated—and sometimes funded—by state legislators. These propositions can also help leaders understand what might be going on when the director of staff development seems to be sabotaging the implementation of a particularly disruptive innovation, the source of which is outside the control of that director or of existing curriculum specialists.

Decentralization, Teacher Empowerment, Parent Involvement, and Site-Based Management

Decentralization, teacher empowerment, parent involvement, and site-based management have become key ideas in most efforts at school reform. Recognizing that the bureaucratic, hierarchical arrangements that typify many school districts create lack of commitment on the part of teachers and lack of responsiveness to the needs of parents and students, reformers generally agree that for school reform to work, teachers must be empowered, parents must be invited into greater levels of involvement, and the school site, rather than the central office, must become the locus of much of the decision-making authority of the school district.

Beginning in the late 1970s, union leaders and school district officials in places like Hammond, Indiana; Miami-Dade, Florida; Toledo, Ohio; and Rochester, New York began negotiating contracts intended to move decision-making authority to the building level and to empower teachers. Over time it became apparent that the need for greater parent involvement and commitment was as important as the need for greater teacher involvement and commitment. The result was that state legislatures, following the lead provided by the Kentucky Education Reform Act, began to mandate or strongly urge the creation of school site councils made up of parents, teachers, and building administrators who were empowered to make many of the decisions once made at the central office.

Most school reformers agree that moving the decision-making authority down the system, as well as moving the authority to enforce those decisions down the system, results in greater commitment to and passion for the decisions that are made. This is not surprising. After all, most people like their own decisions better than they like decisions made by others. Indeed, one of the reasons bureaucracies are so intractable is that those who are empowered by the bureaucracy to make decisions like the decisions they make better than they like the decisions that might be made by those below them. What is often lacking in discussions of site-based management, however, is serious consideration of the quality of the decisions that are made, regardless of where they are made or by whom. Bad decisions are bad decisions, whether made by a far-removed board of education or an up-close-and-personal school site council.

What, then, are bad decisions and what are good decisions? The answer depends in large measure on how authority is distributed in the system.[5] If authority is highly centralized, then a good decision is a decision that satisfies central authority. If authority is decentralized, then a good decision is a decision that satisfies the culturally embedded standards and norms that bind the group together and that define the social identity of the group.

Unfortunately, common programs and common rules more than common values or a common culture hold most school districts together. Therefore, when decentralization is intended, the first step should be to build enough consensus around beliefs and standards to sustain the effort. Leaders who attempt decentralization without attending to building common beliefs and values are

---

[5] In a moral or technical sense, a decision that is good within the context of a given authority system may be objectively bad. In the real world of organizations, however, what is good and what is bad is defined in the context of the authority system. That is why the moral leadership issue is so important. See, for example, M. Fullan, *The Moral Imperative of School Leadership* (Thousand Oaks, Calif.: Corwin Press, 2003).

almost certain to have bad results. Lacking common commitments and a common set of standards, decentralization is likely to become divestiture, making each school site independent from any but the narrowest slice of the community. When this happens, good decisions are decisions that satisfy the needs of a small group of parents and teachers and give little or no attention to the needs of the larger community that is asked to support the schools (for example, nonparent taxpayers) or to the long-term welfare of the school community itself.

To try to counter this tendency, policymakers resort to various forms of accountability measures, which reintroduce centralized bureaucratic authority in even more powerful ways. Thus schools and school site councils are held *accountable* for ensuring improvement in test scores. If a school does not improve, it is subject to a takeover by the state, and the decision-making authority that has been delegated will be taken away. *In effect, decentralization may result in recentralization at a higher and even more remote level than the central office of the local school district. Centralization at the state or national level, regardless of the name given to it, is still centralization.*

In a bureaucracy, assuming it is well managed, people know the rules—they understand where authority is located, and they understand generally what is expected of them and what they can expect of others. Issues of direction are largely issues of concern to those higher up in the organization. Those higher up in the organization also promulgate the rules by which those lower in the organization are to maintain control, and those lower in the organization are, in theory at least, delegated the authority needed to support these rules. The problems of bureaucracy arise when the rules do not fit reality or reality does not fit the rules. The subtleties of human interaction are such that rules must always be subject to modification and interpretation. Who, then, is to be the interpreter? Who is empowered to authorize a modification or an exception? Bureaucracies handle these problems by passing problems up and expecting solutions to come down—which they may or may not do. This is one of the reasons bureaucracies seem slow and cumbersome.

The idea behind site-based management is that those who are in a position to see the problems will be empowered to develop the rules by which the problems will be solved, thereby making the organization more flexible and responsive. This thinking is fine insofar as it goes, but it does not go far enough. Unless the values that will guide decisions are clear and unless the commitments these values demand are understood and shared, sad consequences can result. For example, there are many students who present a potential problem to the typical school. One way to handle this problem is to set admission standards that ensure such students do not get into the school. This solves the problem for the local school unit, but it does not solve the problem for the district generally. The opposite response is to bureaucratically mandate that all schools must be open to all children and to insist that inclusion is of greater value than academic excellence. Neither solution is in fact a solution. Rather, each purported solution is simply a way of dislocating or masking the problem.

What is needed is a system of shared values, beliefs, and meanings as well as a shared understanding of the business of schools. Given these shared beliefs, self-control and informal control rather than control by rules, procedures, and formal sanctions would be commonplace. Such a development is not likely, however, unless top-level leaders develop and convey a clear understanding of the primary business of schools and the standards by which that business is to be conducted and assessed. Without such an understanding, site-based management does not hold many prospects for substantial improvement in the performance of our schools. Furthermore, satisfying the needs of a few newly empowered people to make whatever decisions they feel good about may relieve enough of the pressure for reform to make life tolerable for a few influential parents but probably does so at the price of further erosion in the confidence most Americans have in their schools.

Despite these concerns I am not suggesting that teacher empowerment, parental involvement, and site-based management are bad ideas. Indeed, I was advocating these things long before it be came popular to do so. What I am suggesting is that unless such changes in the power and authority system are accompanied by changes in other systems as well, there are likely to be unanticipated and unwanted consequences that will overwhelm the good that the changes are intended to produce. Consider the following examples:

- Local newspaper editors generally strongly support open meeting laws and are adamant that public organizations should hold open meetings. In urban communities, editors typically assign a reporter to watch and report diligently on the activities of the board of education and central office personnel. As real power devolves to the school level (for example, as charter schools become widespread), will the press be able to keep up with what is going on in each little governing unit, or will it be necessary to wait for whistle-blowers to reveal problems, as is now the case in the health care industry?

- It is commonplace to complain about the factionalism and special interest orientation in local boards of education. (I have complained often and loudly myself.) Is it really reasonable to expect that governing structures that include only parents, teachers, and other school personnel will be any less oriented toward special interests? The difference may be only that it will be the special interests of teachers and of activist parents that are brought to the table as opposed to the special interests of land developers, nonparent taxpayers (who make up the majority of taxpayers in many communities), the local chamber of commerce, and community-based groups like the NAACP, the Urban League, and so on. Representing the interests of teachers and activist parents may be better than the alternative of not having these interests represented at all (as often occurs under present arrangements), but it still does not solve the problem of getting the schools to focus on their primary business, which is providing quality experiences for *all* children.

- If the schools of a community are to serve the interests of the community, how can those interests be served if each faculty and each group of parents can pick and choose whose interests will be served and if much of this picking and choosing can be done outside the light of public scrutiny?

- It is commonly observed that one of the greatest barriers to school improvement is the lack of persistence in direction. Is it really reasonable to assume that schools will be any less fickle in terms of fads adopted and directions taken than is now the case when school governance is under the control of persons who have only a short-term interest in the school (as is typical of most parents) and a special interest as well (the interest of their own child or children)? When this is compounded by the fact that in some instances these parent-teacher councils are empowered to exercise the ultimate in remunerative power (dismiss the principal), is it not likely that traumatic palace coups will occur and short-term wants will overwhelm long-term needs?

None of the outcomes anticipated in these queries is inherent in teacher empowerment, parent involvement, and site-based management. Furthermore, there is no question that the idea of having teachers, parents, and others more directly involved in shaping the decisions that affect their lives is sound, both ideologically and operationally. In the modern world, whether in schools or in industry, old top-down management styles are giving way to more responsive styles of leadership. This does not mean, however, that there is no longer a need for a centralized source of *direction*. What it does mean is that centralized *control* is no longer seen as either necessary or desirable. *The ability to maintain direction from the center while devolving control to those who must carry that direction forward is the key to effective decentralization.* The choice is whether to manage by rules or to lead by values, beliefs, and commitments. This is why it is so important that leaders have a clear understanding of the business of schools and a clear, compelling, and well-articulated vision of how that business is best conducted in the environment in which the schools are located.

To move from a system of external control based on adherence to common rules, procedures, and practices to a system based on self-control and control by small groups requires that direction be maintained by a commitment to common values and standards. Such commitments do not just happen; they are caused to happen. The ability of school leaders to cause these commitments to happen will determine whether or not teacher empowerment, parent empowerment, and site-based management actually deliver what they have the potential to deliver. More than that, it will also go far to determine how adept schools will be at bringing about the kind of systemic changes that will be required if the American system of public education is to survive and thrive.

Sanctions and Rewards

One of the first matters of concern in the effort to lead change should be the nature of the rewards available to support coordinated action that moves in the direction indicated by the change. These rewards come in a variety of forms. For some persons the act of participating in a change effort is its own reward. These persons, whom I refer to elsewhere as *trailblazers* and *pioneers,* are often motivated to change precisely because they find change invigorating and the taking of risk exciting.[6] The primary problem such individuals present to the change leader is ensuring that the passion they have for change and innovation moves in directions supportive of the school's business. Ancillary rewards such as status, access to power and privilege, and collegial affiliations are also important. Change, especially when it has major effects on the power and authority system, always introduces a great deal of uncertainty regarding the kinds of rewards that will be available and the ways they will be distributed as the change takes place.

It is important, therefore, to know whom the present power and authority system rewards and for what reasons. It is equally important to know the basis on which rewards (including access to authority) are awarded and by whom they are awarded. Finally, it is important to understand what parts of the existing social systems (for example, the evaluation system or the induction system) are maintained by the present system of rewards, so that the effort to reallocate rewards to support change does not destroy parts of the system that need to be maintained.

In public organizations, unlike in private ones, the use of monetary incentives to support change is limited. For example, it is not unusual for private organizations to offer small monetary bonuses, trips, and other rewards that offer some lifestyle enhancement to people who suggest changes that result in improved performance. Private corporations also have considerably more flexibility in the way they distribute more substantial rewards like profit sharing, which actually affect standard of living.

---

[6] See Schlechty, *Schools for the 21st Century.*

The use of monetary rewards is more problematic in schools than in business for at least two reasons. First, as discussed earlier, flexible dollars are much more difficult to come by and more narrowly accounted for in schools. The superintendent or principal who gives a teacher a paid vacation for a high-quality idea in a suggestion box is risking more than the executive who takes a comparable action in the private sector.

A second reason that the use of monetary rewards to support change is more problematic in schools than it is in the private sector is found in the preachments that surround the role money should play in decisions made by teachers. Both the general public and sometimes teachers themselves place high value on the belief that teachers are, or should be, committed primarily to the welfare and benefit of students. In this view teaching is a calling rather than an occupation. The upshot is that the too-obvious use of bonuses, pay differentials based on performance, and incentives for change presents a major challenge to some of the most sacred preachments that define what teaching is supposed to be. Teachers are supposed to be dedicated, self-sacrificing, and willing to do whatever it takes to make life better for students. For teachers to respond enthusiastically to monetary incentives, to compete with each other for these incentives, and to endorse the use of such incentives, they would have to abandon these preachments that have a long tradition in education. To introduce money into the equation is to call into question the service-oriented preachments that for many define the teaching occupation. It suggests that teachers, like many others, are in practice motivated more by money than commitment and that they would be willing to compete with their colleagues for money. Many teachers and many others reject the notion that those who teach do so only for the money or even primarily for the money. This is not to say that teachers are not just as concerned about salary issues and welfare issues as are other occupational groups. The difference is that the public, and sometimes teachers themselves, find the notion that they would teach better if they were paid more disquieting, just as I would find it disquieting if I thought the pilot in the front of the plane I am on as I am writing these words would fly better if he were given a bonus for doing so. Those who would use monetary incentives to encourage support of change initiatives need to be extremely sensitive to matters such as these.

Norms of Continuous Improvement

Change-adept schools (like all other change-adept organizations) embrace change as a positive good rather than a necessary evil. Leaders place high value on seeking alternative solutions to problems, and they find ways to reward and recognize those who provide such solutions. Indeed, leaders in change-adept schools often point to the most change-responsive persons in the school as models and exemplars, and they make it very clear that what they are modeling is an *attitude* toward change as well as the willingness to develop or create the technical skills needed to bring the change about.

Because of this commitment, leaders in change-adept schools read widely, and they encourage those around them to read widely as well. They are especially attuned to literature that has the potential for illuminating ways of doing the business of the school better. Rationalized rules and procedures, although important to daily operations, are understood to be conventions created to increase efficiency rather than commandments passed down as standards to judge effectiveness. Local customs and traditions, although valued, celebrated, and understood, are more likely to be stated as general principles than as narrow and specific commands for action. An example of the former is, "We treat students with respect around here, and we expect to be treated with respect in return." An example of the latter is, "Touching students is not permitted, and talking back to the teacher is a suspension offense." These are very different statements.

In change-adept schools the operational norms are widely known in the school and are enforced not only by designated officials but also by nearly all members of the school. Indeed, most participants even understand that there are some specialty norms that apply only to some groups or individuals but that must be upheld by all. For example, it might be understood that those teachers who are leading a particularly arduous change effort or those schools that are piloting a new program may well receive special attention and special resources, for "they are working on behalf of all of us."

Unfortunately, this is not a common occurrence in America's system of education. Far more common is the complaint that those who are teaching in pilot programs are receiving unfair advantages and that the resources used to support innovations would be better spent to help maintain present programs. I sometimes wonder if those who would introduce more competition into schools know how much harm competition is doing in our schools even now.

Key Questions

Leaders should ask these key questions when trying to understand the power, authority, and norm enforcement systems in their schools.

- *How many authority levels presently exist, and how many are needed?* Moral authority can be shared, but it cannot be delegated. To the extent that moral authority is required to support norms or changes in norms, excellent communication between the source of the moral authority and those who must support the change is critical. The more profound the change, the flatter the organization must be that supports that change. Systems with many levels of authority may be quite good at managing routine tasks, but they are not good at encouraging and supporting inventiveness.
- *Which persons or offices have control over the resources that provide the bases of power (for example, who can hire and fire, bestow status, or confirm reputations), and how diffused or centralized is this control?* Centralized organizations are less adept in encouraging systemic changes than are organizations where authority for decisions is diffuse and where authority is shared rather than delegated.
- *To what extent do those who are called on to act on decisions feel that their views are taken into account in the decision-making process?* Making decisions is quite different from implementing them. Those who are called on to implement decisions are more likely to be committed to the decision when they know that decision makers have taken their views and concerns into account.

- *To what extent is feedback from those called on to implement decisions sought and taken into account when leaders consider modifying decisions?* The best sources of information regarding the impact of decisions are those who are called on to implement them. Ensuring communication and dialogue between decision makers and those who must act on or who are affected by decisions is essential to creating a shared leadership framework.

- *How independent are the decision makers? For example, do they depend on others for resources and approval of actions?* Persons called on to act on decisions must have ready access to the resources they need to support their actions, and those who are in positions of authority are obliged to assign these resources or the authority to command such resources to them.

- *Who are the persons of influence among those whose support will be needed to initiate and sustain the proposed change?* Influence persuades. Power controls. Systemic change requires an adequate supply of influential leaders who are favorably disposed toward the proposed change. Influential leaders who are not favorably disposed are likely to become saboteurs.

- *What rewards are available to support the change effort?* Trailblazers and pioneers often find participation in a change effort intrinsically rewarding, and they get a great deal of personal satisfaction out of being among the first and being recognized as risk takers and leaders. For them the gain is the psychic reward. For others, especially those less prone to risk taking, ancillary rewards such as opportunities to work intensively with colleagues, to attend conferences, and to enjoy other lifestyle rewards may have more meaning.

- *How are the current rewards linked to the maintenance of the current system for setting direction and maintaining coordination?* For systemic change to occur, those who are responsible for leading the change must ensure that the rewards for supporting the change are at least as great as the rewards gained by supporting the present system.

- *If these linkages were altered, what effect might the changes have on direction and coordination efforts?* Short-term confusion and uncertainty almost always accompany significant change efforts. Rosabeth Moss Kanter has observed that most changes appear to be failures in the middle stages. Michael Fullan refers to this stage as the *implementation dip*.[7] Leaders need to anticipate these problems so that they do not panic in the face of them and alter direction when the school should be staying the course. As Robert Herriot and Neal Gross have observed, "school officials who ignore the potential organizational and human costs of a major change effort, and treat the highly complex task of instituting fundamental changes . . . simply as routine matters are engaging in irresponsible administrative performance."[8]

- *What, if any, monetary awards are available to support change, and how flexible are they in the uses to which they may be put?* Systemic change requires flexible resources. An accurate assessment of the availability of such resources is critical for leaders of change.[9]
- *Who controls the flexible resources that are available, and how are these persons presently using these resources?* For reasons outlined earlier, persons who control flexible resources are in a unique position to generate influence. An understanding of the manifest and latent ends currently served by flexible resources is critical information for change leaders.
- *How do teachers feel about differential rewards, and what is the basis of that feeling?* Generally, teachers are more favorably disposed toward differential pay and support for teachers who fulfill difficult assignments than they are toward differential pay based on some assessment of results. This has important implications for those who would design reward systems that support sys-

---

[7] R. M. Kanter, *Rosabeth Moss Kanter on the Frontiers of Management* (Boston: Harvard Business School Press, 1997), p. 129; M. Fullan, *Leading in a Culture of Change* (San Francisco: Jossey-Bass, 2001).

[8] R. E. Herriot and N. Gross (eds.), *The Dynamics of Planned Educational Change* (Berkeley, Calif.: McCutchan, 1979), p. 363.

[9] Herriot and Gross, *The Dynamics of Planned Educational Change*, present five case studies that clearly illustrate this point.

temic change efforts. Systemic change requires effort well beyond the effort usually expended in introducing sustaining innovations in environments that are well understood.

- *How do teachers and students feel about the rules that govern action in the district and the school? More specifically, do they see the rules as legitimate (that is, rightful and correct), or do they see them as nonlegitimate (that is, based on values other than those that officially guide the schools)?* Teachers and students can be involved in a school in at least three ways. They can be morally involved, in which case they will have considerable confidence in the school and its leaders and will be prone toward a great deal of volunteerism. They can be calculatively involved, in which case they are unlikely to act unless they perceive some relatively immediate personal benefit attached. They are also likely to be skeptical about the motives of leaders and to assume that these leaders, like themselves, are calculatively oriented. Finally, participants can be alienated. If their loyalties can be transformed from negative agendas to positive ones, they can serve as power resources for systemic change. If, however, their loyalties cannot be transformed, alienated individuals can be a source of major difficulties for change leaders.

- *How consistent is the pattern of enforcement of key norms related to change, and how visible is that enforcement? For example, are persons who make unusual contributions to change efforts routinely identified as exemplars and presented in ways that produce positive regard for them and their efforts, or are such identifications sporadic and ritualized (for example, made during the annual school board mass recognition night)?* Recognition, involvement, assured support, and opportunities for collegial interactions are key determinants of the likelihood that a change initiative will be supported. Linking access to these values in a way that is both public and meaningful is among the more important actions change leaders can take.

- *When the requirements of a change endeavor require that some persons or organizational subunits receive differentiated or special treatment, is this difference understood and supported by those who might be adversely affected by the action?* Too often, change initiatives become associated with a special project or special school that is viewed by others in the school district as receiving special resources at the expense of ongoing operations. Care must be taken to link changes to benefits for those in charge of present programs and to enlist their support for the new initiative, even when the short-term benefit for their own unit is minimal and even when that initiative requires some sacrifice. Open and honest communication about such matters is essential.

Chapter Seven

The Evaluation System

Evaluation systems involve more than technically defensible measures of what students learn or what students have failed to learn. Such measures are a part of the evaluation system, but they are not all of it. Decisions regarding what is worth knowing—and therefore what is worth teaching and testing—are equally a part of the evaluation system. Agreement on answers to the questions, How do we know? and, How do we know what we know is so? are also a part of the evaluation system.

Arguments over the technical aspects of evaluation are, implicitly at least, embedded in moral and aesthetic assumptions as well as in technical ones. Looked at as a technical issue, the creation of standards and ways of assessing standards has mainly to do with validity and reliability. Looked at as a moral and aesthetic issue, evaluation has to do with believability and credibility. If men and women are to be persuaded to act on the results of evaluations that are conducted, those evaluations must be of moral authority as well as technical or rational authority; they must be credible and believable as well as valid and reliable.

When evaluations are not grounded in the moral and aesthetic knowledge that guides the school or when the processes employed and standards set run contrary to that base, getting people to act on the results of evaluations requires the use of remunerative power and sometimes coercive power as well, because the moral commitments that would lead to self-directed continuous improvement will be lacking. Moreover, evaluation systems that must rely on the application of coercive and remunerative power to change behavior do not create the conditions needed to ensure that systemic change will occur or that when it does occur the change will persist. Rather, what is likely to happen is that participants will comply at minimal levels with the intents of the innovation and abandon it as soon as the coercive measures or remunerative incentives are removed.

Unfortunately, many states and school districts that move to a more rigorous and "scientifically" defensible mode of evaluating school performance and teacher performance seem oblivious to these facts. Some go so far as to couple moves toward more rigorous evaluation with performance-based pay, and in some instances they even threaten the loss of tenure and position for failure to perform up to standard. Apparently, the designers of these evaluation systems are willing to accept the fact that the systems they have designed are not morally compelling to those whose behavior they want to direct with these systems. The consequence is that they use the only kinds of power available to them—coercive power and remunerative power. Such systems will be almost totally devoid of attention to the conditions that produce moral authority. And without moral commitments the prospect of increasing either staff or student engagement diminishes.

The difficulty with an exclusive reliance on coercive power and remunerative power is that it inspires more attention to minimums and ritual compliance than to commitment and concerns about excellence. Rather than encouraging people to ask, "What can we do to make things better?" a reliance on remunerative and coercive power encourages them to ask, "What must we do to escape punishment and gain rewards?" Such strategies may drive bureaucracies to higher levels of mediocrity, but they will not produce a commitment to excellence.

Mastery and Continuous Improvement

In Chapter Three I introduced the distinction between mastery and continuous improvement. This section looks more closely at that distinction and its significance for evaluation.

Standards and tests designed to assess the degree to which standards are met will do little to inspire action beyond minimal compliance unless and until the idea of continuous improvement is embedded deeply in the moral knowledge base that guides action in the school. Indeed, without a commitment to the idea of contin-uous improvement and a belief that continuous improvement is possible, it is likely that technically sound evaluation procedures will be viewed as but one more distraction from the main effort of the school as that effort is defined in the existing moral order.

This is precisely what happens in many state and regional accreditation efforts and in many strategic planning efforts as well. Too often such efforts become ritualized events intended to meet the needs of some outside group of higher-level authorities, whereas most insiders view these efforts as having little relevance to what is really going on in the school or in the classroom. The consequence is that it is often difficult to gain serious attention to matters that accreditation assessments focus on, and much of the work toward accreditation is done by people who have little hope that what they are about to undertake will do much good. To try to offset this tendency, many states and some regional accrediting agencies are moving to what is sometimes called *performance-based accreditation,* by which is usually meant emphasizing measures of student learning as a way to determine how well the school is doing its work.

Attention to student learning is, as I have noted many times earlier, a critical concern, and any process of accrediting schools or evaluating teachers, principals, or superintendents must attend to measures of student learning. However, those who create eval-uation systems that focus on student learning must understand that most teachers have been socialized to the view that teaching is an art that can be mastered and a science that can be learned. This means that if optimal or desirable learning results are not forth-coming, the implication is that teachers and perhaps the principal have not mastered their craft. This being the case, the focus of im-provement becomes the teacher or the principal or both.

The deficit model that grows out of such thinking is one of the primary barriers to school reform. It is also one of the major rea-sons why teachers are often unwilling to take ownership of test scores. To take ownership of these scores, especially when they are low, means to accept blame for being less proficient at one's craft than are teachers in schools where test scores are better. The result is that teachers in schools where test scores are high or are clearly improving are prone to take test scores seriously, whereas those who teach in schools where test scores are low create fictions to explain these results away. Among other things, these fictions permit competent teachers to maintain their view of themselves as masters of their craft, whereas to embrace the low test scores as revealing the true state of things would cause them to admit personal failure.

Continuous Improvement and Accountability

One of the concerns of many teachers regarding the present accountability movement is that the emphasis placed on standardized testing—especially multiple-choice tests—forces teachers to teach things that should not be taught, that is, it trivializes the curriculum. Equally damning is the widespread belief among teachers that such tests do not measure many of the important things that are taught.

I have no doubt that some of the teachers who discount the ability of standardized tests to accurately measure what their students are learning do so out of defensiveness and fear. There is, however, the possibility that for many teachers what appears to be defensiveness has its base in a conflict between, on the one hand, the moral knowledge and aesthetic knowledge on which the operation of schools is currently based and, on the other hand, the moral and aesthetic knowledge base from which the standards and testing movement derives. Those who design tests tend to come from research environments, and they carry with them to their tasks the moral knowledge of these environments, which give strong allegiance to those ways of knowing that are, or appear to be, scientific. Validity and reliability, as contrasted with believability and credibility, are the values of primary concern. These scientific ways of knowing are deeply embedded in the moral knowledge that guides much of the present standards movement, especially as that movement is reflected in the No Child Left Behind legislation, and, as I observed in Chapter Five, the brand of science that is given preference is especially narrow and restrictive, relying as it does on experimental studies only. Teachers, in contrast, often have more confidence in instinct and intuition than they have in scientific knowledge, at least as science is defined in the No Child Left Behind framework. Indeed, many teachers disparage educational research derived from experimental models as irrelevant to their needs. "B. F. Skinner never put thirty rats in the maze at the same time" is a line certain to get an approving response from most teacher audiences.

The fact is that most present efforts to assess student performance grow out of a moral tradition that has, at best, a tenuous hold on the hearts and minds of teachers and school principals. These systems are usually installed at the behest of outside sources and forces (for example, the state education agency or the state legislature). Those inside the schools—teachers and administrators in particular—may be sufficiently threatened by the punishments (for example, loss of tenure, the public humiliation of being labeled a low-performing school) to invest considerable time and energy in efforts to *comply* with the standard. They will not, however, be inspired to undertake the kind of rigorous analysis of what they are doing that would be required to move toward continuous improvement as a goal. In a mastery context, low test scores and the failure to meet standards can be debilitating and fear producing rather than enabling and inspiring because to embrace the scores is to accept the fact that one has violated the mastery norm.

For the standards movement to have the effects that proponents hope it will have, leaders must first transform the moral knowledge base of schools from a mastery orientation to a focus on continuous improvement. The way the evaluation system is shaped and performs goes far toward determining whether and how this transformation will occur.

Performance Visibility

Performance visibility is critical to the evaluation process.[1] People are more likely to take into account the evaluative judgments of those whom they believe to be in a position to truly *see* what is going on than they are to take into account the evaluations of those whom they believe cannot see. It is for this reason that strategies

---

[1] See, for example, S. M. Dornbusch and R. W. Scott, *Evaluation and the Exercise of Authority* (San Francisco: Jossey-Bass, 1975).

to open up the classroom and provide teachers with opportunities to observe other teachers and carry on detailed discussions about what they see is so important to the building of an effective improvement-oriented evaluation system. It is for this same reason that those officially responsible for evaluating teachers (or principals or central office staff or the superintendent) must be perceived by those being evaluated as knowledgeable about what is going on and in a position to observe what is going on. This simple truth has not escaped those who design teacher evaluation systems, and that is why so much reliance is placed on *classroom observations* and *observation instruments* as means of evaluating teaching and the teacher performance.

Such observations are useful, but they are also limited. Much that improvement-oriented evaluations need to assess is not visible through simple, direct observation. Assessing the effectiveness of a principal or a superintendent by sitting in his or her office for a few hours filling out an evaluation instrument would be considered patent nonsense. Yet that is precisely what happens in assessing teacher effectiveness when principals are compelled to limit their evaluations to what can be seen in a classroom. What goes on in the classroom is important, but it is not the only thing that is important. How students feel about what is going on in the classroom is equally important. What the teacher wants students to do and what students in fact do are important as well. The ways teachers propose to get students to do what the teachers want them to do are important data for improvement-oriented evaluations—at least as important as evidence that teacher intentions are realized.

There are of course reasons why so much teacher evaluation is based on classroom observation and so little on other forms of data such as interviews with students and parent surveys. Teacher classroom performance is clearly visible and controllable—*so much so that in schools where systematic classroom observations are the only form of evaluation, teachers sometimes develop evaluation lessons that they pull out whenever a supervisor or the principal is present.* More important, however, is the fact that to make other aspects of performance visible to observers, the present moral order of the school needs to be changed. The norm of the closed classroom door must give way to norms that promote collegiality and shared responsibility—including responsibility shared between the principal and teachers for what goes on in the classroom. The view of the teacher as an independent member of an autonomous profession, based on the model of medicine or law, must give way to a view of the teacher as a leader in an organization where it is understood that each is accountable for the performance of all. The *logic of confidence* (the idea that everyone knows what to do and is doing it, even if the performance cannot be observed and verified) that typifies schools must give way to a *logic of public verification, analysis, and discourse.*[2] Such changes are more than technical, and the kind of leadership required to bring them about goes beyond the kind of leadership needed to lead technical changes and modest improvements that are relatively consistent with the existing moral order of the school.

Evaluations That Count

Evaluations that count are conducted by people who count. Those who design evaluations for schools often assume that those who count most are those who have official authority to evaluate, authority that entitles them to use whatever remunerative and coercive power is available in support of the judgments they make. Indeed, a frequent lament of those who would have more accountability in schools is that those who have evaluative authority do not have access to enough rewards and punishments to make the evaluations "really count."

However, a traditional view in sociology and social psychology, dating back to the work of George Homans carried out around 1950, states that it is futile to depend on remuneration or even coercion as a strategy for continuous improvement of performance.[3] As Homans and others have shown, in settings where piecework is conducted and pay is based on the number of items produced, workers generally establish a norm well below what they could

---

[2] The logic of confidence is discussed by J. W. Meyer and B. Rowan, "Institutionalized Organizations: Formal Structures as Myths and Ceremony," *American Journal of Sociology,* 1977, *83*(2), 340–363; J. W. Meyer and B. Rowan, "The Structure of Educational Organizations," in J. V. Baldridge and T. Deal (eds.), *The Dynamics of Organizational Change in Education* (Berkeley, Calif.: McCutchan, 1983).

[3] G. Homans, *The Human Group* (Piscataway, N.J.: Transaction, 2001) (Originally published 1950).

achieve if they exerted maximum effort. Furthermore, when some workers exceed this norm, they are sanctioned, first by humor and later perhaps through more direct physical means. Ideas about good and bad, just and unjust, operate in the factory as well as the schoolhouse.

The point here is a simple one. Commitment to continuous improvement requires commitment to continuous evaluation and continuous learning. Such commitments cannot be mandated, and they cannot be caused to occur, not even through the most rigorous applications of remunerative and coercive power. Indeed, when such strategies are employed without attention to the moral order, the most likely consequence will be the emergence of new norms of evasion (right ways to do the wrong things) that will make it possible to keep on doing what has always been done, though what is being done will now be explained differently.

If those with authority in the school want norms supportive of continuous improvement and continuous evaluation to develop, they must model the behavior associated with these norms. It is for this reason that I would argue that one of the most important single acts a leader who is committed to systemic change can engage in is the act of making his or her own performance highly visible to subordinates and inviting their help in improving what he or she does. For example, leaders who make the basis for their decisions visible to followers and invite critical reviews of their reasoning will do more to promote data-based decision making than will leaders who simply share with others the decisions they have made or the leaders who simply invite others to participate in the decision, uninformed by facts though that participation may be.

Knowledge of Expectations

In the simplest of terms, evaluation is the process of comparing standards to actual performance and rating the performance relative to the standards. Those standards embody people's expectations. Evaluations are, therefore, conducted in terms of expectations. This fact becomes critically important to understand when one is considering the standards that should be applied when assessing the internal operations of schools and when designing an effort to modify these operations.

When leaders are setting about systemic change, they need to know the content of the norms that will be affected by the planned changes. They need to understand as well the way these norms are distributed and to whom they apply. Sometimes norms are widely distributed through a group yet apply to only a narrow segment of that group. The expectation that the high school principal will always be present at major athletic events is but one example of such a norm. Sometimes norms with which leaders expect all to comply are in fact known to only a few persons. This condition often gives rise to mistaken diagnoses. Noncompliance is observed, and it is assumed that the noncompliant are unable or unwilling to comply when in fact they simply do not know what is expected. Such *structurally based ignorance* is likely to be prevalent in times of substantial change, especially when the changes affect the way power, authority, and prestige are afforded.

For example, one of the common effects of efforts to flatten an organization is that those who once occupied positions of authority (usually central office supervisors, coordinators, and so on) no longer know what is expected of them and what they are to do. Simultaneously, those who once depended on the occupants of these offices for services and support (especially for direction) sometimes feel abandoned. The upshot is that in the midst of such reforms it is typical for principals to complain that "nobody downtown knows what is going on" and for former supervisors to complain that they no longer have the authority they need to ensure that principals and teachers do the right things.

Unless leaders attend to issues like these and unless new expectations are clearly articulated and widely disseminated, it is likely that old patterns of behavior will reemerge and the system will go on pretty much as it was before it was reformed.

Inspiration and Compliance

There are at least two types of evaluation standards: standards that are defined in practice and standards that are defined by preachments. Practice-based standards (or operational standards) take the form of statements about what is really expected and what kind of compliance is required. Preachment-based standards are intended to inspire, but some range of deviation from these standards is considered acceptable. Practice-based standards are *realistic* in that they indicate the level of performance expected and required. Preachment-based standards are *heroic* in that they describe "the way it is supposed to be." An assertion such as, "Parents, teachers, the principal, the board of education, and others who have a stake in the performance of the schools are satisfied with the level and type of learning that is occurring in the school" is a preachment-based standard. Such a standard suggests that all those who have a stake in the performance of the school are in agreement regarding what children should learn, and have access to data and facts sufficient to satisfy them that they know what the level of student achievement is and are content with it. An operational standard indicates how far the school system can deviate from this preachment and still be assumed to be operating within acceptable limits. For example, state legislatures that mandate minimum test scores are attempting to ensure that the state can be satisfied with the level of learning in the schools. Does this mean that if the state is satisfied, parents will be satisfied as well? Probably not! Indeed, there is some reason to believe that some parents are coming to the view that the effort to satisfy the state is trivializing the curriculum and that their children are not learning as much as they did before this effort was launched. One of the functions of preachment-based standards is to maintain balance in the system and to ensure that the systems do not become so fixated on one operational dimension that other dimensions are overlooked or looked past. Goal fixation can, and often does, lead to goal displacement.

Key Questions

It is of course necessary to know the content and substance of evaluation expectations as well as to understand the systems designed to support them. There is no question that high expectations for student performance have a real impact on the way students perform, just as high expectations for teachers and principals affect their performance.

- *How clear are the performance expectations for various role groups in the school (including students and teachers), and who knows about these expectations?* It is often the case that individuals do not perform as expected precisely because they do not know about or are unclear about expectations or because they have no understanding of how they are supposed to perform to meet these expectations.

- *How close is the fit between the official expectations of various groups in the school and the operational expectations?* When the discrepancy between preachments and practices become too large, distrust of the evaluation system is likely to increase. Indeed, distrust is almost always generated by the perception that there is simply too much variance between what is and what is supposed to be.

- *What is the knowledge base used to validate expectations, and how much confidence do the different groups have in this knowledge base?* Scientific knowledge is intended to convince a universal audience. Scientific knowledge may persuade people to alter technical norms, but when a technical change is disruptive and requires changes in structure and culture, the arguments are no longer simply technical ones; they are moral and aesthetic as well. For example, getting high school teachers to embrace the idea of collegial support groups sometimes requires that these teachers first be persuaded to give up allegiance to the norm of the closed classroom door, a norm deeply embedded in the culture of many high schools and long a defining feature of the moral order of the high school.

- *To what extent are expectations universal (applying to all members of a group), and to what extent are they specific (applying only to some members of the group)?* One of the problems with pilot programs, experimental programs, and even the idea of schools within a school is that they all require the creation of sets of specialty norms that are neither widely shared nor widely supported throughout the school district. The result is that rather than being seen as a special and valued part of "our school," the experimental or pilot program becomes a world apart—and a deviant world at that.

- *When expectations have major exceptions built in, how is this justified, and who believes and who doubts the justification? For example, if beginning teachers are forgiven offenses that would be sanctioned in an experienced teacher, do the experienced teachers believe the forgiveness is justified? If persons who are early adopters of an innovation are given special privileges or special treatment, what meaning do others attach to this action?* Exceptions, properly used, can serve as a source of inspiration and motivation for early adopters, but they can also create debilitating competition if the reasons for them are not carefully and persuasively communicated. If special norms are to have positive effects, they must be endorsed by those to whom they do not apply as well as by those to whom they do apply.

Chapter Eight

| The Directional System

Moving a school system from a focus on compliance and attendance to a focus on attention and commitment clearly involves a
change in direction. And once the new direction has been set, participants must maintain it in the face of strong pressures to return
to the more comfortable past. This is especially hard to do because
this is a disruptive change, and much that happens will feel like a
failure, especially in the middle stages.[1]

To establish and maintain direction, therefore, it is necessary
to deal with those systems and subsystems that define the way goals
are set, priorities are chosen, and resources (time, people, space,
information, and technology) are distributed. It is also necessary
to deal with the beliefs and values that legitimize and give meaning to the goals selected and the priorities set. To coordinate effort,
the linkages between and among systems must be understood, and
provisions must be made to ensure that changes made in any
one system are accompanied by complementary changes in the
other systems that make up the school or school district. To fail to
bring about these related changes is almost certain to lead to failure in the change intended in the first place. Matters like these are
the subject of the present chapter.

Establishing and Maintaining Direction

The problems that confront leaders who are intent on creating systems capable of establishing and maintaining direction occur in
these four areas:

---

[1] See R. M. Kanter, *Rosabeth Moss Kanter on the Frontiers of Management* (Boston:
Harvard Business School Press, 1997), p. 129.

- Competing loyalties
- Goal clarity
- Goal consensus
- Goal displacement

Competing Loyalties

Competing loyalties have to do with the tendency of individuals inside an organization to develop loyalties to projects, programs, and sub-units within the organization and to outside agencies that are making competing claims on the organization's resources. These competing interests affect the way goals are established and priorities are set. Sometimes the effects are obvious; sometimes they are not.

Sometimes, for example, competing loyalties are reflected in things as simple as competition between the football coach and the band director for the services of a star athlete who is also an accomplished musician. At other times this competition might be seen in the demand that a principal attend a meeting at the central office at the same time he or she is expected to be present in the school office to deal with a real or perceived crisis. Competing loyalties might be an issue in a politically, legally, or socially controversial group's request for recognized status and a place to meet in the school. Regardless of their sources, competing loyalties have important implications for those who would lead systemic change in schools.

For example, it has often been observed that high schools are more difficult to change than are elementary schools. It is commonplace to explain this fact by reference to real or perceived differences between elementary teachers and high school teachers, usually implying that elementary teachers are more compliant. Without denying that such differences may exist and may account for differences in the ways elementary and high school teachers respond to change, a person oriented toward systems analysis might also suspect that at least part of the explanation lies in the fact that high schools are much more subject than elementary schools to competing forces with origins outside the authority structure of the school. In the case of the high school, local employers are concerned about the school calendar because they want to employ students in summer jobs, alumni want the school to have a winning football team, various interest groups want to ensure that their views are reflected in the curriculum, the chamber of commerce wants a trained workforce, and colleges and universities want the school to support academic standards consistent with their needs and expectations. Though the capacity to respond to each of these interests may have its origins in the elementary schools (children who cannot read are not likely to meet college requirements, for example), it is in the high school that shortcomings become visible to many outside groups, and it is the high school that is looked to for solutions to these shortcomings.

In addition to the competing loyalties that have their origins in outside groups, there are sources of competition that originate inside the school. For example, the nature of the programs conducted by high schools means that high school teachers are more likely than are elementary teachers to occupy *boundary-spanning* positions (that is, positions that require interaction with outside groups and agencies and that make the performance of the teacher occupying the position visible to outside groups). Teachers in such positions not only become conduits for outside interests into the school's internal operation but also have access to forms of community power that directly affect how decisions are made in other areas of school life. Examples of persons who occupy boundary-spanning positions are band directors and coaches in high schools and agriculture teachers in rural schools. Union leaders, who have historically been disproportionately drawn from the ranks of secondary teachers, are also boundary spanners. These conditions, combined with such internal structures as departmental organization, make the high school especially vulnerable to problems associated with competing loyalties. In high schools any change that occurs is almost certain to affect competing forces in ways that are perceived to bestow advantage to some and disadvantage to others.

Elementary schools exist in a somewhat more protected environment. Until recently the primary interests served by the elementary school were those of the students, parents, and faculty, with an occasional need to respond to the central office or the board of education. Thus those interested in introducing an innovation in the elementary school had fewer competing interests with which to contend than did high school reformers. However, the standards and accountability movement that is now underway in education may be in the process of changing these conditions. Nowadays, elementary school faculties must be as concerned with responding to the demands of the business community and newspaper editors for higher test scores as the high school coach is with the demands of athletic boosters for a winning team.

Proponents of this new arrangement often argue that increasing the public visibility of evaluations of school productivity will lead to greater goal clarity and more focused action. Perhaps, but it is just as likely to lead to goal displacement, the substitution of test scores for standards, and the confusion of test performance with profound insight. Should this happen, and there is reason to believe it is already happening, some teachers will become less concerned with meeting the needs of children and parents and more concerned with producing high test scores, regardless of the cost to students or to the teachers' own integrity. After all, competing loyalties have a great deal to do with how power and status are distributed in the system and how the boundary system is organized. In the competitive arena the demands of the more powerful are likely to have greater effects on direction than are the needs of the less powerful.

For example, in the high school and in the elementary school, it is commonplace for teachers to gain status through the status of the students they teach. Thus the chemistry and foreign language teachers, who are likely to teach the higher-status students in schools (that is, the college bound), are likely to enjoy a higher status among their peers than the vocational teacher does. The teacher of the gifted and talented in the elementary school is likely to have a higher status than the teacher of a self-contained special education class does. Teachers who teach high-status subjects will likely have more impact on the direction of the high school than will those who teach subjects that have lower status. Similarly, the high school history teacher or the first-grade teacher who is also a union steward will have a status different from that of most other teachers, and the power of these persons to influence internal decisions is likely to be enhanced as well. The special education teacher who chairs a parent advisory group and the kindergarten teacher in a self-contained classroom will also be seen through different eyes.

Furthermore, this special education teacher is likely to be able to mobilize an advocacy group to support his or her claims on the direction of the organization. Teachers and others who hold positions in powerful outside organizations are better positioned to influence direction than are those who are not members of such groups.

Over the past fifty years, and at an accelerating pace over the past decade, the impact of outside sources of internal competition in schools has increased. Among the sources of these tensions are the growing numbers of advocacy groups who represent special interests (such as special education advocates) and who have succeeded in making these interests a consideration in the internal operation of schools. Indeed, many special educators see themselves as inside advocates of the interests advanced by special education parent organizations. Another source of competing loyalties is the increased factionalism among the adult populations served by the schools, and the increasing sophistication of these groups in ensuring that their voices are heard.[2] In addition the growing willingness of state legislators, and now the federal government, to mandate the types of innovations that will be supported in the effort to improve schools has created competing loyalties. Many teachers and critics believe that these state and federally mandated programs are moving schools in the wrong direction, and they find themselves in the position of being required to violate moral and technical norms they hold dear, a particularly clear example of competing loyalties. One can gain some appreciation of the likely effects of competing loyalties by reading recent articles in professional journals that suggest detailed strategies for developing norms of evasion or fomenting outright rebellion in the face of innovations associated with the standards movement.[3]

In the not too distant past, when competing loyalties surfaced it was common to treat them as boundary problems. The complaining teacher was suppressed, transferred, or suspended. Nowadays the

---

[2] See M. Gerzon, *A House Divided: Six Belief Systems Struggling for America's Soul* (New York: Putnam, 1996).

[3] See, for example, A. Kohn, "Fighting the Tests: A Practical Guide to Rescuing Our Schools," *Phi Delta Kappan,* Jan. 2001, pp. 348–357.

complaining teacher is likely to be a union steward waving a con-tract. In the past the parent who wanted special treatment for his or her child had to stand alone in making the case. Now that same parent is likely to be a member of an organization that retains paid staff members skilled in advocating for special interests in the con-text of public bureaucracies. These developments mean that lead-ers who would provide or maintain direction in a school need very different skills than were required of school leaders in a more docile environment.

Some school leaders are quite skillful at excluding persons and groups from positions where they might affect decisions in ways these leaders do not want. I first became fully aware of this fact in the course of conducting a line of research intended to illuminate the strategies educators used to establish and maintain organiza-tional boundaries. In the resulting paper, "Strategies of Boundary Maintenance in Complex Social Organizations: The Case of the Public Schools,"[4] I developed a typology of the strategies school leaders used to protect the social boundaries of the school and ward off sources of competing loyalties. One of the many strategy categories I identified was *co-optation,* by which I meant the ten-dency of school leaders to offer potential critics special places or positions in the schools in exchange for support. Booster clubs were sometimes used to this end, as were parent organizations. I recall that one superintendent I interviewed said something to the effect of, "I give them the band and the football team, and they [the activist parents] leave me alone in the areas I am concerned about [teaching and learning]."

The cultural contexts in which schools are now located are quite different from the contexts I observed at the time I con-ducted this study. Shifts in the external environment mean it is no longer possible to keep the boundaries of schools as impermeable as they once were. The question is whether school leaders will

---

[4] Although I no longer have a copy of this paper, I wrote it as part of the graduate seminar that planted the seed for this book, as I discussed in the Introduction. Parts of the paper were used by Ronald Corwin in "Education and the Sociology of Com-plex Organizations," in D. Hansen and J. Gerstl (eds.), *On Education: Sociological Per-spectives* (New York: Wiley, 1967), pp. 156–223.

learn to lead in organizations characterized by the chaos resulting from more permeable boundaries or whether they will continue to try to employ boundary maintenance strategies that are increasingly less effective and more dysfunctional.

To provide direction in the midst of conflict and chaos, school leaders must come to understand that competing loyalties are not in themselves the problem. Competing loyalties are symptoms of other problems. *Competing loyalties emerge when the moral order of the school is not sufficiently inclusive to respond to the needs of all those who have legitimate claims on the organization and whose needs must be satisfied if the organization is to succeed.* To address this problem, leaders must change not only the boundary system (so that some now defined as outsiders become insiders) but also the power and authority system, which ensures that whatever boundaries are established can be defended and maintained. *The place to begin this task is with ensuring goal clarity and goal consensus among those whose support is needed to maintain the viability of the school.*

Goal Clarity

Goal clarity involves more than clear statements about intentions. It also involves more than ensuring that goal statements are articulated in measurable terms. Goal clarity includes ensuring that those expected to act in ways supportive of the goals are clear about what they are to do and how what they do—or refuse to do—will affect the achievement of the goals. Goal clarity also requires the goals selected to be consistent with the direction set by the values, beliefs, and purposes of the school. To tell teachers that "our goal is to improve student learning as that learning is measured by state-mandated tests" moves toward goal clarity, but it does not achieve clarity. For such a goal to be clear, teachers must have an understanding of what they are expected to do to achieve it. Then and only then will there be sufficient goal clarity to inspire action. When teachers are simply expected to ensure student compliance with some relatively low-level task, then that is one kind of goal, and it will inspire one type of action. When teachers are expected to ensure that on each day each student is provided with engaging schoolwork that brings him or her into significant contact with rich and important content and intellectual processes, then that is another kind of goal, and the action it will inspire will be very different from the action inspired by the first goal example.[5]

It is unfortunately too often the case that official goals are selected seemingly out of thin air, without much attention to how consistent they are with the direction of the school or with the values, beliefs, and understandings that undergird that direction. Too many people involved in strategic planning in schools fail to understand that direction setting and goal setting are not synonymous. Setting direction requires a clear vision: an understanding of where the organization should be headed and why this direction is important. It is more basic, and has a longer-lasting impact on the organization than does goal setting.

Given a clear vision, powerful goals can be set, but the goals set do not determine the vision. The vision is a template that makes it possible to answer questions like these: Would the successful pursuit of this or that goal result in our having more fully realized our vision of who we are and what we are about? and, Will the pursuit of this or that goal detract from or enhance the core values that guide us?

Properly conceived, goal setting is a tactical action that occurs within a larger strategic framework. School leaders must be able to clearly articulate answers to questions like these:

- Who are we?
- What accomplishments will make us most proud?
- What do we want to be like five years from now?
- If we present ourselves as who we say we are and accomplish what we propose to accomplish, is there reason to believe that those whose support we need will value our accomplishments as much as we do?

Without leaders who ask such questions, goal setting is nothing more than a crapshoot in an environment where various factions each have an interest in loading the dice.

---

[5] This issue is discussed further in several of my other books, especially P. C. Schlechty, *Working on the Work: An Action Plan for Teachers, Principals, and Superintendents.* San Francisco: Jossey-Bass, 2002.

Clear goals, if they are consistent with each other and with the principles contained in a clear vision of the future, are important to continuous improvement. However, goals, even clear goals, that are not disciplined by a clear vision can move an organization in multiple directions simultaneously, resulting in antagonistic actions that produce no improvements at all. For example, a number of states have passed laws mandating the creation of site-based councils and mandating as well that these councils be composed predominantly of parents and teachers. At the same time, many of these same states have the goal of increasing citizen involvement in and support for public education. What the policymakers in these states seem to have overlooked is that the mandated actions may be antagonistic to the goal of citizen involvement in the schools. In many communities, parents no longer represent a majority of the adult citizens, a trend expected to continue for the foreseeable future. Unless carefully conceived, the pursuit of the goal of empowering parents and teachers may have the effect of ensuring that most citizens will not have the chance to participate in some of the most vital decisions made and will be excluded from discussions that affect the future of communities and the lives of children. This surely does not bode well for the survival of public schools, especially if one believes as I do that one of the most important functions of schools in the future will be building communities to serve as well as serving communities.

Goal Consensus

Goal consensus is at least as important as goal clarity. Goal consensus involves two matters. First, there is the matter of agreement, among those whose support is needed to pursue the goals, about what the goals are and what needs to be done to achieve them. Second, there is the matter of gaining individual commitments to goals and agreements to act in ways supportive of the goals.

It is unfortunately the case that one of the easiest ways to gain consensus on goals is to state them in such vague and unclear terms that people can attach multiple meanings and intentions to them. As a general rule, *the more clearly a goal is stated, the less wide will be its appeal.* Goals that have wide appeal will therefore necessarily be vague and will serve only to signal direction. Goals that inspire action will appeal only to a narrow segment of the participants, and widespread consensus on these goals should not be expected. What is required is that leaders evaluate these goals in terms of their consistency with the overall direction of the organization, and ensure that the goals that do inspire action are in fact goals that will support the direction set.

For a goal to have an impact on action, it must be stated so as to encourage and sometimes compel specific action. For example, a statement like, "our faculty will design more tasks that students find engaging and from which they learn important things," is very different from a statement like, "test scores will increase by 5 percent over the next two years." It may be that increased test scores can be selected as an indicator of goal achievement, but indicators are not goals. Sound goal statements focus on what will be done (for example, designing engaging tasks) as well as what will be directly achieved (increased engagement and increased learning).

Given this view of goals, it is imperative for those who are assigned responsibility for a goal to be clear on the meaning of the goal and committed to the actions described by the goal. For leaders the critical question is whether or not this goal, if pursued, will move the organization in the direction suggested by the vision that guides the organization, its members, and its constituents. For others in the organization, all that is required is that they do not see the goal as antagonistic to interests they hold dear and that where the pursuit of this goal intersects with the pursuit of goals they value, they understand and are prepared to act upon the connection. At the organization-wide level, it is more important to have consensus on beliefs, vision, and direction than on specific goals. Goal consensus is required only among those persons who are directly called on to act.

Selecting or creating goals that are compelling to others, consistent with vision, and in conformance with the beliefs is a key act of leadership. Creating consensus around these goals and gaining commitment to the pursuit of these goals is critical as well. Unfortunately, the way most schools and school districts are put together makes it very likely that strategic plans will become nothing more than voluminous documents that rest on a principal's or superintendent's desk for all to see but few to heed. Among other things, the kind of cohesive team needed at the top of an organization to shepherd a strategic plan is often absent. The tendency toward episodic rather than routine interactions between superintendents and principals can be a problem as well. As I have argued elsewhere, a critical link in any effort to improve schools is the link between the office of the superintendent and the building principal. The superintendent should be positioned to send clear, personal messages about direction, and principals should be positioned to respond with clear input into that direction. Without this ongoing interaction, attempts to move any change effort to scale are almost certain to fail.[6] Finally, either before developing a strategic plan or as a part of the planning process, school leaders need to ensure that the systems in place have the capacity to sustain strategic action. As I have observed on numerous occasions, this capacity is too often lacking in most schools and school districts.[7]

Goal Displacement

Goal displacement occurs when operational goals (doing things right) replace substantive goals (doing the right things). When the procedure by which things are accomplished becomes more important than the accomplishment of the result the procedure was intended to produce, goal displacement has occurred. For example, among the goals of school reform are the following:

- To increase the number of students who are learning what it is intended they learn
- To improve the quality of that which is learned by all students

In the context of the accountability movement these goals are sometimes displaced by a much more compelling goal—increasing test scores. The strategies appropriate to producing higher test scores, especially among low-scoring students, often have little to

---

[6] See Schlechty, *Working on the Work.*

[7] For a more detailed discussion of these issues, see two of my earlier books: *Inventing Better Schools: An Action Plan for Educational Reform* (San Francisco: Jossey-Bass, 1997); *Shaking Up the Schoolhouse: How to Support and Sustain Educational Innovation* (San Francisco: Jossey-Bass, 2001).

do with improving the quality of what students learn. Paper-and-pencil tests can determine only whether or not students have some grasp of the "right stuff" at a given point in time and are capable of displaying this knowledge in a special context. Such tests say nothing about whether students are likely to remember what they can presently display (retention) or whether they will be able to use what they have learned in novel contexts (transferability). So the emphasis on standardized testing may push teachers to a strategy of preferring knowledge that is superficially held (low on retention and low on transferability) as opposed to knowledge that is profoundly held (high on retention and high on transferability). Similarly, coaching in test-taking skills does little to improve student learning, though it does improve test scores. Providing students with incentives to attend more carefully to the test does not improve learning, though it may reveal that students know more than they typically show when they do not care about the exhibition they are asked to produce. Yet such improvement strategies are highly touted in some school districts. Seminars and workshops are conducted to help teachers use such strategies to improve test scores.

It is not my intention to suggest that test scores are meaningless or irrelevant. But test scores in education (like profit in business) can serve to distract attention from those things that must be attended to if improvement is to occur. Setting test score goals (like setting profit goals) makes sense only if one attends also to setting goals that define what will be done to increase test scores (or increase profit). If it is expected that test scores (or profits) will improve simply by willing it so, there will be strong pressure to cheat in some way—to adopt a new test (or employ new accountants and accounting procedures).

To avoid goal displacement, leaders must be very clear about the business they are in and the results they expect that business to produce. They must understand as well that people who work with them will respond to the most subtle cues regarding that business, and they will work diligently to figure out "what is really important around here." One of the ways teachers and students discover what is really important is by watching who receives honors, rewards, and privileges; who is talked with and who is talked at; and what is talked about. The superintendent who emphasizes instruction and quality experiences for children in his or her annual message, but comments only on the cleanliness (or lack thereof) of school halls when visiting schools, is setting the stage for goal displacement of the first order. To maintain direction and to avoid goal displacement, leaders must use every system resource available to point the way.

Coordinating Effort

Coordination requires that people do what is needed when it is needed. It also requires a reasonably well understood way of doing things and a means of enforcing this method and avoiding serious deviations. One strategy for fostering coordination of effort requires a system of rationalized rules and procedures combined with a formal set of rewards and sanctions that support compliance with expectations. A second strategy for fostering coordinated effort requires the development of shared beliefs, commitments, and values that have become sufficiently internalized by group members that they are routinely applied to almost all decisions, combined with heavy reliance on informal control and self-control as the primary mechanisms for enforcement.

The first strategy leads to the creation of elaborated bureaucratic structures with detailed rules and formally defined roles and relationships. The effective operation of the second approach requires detailed attention to the creation of powerful knowledge transmission systems, complex systems of induction, and evaluation systems that encourage a great deal of vertical and horizontal communication, that is communication between superordinates and subordinates as well as among peers.

One criticism of America's schools is that they are too centralized and bureaucratic. Faced with this critique, many have suggested that the schools should be moved to a more decentralized model, where power and authority for making critical decisions are lodged closer to the point where implementation is to occur. What is sometimes overlooked is that altering the power and authority system in this way, without supporting changes in the knowledge transmission system, the induction system, and the evaluation system, can be dysfunctional. Rather than increasing effectiveness, decentralization may lead to chaos, confusion, and a further deterioration in coordination of effort.

In the face of this confusion, decentralization may be abandoned or domesticated, in which case it is likely that the preachments of decentralization will be upheld through an elaborate set of pretenses. The ongoing implementation of the Kentucky Education Reform Act (KERA) of 1990 is an illustration.

At the time KERA was passed it was clear that the intention of the legislature was to decentralize decision making at the local district level and to use a program of rigorous statewide testing as the primary means of ensuring that all schools were moving in the same direction and were oriented toward essentially the same goals. Taking power away from school boards and local superintendents also appeared to be a priority concern. Decreasing the regulatory power of the existing state education agency was another apparent goal.[8]

From the beginning the decentralization involved the authority of the state education agency as well as local school boards and local superintendents. Indeed, one of the most radical moves in the reform legislation was the dismantling of the existing state education agency, which was said to be too large, too bureaucratic, and too much involved in regulation. What was needed, it was argued, was a state education agency committed to support and to the provision of technical assistance. As a result of this mandate, leaders of the newly established state agency, operating under an appointed commissioner rather than an elected state superintendent, resisted issuing official directives. They also resisted indicating precisely how various aspects of the new legislation should be implemented. The argument was that local education agencies should have maximum flexibility in interpreting these matters. However, because they were used to a system where legislative intent was interpreted by the state agency, local superintendents pressured the new state agency to tell them what to do, what programs to adopt, what consultants to use, and so on. And because many of those who occupied positions in the new state agency had been socialized in the values of the old

---

[8] To my knowledge, these were never officially stated as goals, but as one privileged to listen in on many backstage conversations during the period when the legislation was being drafted, I can attest that many legislators left no doubt that among their intentions was to reign in the power of local school boards, to decrease the power of superintendents, and to create a state education agency that was more oriented to service than to regulation.

agency, there was considerable willingness among some of these employees to comply with these requests. The result was that very shortly, the state agency began to offer *advisories* suggesting what should be done. Many superintendents treated these advisories as they had once treated regulations and mandates, and over time these advisories began to function as regulations. As a consequence, there is today much less difference between the way the present state education agency operates and the way other state agencies with more regulatory intent operate than was initially envisioned.[9] In addition, as budget difficulties have confronted the Kentucky legislature, the nonregulatory support systems that were initially put in place are being stripped away. For example, regional support agencies were recently cut out of the state budget, as was a substantial amount of money intended to provide new performance incentives for teachers. This is producing an interesting paradox. The state agency is gaining ascendancy over the local school district operation but so are local school site councils, made up primarily of teachers and parents. (For example, there is presently a struggle between some superintendents and some school site councils over who is empowered to employ principals. To date the courts have held that the legislature has granted this power to school site councils.) What seems to be happening is that education in Kentucky is becoming more centralized at the state level and simultaneously more decentralized at the local level—but the local decentralization is due to a mandate from the state—something akin to centralized decentralization.

There is no question that as initially conceived the Kentucky Education Reform Act was a bold and radical approach to many of the issues that beset the schools of Kentucky. Furthermore, there is no doubt that the effort to implement this act has had positive

---

[9] It is likely that many in Kentucky, especially in the state education agency, will disagree with this analysis. I acknowledge that I have not systematically investigated the matter, but I do keep a pretty close eye on what is going on and I have many contacts among Kentucky educators both inside and outside the state education agency. In fairness, I also need to point out that federal actions under the No Child Left Behind legislation are encouraging increased centralization at the state level and decreased authority at the school district and schoolhouse level, official claims to the contrary not withstanding.

effects for many students and has strengthened education in many Kentucky communities. However, bringing about the kind of massive shifts in power and authority envisioned by KERA's designers and having that shift last over time called for a heavy investment in the induction of new employees in the state education agency and the reeducation of those who were retained. Indeed, it called for a massive overhaul of the entire knowledge transmission system and the evaluation system as well as a revisioning of the way education would be delivered to the citizens of the state. It required that local superintendents and local boards of education be brought to understand and embrace the values and beliefs that were giving rise to the new system. And these systemic changes did not occur. Instead, the legislature relied heavily on the imposition of formal sanctions for violations of the rules promulgated to support the new system. For example, the legislature created a special department— the office of educational accountability—to support these enforcement procedures. The idea was to take enforcement out of the hands of the state department of public instruction so that that department could commit itself to its role as a support agency. As I have indicated, this intent has been only partially realized. It is in fact increasingly clear that good though the effects have been, the changes wrought in Kentucky's system of education are nowhere as grand or as profound as the original designers assumed they would be. For example, two of the most disruptive innovations envisioned by the designers were the nongraded primary school and the comprehensive testing intended to test students in a wide range of heretofore untested areas. Both of these efforts were modified, and for all practical purposes should be considered abandoned. The Kentucky education reform effort was comprehensive in that it touched many parts of the existing school organization. It was not, however, systemic in that it left relatively untouched many of the systems that would have needed to be changed if the disruptive innovations that the designers intended to install were to be sustained.

Structural Lag

One of the most important coordination issues confronting change leaders is a problem sociologists refer to as *structural lag*. Structural lag has to do with the tendency for rules, roles, and relationships to get out of synchronization with beliefs, values, and commitments, thereby pushing and pulling the school in competing directions simultaneously. Sometimes the pace of structural change outstrips the pace of cultural change. The situation in Kentucky that I described earlier is illustrative of this type of structural lag. Sometimes new beliefs arise and new values emerge that are incompatible with existing rules, roles, and relationships. Then the pace of cultural change outstrips the structural changes that school leaders are capable of imagining, or perhaps they can imagine the right changes but cannot see their way clear to bringing these changes off.

For example, as I discussed at the beginning of this book, up through the 1980s it was generally held that the obligation of the schools was to ensure that every child had an equal opportunity to learn. Though the structures that were in place did not always achieve this and many pretenses were used to explain away the discrepancy between preachments and practices, there was general consensus on the preachment—all children should have an equal educational opportunity. The *Brown* v. *Board of Education* decision was based on the argument that separate is inherently unequal. It was not assumed, however, that the provision of equal opportunities would guarantee that all students would learn—at least not at high levels. Indeed, up through the 1950s it was commonly accepted that curriculum design should take into account the fact that some students were more likely than others to benefit from academic studies.[10] Nowadays it is commonplace to assert that "all students can learn at high levels" and that schools should be held accountable not only for opportunity but also for results. Moreover, schools are being held accountable for ensuring that all students learn things that in the past were assumed to be unteachable, unlearnable, or unnecessary for certain students—especially the children of the poor and laboring classes. Diane Ravitch puts it this way:

---

[10] Diane Ravitch, *Left Back: A Century of Battles Over School Reform* (New York: Simon & Schuster, 2000), makes the point that in some ways the progressive education movement was fueled by the notion that some—perhaps many—children could not benefit from an academic education but could benefit from such alternatives as vocational education or a "life skills curriculum."

Perhaps in the past it was possible to undereducate a significant portion of the population without causing serious harm to the nation. No longer. Education, today more than at any time in the past, is the key to successful participation in society. A boy or girl who cannot read, write, or use mathematics is locked out of every sort of educational opportunity. A man or woman without a good elementary and secondary education is virtually precluded from higher education, from many desirable careers, from full participation in our political system, and from enjoyment of civilization's great aesthetic treasures. The society that allows large numbers of its citizens to remain uneducated, ignorant, or semiliterate squanders its greatest asset, the intelligence of its people.

The disciplines taught in school are uniquely valuable, both for individuals and for society. A society that does not teach science to the general public fosters the proliferation of irrational claims and antiscientific belief systems. A society that turns its back on the teaching of history encourages mass amnesia, leaving the public ignorant of the important events and ideas of the human past and eroding the civic intelligence needed for the future. A democratic society that fails to teach the younger generation its principles of self-government puts these principles at risk. A society that does not teach youngsters to appreciate great works of literature and art permits a coarsening and degradation of its popular culture. A society that is racially and ethnically diverse requires, more than other societies, a conscious effort to build shared values and ideals among its citizenry. A society that tolerates anti-intellectualism in its schools can expect to have a dumbed-down culture that honors celebrity and sensation rather than knowledge and wisdom.[11]

This clearly reflects a fundamental shift in the assumptions on which schooling in America is based. *A system designed to provide opportunity is not the same kind of system required to ensure results,* especially where the results intended are not especially valued and supported by some of the parents whose children are to be so educated. Moreover, many in American society, when put to the test, really do not believe that such results can be achieved by all children. To create schools that achieve such results, school leaders must find designs that take into account the fact that anti-intellectualism is still a real-

---

[11] Ravitch, *Left Back,* p. 466.

ity in American society and that this anti-intellectualism is to be found not only among the poor and those whom the schools of an earlier generation failed to educate but also among leaders in the broader society, many of whom are not persuaded that all children can—or should—learn those things that have historically been reserved for the elite.

If reformers are to be successful in the effort to ensure that all children learn at high levels, the systems they create must also take into account that in practice there is only limited support for the preachment that every child can learn at high levels. These are tough words, but I believe they are true. Many Americans view academic education with some degree of suspicion.[12] To expect all communities to embrace the value of a fine *academic* education for every child, without first engaging in a great deal of community building and producing a fundamental shift in the moral order that undergirds schools, is to expect something that never was and never will be. The coarsening of our culture is reflected not only in the school curriculum but also in the style of discourse that is becoming increasingly common in school board meetings and community forums where concerns about schools and schooling are being addressed. Without systemic change problems such as these cannot be addressed, and unless these problems are addressed schools will not survive as vital social institutions.

Creating a system of rules, roles, and relationships that prevents, or at least ameliorates, structural lag requires major leadership efforts. It requires that leaders take into account the entire range of systems likely to be affected by the change, not just that part most visibly the target of the change. For example, it is clear that if the change from providing equal opportunity to learn to providing learning at high levels is intended is to be effective, there must be fundamental culture shifts in the community served. Also, changes in the moral norms and technical norms that shape relationships between the school and the community as well as behaviors within the schools are essential. The ability to engage in dialogue and to see the views of others must become at least as

---

[12] See, for example, R. Hofstadter, *Anti-Intellectualism in American Life* (New York: Random House, 1966).

valued as is the ability to articulate one's own views and to persuade others to yield to those views.

Reducing structural lag also requires that some means be developed to ensure that the programs and projects nominated as desirable changes are evaluated prior to implementation to determine if they are consistent with the direction set for the district and compatible with the values expressed in the present culture. If they are not, what would the new direction look like, and why is it better than the present direction? Are there values of significance that are threatened by the new direction that are so important they cannot be abandoned? Are there values served by the new direction that cannot be served by the present direction?

There are, for example, many critics of the present standards movement who hold that the imposition of high-stakes testing without compensatory action in the delivery of programs will result in further erosion of the value placed on equity in the educational context. For these persons the value of equity is at least as important as the value of excellence. For them, efforts to introduce new standards of excellence must be accompanied by changes that will ensure that such standards do not have an adverse impact on any identifiable group or subgroup.

Diane Ravitch and many others believe that the values of equity and democracy would be much better served if all children had sound academic educations, regardless of their backgrounds or likely trajectories in life. Others would argue that highly differentiated educations would be preferable and more in keeping with the notion of democracy. Such debates must be joined by those who would lead reform in America's schools.

Key Questions

In addition to the specific questions about goals and structural lag issues offered in the context of the substantive discussions presented in this chapter, I have found it useful to ask and answer these questions in my efforts to understand how schools establish and maintain direction and coordinate efforts.

- *To whom are the goals, regardless of their clarity, important?* The selection of goals almost always serves some interests and threatens others. Change leaders need to understand who is served and who is threatened, so that they can better understand and deal with reactions to the pursuit of given goals.

- *Are some goals more important to some groups than to others, and if so, what is the relative power of these groups?* When goals become the property of groups as well as individuals, organizational power is likely to come into play. The consequence is that sometimes relatively trivial goals receive an inordinate amount of attention because powerful groups own them, and goals more central to the life of the school are resource starved. Because power is almost always organized in support of the status quo, anyone who wants to introduce an innovation that requires substantially new goals must be prepared to disrupt existing authority systems and systems of power and status.

- *Do those who control the resources needed to support the pursuit of the goals know about the goals, and are they committed to the pursuit of these goals?* Frequently, those who control the flow of funds and establish budget categories (finance officers, for example) are not involved in the goal-setting processes and are therefore naïve about or not committed to the actions needed to support the goals. As a consequence, those who control budgets often become barriers to change rather than facilitators of change.

- *Do those who control organizational resources (that is, those who have authority and power) agree on the importance of specific goals and the priority the pursuit of these goals should receive?* For example, school boards sometimes endorse goals and priorities but then establish budgets that reflect little or no attention to these decisions.

- *How widespread in the school is awareness of the goals that are of concern, and how much commitment is there to these goals?* Sometimes goals are not met because those in charge of the actions needed to achieve the goals are unable to gain the cooperation of others whose support they need, precisely because these others were not made aware of the demands the goals would make on their own operations.

- *In terms of time spent and resources allocated, how much consistency is there between official priorities given to goals and actual school and school district operations?* One of the ways to detect the presence of structural lag, goal displacement, and lack of goal consensus is to develop detailed answers to this question.

- *How many different groups and agencies are ordinarily involved in or responsible for decisions and tasks in the area that is the target of the change?* The more groups that are involved, the greater the chances for competing loyalties.

- *To what extent are rewards (time, money, and status) provided to those who are asked to support the change?* People know what is expected by what is inspected, respected, and rewarded.

- *What proportion of the time of staff members expected to be involved in the change is committed to the change effort, and what proportion is given over to routine school activity?* Maintenance needs usually overwhelm developmental needs, and, given a choice, persons will give priority to doing what they have always done.

- *What is the supply relative to demand of persons with the leadership skills and commitment needed to persuade others to support and sustain the initiative?* Disruptive innovations require passionate advocates. The failure to develop such advocates often results in the abandonment of the innovation once the initial set of advocates disappears or loses enthusiasm.

- *What is the supply relative to demand of staff with the technical competence to support the new program or project and to do what needs to be done to ensure fidelity of implementation?* Disruptive innovations often fail because those who are expected to install the innovation do not possess the skills they need to act with fidelity and they are not given the training and ongoing support needed to ensure the success of the effort.

Chapter Nine

The Boundary System

The boundary system defines the resources and activities that the school (or any other organization) controls or attempts to control. The boundary system also defines the relationships between the school and individuals. For example, it defines who is a member of the life of the school and who is not. The boundary system also defines the areas of members' lives over which the school is entitled to exercise authority. The social life of the superintendent is more likely to be of concern to community leaders than is the social life of a part-time school bus driver. Similarly, this system is likely to place a wider range of demands on the building principal than on a classroom teacher.

Boundaries are almost always under dispute. Schools and other organizations frequently try to regulate the behavior of members and nonmembers in ways that some or all find undesirable enough to resist. Dress codes are examples of such regulations, as are requirements that teachers attend an in-service activity after school or on Saturday. Similarly, schools frequently make claims on resources that are resisted from within and disputed from without. For example, shifting from a ten-month calendar to a year-round school calendar may be resisted by some parents as an invasion of their private time with their children (time is a resource), and resisted by some teachers as a violation of the "rules" under which they entered teaching in the first place (specifically, the "rule" that long summer vacations would be a fringe benefit). Given these disputes, boundaries are almost never static.

Indeed, as things now stand the boundary systems of most schools and school districts require members, especially top-level leaders, to spend too much energy establishing and maintaining boundaries, which results in too little energy being left to support serious efforts at continuous improvement. The intent of the present chapter is to focus attention on these important matters.

Organizational Set

The way an organization is situated with regard to its external environment is a critical determinant of how life inside the organization can and will proceed. Some organizations are relatively isolated from the outside world; others have routine interactions with many groups and organizations. The number of organizations—that is, the *organizational set*—with which a school or school district interacts can have a dramatic impact on the way those in the school respond to change. Furthermore, the number of organizations with which schools and school districts interact varies much more than is commonly understood. For example, as I discussed in Chapter Eight, high schools generally have more difficulty establishing and maintaining direction than do elementary schools. In part this fact is attributable to their organizational set. High schools generally interact with many more powerful community organizations than elementary schools do.

The office of the superintendent, even more so than the office of the high school principal, must interact with a very wide range of groups and organizations, and many times these interactions contain the threat of real or perceived boundary invasions. Consequently, the office of the superintendent is confronted with particularly perplexing boundary problems, problems that in my experience, executives in private organizations find hard to understand. I have had many occasions to engage corporate executives in conversations about school governance, and almost without exception they are amazed that superintendents can get anything done inside the school district, because they must spend so much time serving the school board.

For example, in the context of corporate life the board is viewed for the most part as a part of the organization's executive structure. It is the function of the board to establish policy, to ensure that this policy is implemented with fidelity, and to hire and fire top-level executives. To the extent that the corporate board has a constituency, that constituency is, *or should be,* the stockholders (of course this ideal is often at variance with reality, as the case of Enron shows). The typical public school board functions very differently. Rather than seeing themselves as school district insiders, board members quite often see themselves as outsiders who represent the community to the district. The school board, as a unit, is not accountable for the operation of the schools. Rather, it is the mechanism by which the community holds the schools accountable. The school district, in this view, begins with the superintendent. The board is not a part of the district. Instead the job of the board is to oversee the schools. The culture of the schools has no claim on board members because their allegiance is not to the schools. Their allegiance (and membership) is to and with the factions and groups they believe they are elected to represent.

The result is that superintendents, unlike effective CEOs in the private sector, spend much more time in efforts to respond to and satisfy the board than they spend in creating organizations oriented toward satisfying customers (students and parents.) Furthermore, given the available research and my personal experience, it is clear to me that most superintendents spend a great deal more time than most of them would like engaged in board-related activity—for example, preparing agendas, conferring with individual board members, investigating issues of concern to individual board members and meeting with the board in general sessions. Indeed, some superintendents (all from large urban districts) have reported to me that they spend up to 75 percent of their time in such activities. Other superintendents report spending less than 15 percent of their time on these activities, but they are always from small, relatively stable rural districts.

High school principals are in a similar situation. Dealing with issues associated with boundary spanning and boundary control consumes much of their energy that could be better spent driving change through the school. Indeed, one of the classic laments of high school principals is that they spend so much time dealing with outside groups and agencies (including the school district central office) that they do not have time to do what they think they should be doing as instructional leaders and as leaders of instructors.

Boundary Extensiveness

Boundary extensiveness has to do with the range of activities and resources over which an organization attempts to exercise control or exert influence and with the level of detail it gives to these concerns. For example, in the early days of basic training the military services make a concerted effort to regulate and control nearly every aspect of the life of the recruit. Thus the boundaries of most boot camps are extensive indeed and bear upon almost all aspects of social life. Other organizations have much less extensive boundaries. For example, to be a member of the Democratic or Republican party, all one needs to do is to register one's name. It is assumed that members have certain predilections toward issues, but there is no requirement that they do, nor is there a mechanism to police and enforce the assumption. Even in the case of political parties, however, there are some people who are more firmly inside the organization than others. Volunteers make up much of the actual workforce in political parties; however, paid campaign workers and support staff are more central to the life of a party, and parties are able to exert much more control over the latter and to use more effective sanctions to move their actions in a desired direction. Volunteers do not have to show up; paid workers do. Volunteers are more apt to stray from the party line than are paid workers. Volunteers are not apt to be brought in on and made privy to high-level strategy sessions; paid employees call such meetings.

Schools, like political parties, vary in terms of boundary extensiveness, define different classes of members, and afford different rights, duties, and privileges of membership to those different classes. Like other boundary matters, the issue of extensiveness is sometimes not adequately attended to when leaders are thinking about issues related to school change. For example, extending the school year or the school day or even changing homework policies involves boundary claims. When more homework is assigned, the school is claiming the right to control more of the students' time than it has controlled in the past. Parents who share the values associated with such initiatives may be supportive of such claims; others may not.

Any assumption that those who are not supportive of such claims are not supportive of the schools or that they do not care about the future of their children may be mistaken. Sometimes there are other values at stake, values that some parents hold more sacred than the values advanced by the schooling enterprise. For example, I once conducted a study of parental reaction to year-round school in a school district that was implementing a year-round program of forty-five-day sessions and fifteen-day vacations. Among the more interesting findings was that the parents most likely to resist the program and find it unsatisfactory were blue-collar parents who had inflexible vacation schedules and who felt the year-round program infringed on family time they held to be sacred.

It is also important to understand that boundary extensiveness has as much to do with the moral order of schools (judgments about what is right and wrong, just and unjust, equitable and inequitable) as with technical issues or even local customs and conventions. For example, what appears on the surface to be simply a matter of local taste and custom (for example, wearing a hat or cap in the classroom) often gets escalated into an issue of equity, justice, and tolerance for cultural differences. Thus changing the extensiveness of school boundaries often, perhaps always, involves changing the moral knowledge on which schools are based.

Boundary Permeability

Permeability refers to the ability of groups and organizations perceived to be outside the organization to direct action inside the organization. One area of marked differences between most private corporations and most schools has to do with the permeability of the boundaries and where that permeability is most likely to be displayed. For the most part, in the corporate world the top or center of the organization is relatively well insulated from *direct* outside influence, including customer influence; some would say too much so. Few corporate board members see themselves as advocates for constituency groups, with the exception of persons placed on the board as a result of a union contract negotiation or consumer advocates appointed to satisfy a drive toward consumerism. (However, recent corporate scandals may result in some changes here, in response to the argument that one of the problems in corporate America is too much unchecked authority.) The result is that those at the top are able to spend a great deal of time developing strategy and communicating and reinforcing intentions throughout the organization.

In schools the situation is generally the opposite. The boundaries of the school organization are more permeable at the top than at the bottom. Indeed, as they are now constituted, school boards are structural mechanisms designed to support boundary incursions and to give full play to the interests others might have in controlling the people and resources over which school officials also want to exercise some authority. Interest groups, ranging from the teachers' union to the religious right, are sometimes organized to elect board members. When board members elected in this manner are seated, they tend to represent the interests that elected them. This does no particular harm if the community in which the school district is embedded is relatively homogeneous in interests and values. It is a disaster when there is wide diversity. It is for this reason that superintendents in small rural districts are often less concerned about governance issues than are superintendents in, for example, Dallas, Los Angeles, Fort Lauderdale, Cleveland, and Chicago.

Some critics of schools see this as an irremediable problem: one that precludes the possibility of real reform in schools as long as the schools are submitted to principles of democratic governance. What is needed, some argue, is a mechanism that makes schools responsive to market forces rather than political forces. John Chubb and Terry Moe are the most persuasive presenters of this argument.[1] Though I do not agree with their recommended solution, I do agree with their conclusion that real reform cannot proceed so long as the present system of governance is in place. *Indeed, I would assert that until this matter is dealt with, all other efforts at reform will accomplish much less than must be accomplished to satisfy the conditions of the twenty-first century.*

Because they are a part of the political fabric of the community, the short-term interests of factions, groups, and parties necessarily influence schools. For example, parents living in one area may find their interest best served by having a new high school built close to them, whereas the senior citizens in the area would prefer to have the high school located elsewhere. Local contractors want the school to give preference to purchasing from local

---

[1] J. E. Chubb and T. M. Moe, *Politics, Markets and America's Schools* (Washington, D.C.: Brookings Institution, 1990).

providers, and the taxpayers' union wants the school district to seek the lowest bidders, wherever they are.

As actors in our economic system, schools are peculiarly vulnerable to being co-opted to serve the needs and interests of the more powerful members of the economic community, sometimes at the expense of those who are less powerful. Similarly, those who would foster social change in the community sometimes try to co-opt the schools to serve their ends and achieve their goals. For example, as one of the largest employers in the community, school boards are likely to be under considerable pressure to make sure that their hiring practices and promotion policies are responsive to the patronage needs of various local factions and local groups. At the same time, they are under pressure to ensure that those who are hired are the most able and most qualified of all the available candidates.

School boards are usually very good at responding to the political and economic pressures exerted by the community, and when their response is lacking the electoral process usually corrects the problem. Where school boards often fail is in looking out for the long-term interest of the community generally and in ensuring that the decisions they make to satisfy the short-term demands of factions and groups also reflect the deepest beliefs and abiding values and aspirations of the community at large. *Put bluntly, school boards are good at balancing the short-term needs of the interests, factions, and groups that exist in the community, but they are not necessarily good at building a larger sense of community among those diverse, competing, and sometimes antagonistic forces. It is as moral institutions that school boards are most likely to fail.* And it is because of this failure that schools are so often judged to be operational failures as well. In the effort to satisfy everyone, the schools wind up satisfying no one.

As moral institutions the schools must be protected from the harmful effects of factions, groups, and parties when these interests threaten core values and the common good. Without such protection, school boards and those who work in schools have little option but to respond to the immediate pressures they feel from this or that constituency, even though doing so may result in doing harm to values they might otherwise want to uphold and embrace.

If systemic change is to occur, it is essential to build systems that support the change. These systems must be sufficiently integrated into the existing boundaries of the school or school district undergoing change that those who operate in it are accountable for being responsive to the needs of those empowered to direct the change effort. At the same time, the systems designed to support the change initiative must be sufficiently independent of the authority systems that maintain the present direction and manage existing programs to avoid co-optation of effort. Without such independence, the maintenance needs of the present system will almost certainly overwhelm the developmental needs of the systems that are struggling to emerge.

In my view there are a number of remedies that might address the real issue involved here—namely, ensuring that schools and school districts are accountable to their individual communities and all the diverse interests represented in those communities and that they maintain a course of continuously improving the quality of the experiences provided to students as well as providing the responsiveness to the needs of parents. Such solutions would, however, call on state legislatures to take actions that would threaten the short-term interests of powerful groups, including some of the more reactionary members of state and national school board associations.

Though I agree with Seymour Sarason[2] when he asserts that the issue of governance is far too complex to be dealt with by any one individual, I have had the audacity to advance a couple of proposals with the potential of addressing this issue. The first proposal is to treat the school district as a regulated monopoly, governed as such monopolies are governed.[3] The second proposal is to move the charter school concept up to the district level and permit the community to charter the district and a board to lead and manage the district, rather than chartering individual schools.[4]

Recently, I have become aware of an embryonic development in Chattanooga, Tennessee, that suggests a system that might be developed that would protect developmental resources while respecting the internal integrity of the existing system (note, how-

---

[2] S. Sarason, "Some Features of a Flawed Educational System," *Daedalus*, 1998, *127*(4), 1–12.

[3] P. C. Schlechty, "Education Services as a Regulated Monopoly," *Education Week*, Apr. 10, 1991, p. 36.

[4] P. C. Schlechty, *Inventing Better Schools: An Action Plan for Educational Reform* (San Francisco: Jossey-Bass, 1997).

ever, that this system is not nearly as formalized as my presentation may make it appear—for example, there is as yet no formal governance structure to support the emerging cooperative action of the various community groups involved). Specifically, under the leadership of a nonprofit corporation established with the express purpose of promoting change and improvement in the Chattanooga schools, two local foundations—and to some extent the mayor's office—have begun to work cooperatively to provide funding and support to a school improvement initiative aimed at improving the performance of ten low-performing schools. The governance of this budding consortium is independent of the school district. The linkage to the district is a type of partnership arrangement that among other things causes the district to make the way developmental funds are being expended more transparent than has been the case in the past. Furthermore, it has caused school district officials to be more aggressive in considering how these funds might be redirected to support the intentions of the new initiative.

What seems to be happening in Chattanooga may appear on the surface to be little different from other consortia arrangements made over the past twenty years in the effort to improve America's system of education. This may be so, but what the Chattanooga experience suggests to me is the possibility of creating a community organization (a consortium formed as a nonprofit organization) that is independent of the school district, and then engaging the consortium in a partnership with the district. This would be quite different from creating a consortium in which the school district is a member.[5]

Boundary Maintenance and Boundary Invasions

Schools, to use Willard Waller's term, are in a state of perilous equilibrium.[6] Schools attempt to control the behavior and sometimes the sentiments of one of the most precious resources in the community—children and young adults. As the educational sloganeers sometimes

---

[5] I have suggested this idea to leaders in several urban communities. So far no one has taken the idea seriously. It is likely, however, that the next book I write will deal with this subject, if for no other reason than that I believe it to be so important.

[6] W. Waller, *The Sociology of Teaching* (New York: Wiley, 1967). (Originally published 1932).

say, "We build the future every day." There are many groups and interests concerned with what that future will be, what students come to know, and how they come to know it. These interests are not always in agreement among themselves to say nothing of being in agreement with the direction endorsed by school faculties and top-level school leaders. The consequence is that school leaders often become adept at resisting efforts by these groups and constituencies to control action in the schools. Under the present circumstances, this may be necessary for organizational survival, but it is certainly not what is needed to create the kind of flexible and responsive organizations required to handle change easily and with style.

Without a doubt, parent groups can be a source of valuable input into school district and schoolhouse policy and a source of valuable information about parents' concerns. Unfortunately, parent organizations can also be a means of focusing parent leaders on those organizations and shifting dialogue about conflicts away from the school door and into committees that have little official authority in the school.

Recall, for example, the superintendent I quoted in Chapter Eight, who told me he had always encouraged activist parents of high school students to join the band boosters and the athletic boosters. He also told me he always gave these organizations much to do and responded almost slavishly to their recommendations for changes in the athletic programs or the music program (including the hiring and firing of coaches and band directors). I have heard many superintendents and many principals make similar statements. The justification this particular superintendent used for this strategy is that it tends to keep more-activist parents occupied and reduces interference with what really counts—the instructional program. As he once put the matter, "Sacrificing a coach or two is a small price to pay to ensure that teachers and principals will be able to do their jobs." Cynical? Perhaps! But it is a cynicism born out of a deep understanding of the way schools are now organized. The threat of boundary incursions at the top makes it hard for schools to do their business even when their leaders have a pretty clear notion of what that business is. Indeed, for many school leaders the business of the school becomes maintaining boundaries so that some modicum of what needs to be done to educate children gets done *in spite of the system.*

The strategies school leaders use to maintain boundaries are usually not articulated and sometimes not recognized, even by those who create and employ them. For example, I know of one school district where there is a particularly militant and adversarial union and where it is common practice to offer executive directors of the union (a National Education Association affiliate) top-level administrative positions in the district. I have no doubt there are good reasons for this pattern; for example, a former executive director is likely to be able to call on some residual goodwill from the union, which might ease tensions in hard-fought negotiations. However, it is also possible that this strategy carries with it the message that if the present executive director does not push matters too far, he or she too can wind up in a corner office with a plush carpet on the floor. Indeed, in this district one of the complaints principals have is that those who were once "big in the union" have too much control of central office matters and tend to resolve issues in the union's interest and sometimes to the detriment of students.

Of course many strategies for maintaining boundaries are recognized and articulated. One is most likely to hear about these strategies in those frequent informal sessions where superintendents and principals share tricks of the trade with each other. I have been a participant in many such conversations for over forty years, and what I have learned persuades me that in many schools and school districts, the situation is pretty much as I describe it here. Indeed, some of these strategies are so patently manipulative that to acknowledge conscious use of them to anyone who is not in the know and similarly situated would be tantamount to confessing to organizational sin. It is, however, a sin many good men and women feel obliged to commit in order to be able to do as well as they can for students.

Schools and Communities

The traditional views of the relationship between schools and the community were formed at a time when the majority of the community consisted of parents who had children in school. This is no longer the case. In many communities, a majority of adults do not have children in school, public or private, and this majority is growing. Thus the ability of the school to respond to the community is conditioned by the understanding school leaders have of the community that is to be served. Those who take an expansive view (as I do) believe that all citizens have the right to make claims on the school and should in turn be obliged to support the schools financially as well as personally; those who take a less expansive view would limit nonparents' support.

The traditional view of students and parents derives from a body of moral understandings in which the function of the school is seen as largely concerned with transmitting a common culture and ensuring that the citizenry is sufficiently literate to fulfill civic functions.[7] This view assumes, therefore, that the student is an insider in the organization of the school, with rights and duties, but that those rights and duties are more like those of a neophyte being inducted into the tribe than like those of an individual in a democratic social order. Our society has changed in ways that make this view difficult to sustain, but it persists in the "tribal memory" as a preferred way of operating. In urban areas, few in the community really know who the teachers are, where they live, where they go to church (or if they go to church), what their lifestyle is, and so on. Indeed, many teachers would argue that such matters are not the business of schools or of parents. Yet teachers lament the fact that teachers no longer get the respect they were once afforded. Teachers sometimes forget that this respect was based partly on the myth that teachers and parents agreed about the welfare of children. This myth has been difficult to maintain when parents sue teachers and when teachers are, by law, expected to report suspected cases of child abuse.

I am not arguing that the legal rights of parents should be abrogated or that teachers should have no responsibility when child abuse is suspected. Rather, I am arguing that if the relationships between teachers and parents and students are to be productive, then the moral knowledge that serves as a base for defining that relationship must change in ways that address present realities.

---

[7] See P. C. Schlechty, *Schools for the 21st Century: Leadership Imperatives for Educational Reform* (San Francisco: Jossey-Bass, 1990).

It must be understood, for example, that unless some proactive strategy is developed to address this matter, teachers and parents will for the most part be strangers to one another. Similarly, unless systematic strategies are developed to address this issue, schools that were once the focal point of much community activity will lose out in the competition for the attention of students and of parents as well.[8] The fact is that many parents, especially of high school age students, do not attend any type of school function. Even participation in the PTA is declining. It seems also that for many students the school has ceased to be the center of social life and social activity. The relationships that seem important are increasingly those established in the shopping mall, on the streets, or in the neighborhood.[9]

There are of course many groups that want to use the schools and their facilities. However, these uses typically have little to do with the core business of the schools, and some have little prospect of being in any way educational. Furthermore, responding to requests to use the schools for noneducational purposes often involves school leaders in conflicts with the very community leaders they are trying to serve. Indeed, one of the reasons that some school leaders give for closing the doors to community groups who want to use the school is that the claims for use are likely to be so disruptive and controversial that it is just easier to say no to everyone. It is not hard to imagine the conflict that might arise from simultaneously considering requests for space from a gay rights group and a newly formed Pentecostal sect. Neither is it hard to imagine one group of community activists protesting because another group that is using the school represents views that the

---

[8] For many small rural schools even today, the surrounding community is sufficiently homogeneous that deciding which religious holidays to honor is simple—Christmas and Easter. The primary scheduling conflict for night activities is the Wednesday night prayer meeting at the local church. Things are not so simple in urban schools and school districts, and they are becoming less so in smaller school districts as well.

[9] This is clearly not yet the case in all schools, but as Patricia Hersch makes clear, this characterization is not limited to large urban high schools; see P. Hersch, *A Tribe Apart: A Journey into the Heart of American Adolescence* (New York: Fawcett Columbine, 1998).

first group opposes, or filing lawsuits because advocacy of the first group's ideas in schools might be judged unconstitutional.

A Need for Redefinition

In spite of the concept of *in loco parentis,* teachers never had the authority of the parent. Furthermore, the authority the community and parents are willing to grant teachers has always been tenuous and in doubt.[10] Today, growing numbers of parents view teachers as nothing more nor less than civil service employees, deriving whatever authority they have from their position in a government-run bureaucracy rather than from their position in the moral order of the community. In many communities, especially urban communities, teachers are moving from being members of the priestly class to being members of officialdom.

At the same time, many teachers define parental support in terms of the degree to which parents are willing to ensure that their children comply with whatever request or demand the teacher imposes on their child. Supportive parents ensure that students do their homework, come to school on time, and speak respectfully to adults; they are willing to accept disciplinary actions taken when their child misbehaves, and so on. Nonsupportive parents are parents who sometimes challenge, on behalf of their children, the meaning and significance of the homework the teacher provides or the assignments given. Nonsupportive parents are parents who challenge the school's right to discipline their child through the application of such coercive means as suspension or expulsion from the school or exclusion from desired activities and programs (for example, making academic performance a condition of participating in athletic programs).

One of the attractions of public schools that function on traditional principles is that such schools promise to go back to a time when teachers and parents enjoyed relatively equal positions in the community authority system that defined the relationship between children, youths, and adults. However, the problem with the traditional school concept in the modern context is that the community

---

[10] See Waller, *The Sociology of Teaching.*

has changed as well. It is adult authority in general that has been eroded, not just the authority of teachers and of parents.[11] Similarly, the professionalization of teaching has tended to reinforce teachers' view that they are, or should be, the experts on what students need to know and how best to get them to know those things. The job of the parent is to ensure that the student's medicine is taken as prescribed. It is not the job of the parent to interfere in the treatment.

All of this results in a situation where teachers see lack of parental support as one of the major sources of the failure of the schools, and increasing numbers of parents see the "educrats," by which they mean unionized teachers as well as administrators, as the source of the problems they and their children are experiencing.

What is needed is a redefinition of the boundary positions of both parents and students. This redefinition must honor the fact that parents have a special position in the constellation of school life. It must also recognize that students have obligations to the school just as the school and teachers have obligations to the students. Students and teachers alike must accept responsibility for performance and achievement, as must principals, superintendents, and boards of education. This means that both parents and students must be defined as types of school district insiders. Two key questions must be answered by this definition:

- Should parents simply be one group among the broad class of persons that policy analysts sometimes refer to as *stakeholders,* or is the relationship between schools and parents more personal and important than the idea of stakeholders suggests?
- Is the student a client to be served (much as doctors and lawyers serve clients), or is it better to think of the student as a worker in the school or perhaps as a full-fledged member of a democratic community? Might children be better served if they were viewed as first-line customers whose interests and needs are at the heart of the enterprise?

There are of course no absolute answers to these questions, but leaders of school reform must work out answers that will satisfy

---

[11] See, for example, Hersch, *A Tribe Apart.*

themselves and the vast majority of the members of the communities of which the schools are a part.

Redefining the Boundary Position of Students

The reader familiar with my earlier books will know how I would answer these questions. The idea that guides my own notion of how schools should be organized (the idea of the student as first-line customer) begins with the assumption that students are volunteers. Whether or not the student and his or her parents chose the school the student attends is beside the point. Even after parents have chosen a school, it is still left to the student to choose whether or how he or she will relate to the tasks assigned and the performance standards set forth. Through coercive measures some schools are more effective than are others at gaining compliance, but compliance is not authentic engagement. Engagement requires commitment, and commitment cannot be commanded; it must be earned.

The traditional view of teachers as coequals with parents, entitled to the same respect and unquestioning obedience assumed by the traditional view of the parent role, reinforces teachers' view that students owe teachers their attention and their commitment as well. Unfortunately, many students are not willing to pay up, or at least not in full. Some simply retreat, some engage in ritual compliance, some redirect their energies to other pursuits (for example, gang activity), and some openly rebel against the expectations of the schools. Indeed, it is the struggle between teachers' assumption of traditional adult authority and the drive of the students for independence from that authority that shapes much of the dynamic of the relationship between students and schools.

The fact that students on some occasions refuse to comply with the authority of teachers is not new. What is new is that compliance and attendance are no longer enough, and even if they were, the coercive measures available to teachers to gain compliance are increasingly limited by parents and the larger society. Corporal punishment did not gain commitment or even increase engagement, but it did beat some rebellious students into submission and set an example for the less rebellious though equally disengaged. Modern schools must engage students, not simply ensure that students submit to authority, because it is only through engagement that the high levels of learning that many in the community want can be achieved.

Properly understood, customers are inside the organization— not apart from it. Customers make demands on the organization, but the organization is in a position to make demands on the customers as well. For example, I am preparing this manuscript on a computer programmed with Microsoft Word. I use this program basically as a substitute for a typewriter with the added benefit of built-in cut-and-paste capacity. Many of those who work with me at the Schlechty Center for Leadership in School Reform have taken the time to learn what they need to learn to get much more out of their computers than I get out of mine. The fact is, in my hands Microsoft Word is not a high-quality product. It represents only slight, though important, improvements over my old IBM electric typewriter. As I watch my colleagues use the same program and get so much more from what they do, I know that the reason I am not getting what they are is that I have yet to find the motivation I need to engage in those tasks through which I would learn what I need to know to use the computer well. I have yet to attend a class, read a manual, or view a training tape on the subject; it is my loss, but also my responsibility.

Defining the student as customer does not excuse the student from responsibility. It simply redefines that responsibility. In terms of schoolwork the bargain is a simple one. The school and the teachers promise students and parents that they will strive to create work that students find to be engaging, and students and parents promise that when such work is provided, they will expend whatever effort is required to learn what needs to be learned to achieve the goals toward which the work is directed. Defining the role of students in this way necessitates a redefinition of the role of parents and the larger community. It is commonplace to apply the word *partner* to parents, hoping, I suppose, to indicate the mutual interest parents and teachers have in the welfare of each child. It is often suggested that the various community groups should be viewed as stakeholders, which I surmise means something like the stockholders in a corporation.

Such definitions, if acted on, would certainly be preferable to the idea of the parent as friendly stranger or natural enemy. Referring to community groups as stakeholders does clearly imply that the interest in what students accomplish goes well beyond the interests of parents. There are, however, some problems with these definitions. To consider parents as partners is to assume that each parent has, and understands that he or she has, an interest in the education of all children, not just his or her own. Some parents may be willing to adopt such an expansive view. Many are not. They see the interests of other children only through the interests of their own child. This is as it should be. To expect parents to put the interests of other children ahead of their child's interests is to expect what never was and never shall be. Furthermore, to expect a teacher to know a child as well as a parent does or to care about and for the child in the same way as a parent does is to expect more than can be or should be.

I know these statements fly in the face of a strong pretense structure that defines the ideal relationship between parents and teachers as always happy, harmonious, and cooperative. It can be so but not if we expect parents and teachers to have the same interests in the child and the success of the child or if we expect that teachers and parents will relate to students and schools in the same way. Parents are not full insiders in the life of the school as their children are. Parents are not direct customers of the school—unless one considers the delivery of custodial care for children the primary purpose of the school and the provision of engaging experiences for children a secondary concern. The interest parents have in the school is always filtered through a second party—namely, their children. The interest teachers have in parents is also always filtered through a second party—namely, their students.

Adults who have no children in a school usually do not have the same interest as parents in what is going on in the school. Teachers who are focused on their students and the needs of those students are naturally more concerned about the parents of those students than they are about other members of the community. What is needed, I believe, is a definition of the role of the parent and other members of the community that will take these realities into account and at the same time honor the importance of parents and the centrality of students in the organization of the school. The idea of the parent as *guarantor* seems to me to fit what is needed.

I first heard about this simple notion in the context of health care. Individuals receiving direct services (such as patients in hospitals or students in schools) are not in a position to carry out all that is required of them to benefit fully from the services provided. They need outside parties to guarantee that the needed supports will be available. For example, for patients in general, private insurance companies, Medicaid, and Medicare are designed to guarantee financial support. For patients who are senior citizens, families, perhaps working in cooperation with extended care facilities, are expected to guarantee reasonable care and support once the patient is dismissed from the hospital. The hospital assumes responsibility for ensuring that the patient has an outside support system in place, but it is that outside system that is expected to actually provide the support. Even though such assumptions and expectations may fall short of reality in this imperfect world, the concept of ensuring needed supports is a good one.

Viewing parents as guarantors would focus attention on the relationship between the parent and the child rather than on the relationship between the parent and the school. The promises (guarantees) the parent would make to the school would address what would be done on behalf of the student and what would be done for the student; they would not be promises as to what would be done on behalf of the school. This idea recognizes that parents are in a unique position vis-à-vis their children, and that they have unique interests in and unique authority over the child. Teachers cannot ensure that children will come to school at all, let alone come to school well fed and properly clothed. Generally speaking, parents can do these things, and when they cannot, there should be community agencies in place to provide the guarantees needed.

Almost all parents are in a position to affirm the importance of school to their children through such simple devices as routinely asking their children to talk with them about school, what the children do there, and so on. Those children who do not have parents who are in a position to guarantee this kind of support should be provided other adults who are willing and able to provide it, and the school should endeavor to ensure that such adults are available. (Mentor programs are illustrative of such efforts.) The key here is that the concern would be with parental and community support of children rather than parental and community support of schools. As citizens, and therefore as community stakeholders, parents have a right to be concerned about the schools themselves, and they should expect the schools to be accountable to them. But the schools should be no more accountable to parents than to any other group of adult taxpayers in the community. The role of parent as guarantor focuses on what the parent will do for the child, and what the community will do for the child when the parent cannot or will not do what the child needs. Parents are, or should be, accountable to the community for guaranteeing that their children have the support needed to do well in school, just as the schools should be accountable to the community for ensuring that the experiences the school provides are responsive to the needs of all children.

If parents were guarantors, the community would have an obligation to articulate what it expects parents to guarantee, and it would then hold parents accountable for providing those things—or seeing to it that those things were provided. However, the point of accountability would be to the community, not to the schools. The schools have no control over parents, nor should they have. But all citizens have, or should have, an interest in children and the kind of support they are receiving—both in the school and in the home. The point of parental accountability should be to the community rather than to the schools. For example, the court system in Jefferson County, Kentucky, takes action against parents whose children have poor attendance records. Though this approach is not without problems—poor parents are more likely to be called into court than are affluent parents—the program does demonstrate the idea of community responsibility for student performance and parent accountability to the community.

What all this means in practice is still to be worked out. My present inclination is to suggest that some sort of a student support standards board should be established and charged with the responsibility of identifying those things all students must be guaranteed to be successful in school—ranging from such subtle things as having some adult who cares about their education and takes the time to express this concern to such obvious matters as being ensured safety on the way to and from school, having adequate food, clothing, and shelter, and so on.

Both schools and parents must be held accountable for meeting the needs of children and, through them, the needs of the future. The only way I know to accomplish this end is to hold parents and other adults in the lives of children accountable for providing the young the support they need to do well in school and to hold schools accountable for providing the young with engaging experiences from which they learn what the community has determined they need to learn. Parents should not be accountable to schools any more than schools should be accountable to parents. Both, however, should be accountable to a community that also has an interest in ensuring that all citizens are well educated and that the society in which we all live is a just and compassionate one ruled by democratic principles rather than principles based strictly on short-term self-interest and instant gratification.[12]

Implications for School Reform

As I discussed earlier, the number of organizations with which schools and school districts interact (the organizational set) shapes the way schools respond to change and to the possibilities of change. On the one hand, having meaningful access to a wide range of groups and organizations can be a source of vitality and tremendous support for those who are serious about change. On the other hand, the threats these organizations can pose to the ability of school leaders to establish and maintain a constant direction is real—so real that some have argued that real improvement in schools cannot occur unless and until this condition is remedied.

---

[12] The idea of *citizenship* has somehow fallen into disuse in recent years. Perhaps that is because citizenship carries with it notions of duty, obligation, and selflessness that seem somehow to have gone out of fashion. I do not think public education can work unless the idea of citizenship is reinstated to a place of prominence. The idea of *stakeholders* places emphasis on self-interests. The idea of *citizens* places emphasis on the common good. Public education is about the common good as well as about individual benefit. As parents, adults are rightly concerned about the benefit of school to their individual child. As citizens, parents and nonparents alike must be concerned about the common good.

The first implication of an analysis of the boundary system, therefore, is that something must be done to ensure that those who lead school reform have enough control over resources and personnel to establish and maintain direction and to be persistent in the pursuit of that direction. At the same time, the boundaries must be defined in such a way that school leaders are accountable to the community at large while also upholding the primary value of being responsive to the needs of students and their parents. This is not an issue that can be dealt with by local leaders alone. It needs to be dealt with at the state level. It will require cooperative action among state and national organizations such as the National School Boards Association, the American Association of School Administrators, the American Federation of Teachers, and the National Education Association. It will require, furthermore, that the leaders of these organizations look beyond the short-term and immediate interests of the more change-averse in their membership and concentrate instead on what is good for students and what is needed to ensure the continuation of local community control of schools while ensuring that no child is denied the benefit of a high-quality educational experience simply because of the locality in which he or she lives or the circumstances into which he or she was born.

A second implication of a serious analysis of boundaries is this: it is likely it will be discovered that for many adults and an increasing number of students the public schools of America, especially the high schools, are no longer in a position to make many claims on those who interact with the schools. Furthermore, the claims that are made are more likely to be maintained through coercion and some forms of remuneration (such as grades) than through persuasion and reference to shared values, what I referred to earlier as the exercise of normative power. For example, fear of physical violence in the schools is changing patterns of interaction within schools and between schools and the larger environment. Requiring students to pass through metal detectors to enter a school may be necessary, but it does little to offset the image of school as a depersonalized environment unfriendly to both those who are known and to strangers. School uniforms may serve some valued functions, but they also run directly counter to the emerging norms of the larger society, which teach adolescents that their personal attire is an expression of who they are and who they see themselves as being.[13]

These problems cannot be addressed successfully until and unless schools become community-building agencies as well as community-serving agencies. It is not enough for schools to be responsive to the needs of parents and students; school leaders must develop skills in helping parents and students develop a sense of community among themselves as well as between themselves and the schools. Included in this equation must be attention to developing among the majority who do not have children in school a sense of belonging in the schools and a sense of ownership for the education of children who are not their own and who in many cases look very different from the way their children might look.

Schools cannot serve communities if there is no community to serve. Community building as well as community serving must become a part of the skill base for anyone who aspires to a position of leadership in America's public schools.

Finally, careful consideration of boundary systems and issues related to boundaries will make it clear that the way the boundary positions of individuals and groups of individuals come to be defined goes far to explain much that occurs within schools as well as between schools and the larger environment. For example, schools that define parents as insiders and schools that define them as outsiders will relate to parents differently. Schools that define parents as partners and schools that define them as natural enemies or as strangers will treat parents differently.

Boundary definitions are not, however, up to the school and its leaders alone. Those who are expected to accept the definitions must be willing to take part in creating them. Otherwise confusion and organizational dysfunction will occur. For example, it is commonplace for school leaders to assert the need for greater parental involvement and to place numerous signs in school buildings to that effect and to hand out bumper stickers that declare, "Parents Are our Partners." Yet when these "partners" make system demands that are perceived as illegitimate by teachers or school administrators, the idea of partnership quickly breaks down, and parents

---

[13] See, for example, Hersch, *A Tribe Apart.*

(at least the offending parents) are redefined as outsiders—and perhaps as even hostile outsiders.

In cases such as these, it is clear that school officials and parents have very different definitions of the meaning of the word *partner.* Conflicts emerge that could have been avoided if the time had been taken to articulate and communicate common definitions of key words that are sometimes used loosely. Preemptive measures such as formulating a clear statement of parent rights, duties, and expectations along with mechanisms for enforcement can go a long way toward resolving conflicts before they occur. It is not a trivial matter to consider how students and parents should be viewed in the schools.

Key Questions

Boundary issues are complex and sometimes difficult to understand. Yet the boundary system, perhaps more than any other system, determines what will go on inside the schools as well as between schools and other groups, organizations, and individuals. What, then, are some of the key questions a leader should ask when trying to get a fix on the nature of the boundary system of a school or school district? The following are the questions I have found to be useful:

- *What is the source of legal control? For example, does state law or federal law apply directly to the school or department, or does it apply only to the school district, leaving the district to uphold the law through policies and other systems of accountability?* Some of the most vexing issues confronting those who want to improve the performance of schools arise from the sometimes contradictory demands made on the schools by the various agencies that exercise some degree of legal control over school operations. For example, in some states, county commissioners control local funding of schools whereas the operation of the schools is under the direction of an elected or appointed school board. Similarly, though local control of schools is still a preachment among educators and politicians, the fact is that over the past fifty years, both the state and the federal government have become increasingly willing to intervene in the operation of schools. Even Orwellian language that suggests otherwise cannot conceal the fact that the No Child Left Behind legislation seriously erodes the power of the state and the local community to give direction to their schools and to reform efforts. As a result many feel powerless to do what they believe they should do to improve the schools, simply because they are too busy doing what they must do. Though I have some sympathy with this view, I also know that school leaders who understand the nature of the business they are leading and who are committed to serving students often find ways to use law and policy to move schools in directions not anticipated, or even understood, by those who have promulgated these laws and regulations. To do this, however, the leader must have a clear understanding of the sources of legal control that affect schools.

- *What are the group and organizational loyalties of the different types of insiders, and to which of these multiple organizations do they give their primary loyalty? For example, do teachers see themselves first as union members and second as school district employees? Is the principal's primary allegiance to his or her school, or does the principal view himself or herself first as a school district employee?* The idea that the schoolhouse rather than the school district should be the focus of concern for school reformers has a long history in education. As reformers are coming to understand, however, the schoolhouse exists in a complex set of relationships within some governmental unit (usually a school district), and the way this unit is related to the school goes far to determine whether there is a school system or a system of independent schools. A case can be made for either outcome, but the case needs to be made rationally and purposefully. Too often, this is not what happens, and persons with powerful loyalties to constituencies outside the schools set the direction of the school system, sometimes without even recognizing that they are doing so.

- *Where does the money come from to operate the schools? For example, how much state, local, and federal money supports programs in a given school, and, conversely, how dependent are local school programs on voluntary contributions by the PTA, affluent parents, private foundations, or businesses?* The amount of private money committed to support public education initiatives increased substantially between 1980 and 2000. Some believe that the motives for this increased funding were not always altruistic and pure, and probably that fear is in some cases justified. Nonetheless there are many instances in which private dollars have made it possible to do positive things in public schools that could not have been done with public dollars. For example, it is very difficult to use government funds for developmental purposes, if for no other reasons than that funding cycles and accountability systems carry with them bureaucratic assumptions that cannot be honored in a full-blown developmental effort where success is uncertain and timelines are at best only estimates. The National Science Foundation and NASA were both created to try to offset the problems inherent in government control of developmental programs. As history has shown, however, when the source of funding is exclusively governmental, there is a tendency for even these agencies to become increasingly risk averse and more and more bureaucratic in their operation. Sometimes communities have taken on the task of creating an extragovernmental agency (for example, an education foundation) that can provide more flexible funding and more flexible timelines than might be available in the existing district. When properly used, such a system can serve as a true catalyst for change. The Chattanooga situation described previously is illustrative of such an effort. What I find most intriguing about this model is that the collaborative is totally independent of the school district and totally dependent on private sources for funding. Leaders of the collaborative use this funding to support programs and projects for which they negotiate partnership arrangements with the schools. Among other things, such partnerships can counter schools' tendency to use developmental resources to support maintenance activity.

- *To what extent are those who are most fully inside the school district (for example, the superintendent, principals, and school board members) expected to be directly responsive to and accountable to various interest groups in the community as well as to parents and to students? How is this responsiveness ensured?* Responsiveness and accountability are two distinct concepts. *Responsiveness* has to do with the willingness and ability to take needs and concerns of others into account when making decisions. *Accountability* has to do with the willingness and ability to do those things that are expected and required. In a community where quality education is an important value, the community at large should hold the schools accountable for being responsive to all parents and to all children. The community should not, however, expect the schools to be responsive to the groups and factions that make up the community.

- *If insiders are not expected to be directly responsive to interest groups and factions, then how is accountability established and maintained, and what mechanisms are in place to protect insiders from dysfunctional conflicts with these outside groups?* This is one of the most perplexing problems to confront those who would redesign America's system of education. To date, I know of no clear answer to this problem, but in the last chapter of this book I will offer some suggestions regarding ways communities and school leaders might move toward developing an answer to this question.

- *What behavioral expectations are assumed to be legitimate for different groups in the employ of the school or functioning in and around the school as relatively independent operatives?* Is the school district inclined to expect the principal to attend athletic events or the teachers to chaperone dances? Are such expectations considered legitimate by those to whom they apply? If so, are such expectations rationalized in terms of their connection to the primary business of the schools, or are they seen as ancillary and perhaps coincidental to that business? Similarly, if outside consultants are employed, are there clear understandings about the way information gained in the consulting relationship may be used by the consultant?

- *How responsive is the district to the claims of students and to shifts in student needs or the student base? For example, does a shift in the community's demographic profile lead easily to shifts in programs and projects to accommodate these shifts, or do programs change only after a period of considerable tension and conflict?* There is probably no area of school life where schools are more reactionary and less anticipatory than they are in dealing with demographic shifts.

Furthermore, there is no area of school life where better data on which to base trend estimates are likely to be found. Yet it is commonplace for schools to undergo dramatic demographic transitions and be totally unprepared for the consequences. Why is this so? Among the reasons is that too few educators fully appreciate the way demographic trends develop, and they typically do not have mastery of the kinds of tools that would permit them to better anticipate these trends and incorporate what they anticipate into their planning processes.

A Concluding Comment

Some of the most significant change efforts in schools today are efforts to change the boundary system. Sometimes these efforts result in greater inclusion of the state in the affairs of the local school unit, as when the state sets forth uniform curriculum requirements. Sometimes these efforts result in greater exclusion of some community members from any real prospect of having a meaningful role in the operation of the schools. (School site councils that are empowered to make decisions about the education of children but that do not include nonparents along with parents are illustrative of this point.)

The growth of the idea of forming community collaborative organizations and community foundations focused on education is symptomatic of the recognition that there is a need to regularize relationships between schools and communities and to do so in a way that is extragovernmental. Governments function by laws, but laws can be upheld only when supported by the moral sentiments of the community. The state can require students to attend school, but the state cannot mandate that these students be attentive. The state can demand that students demonstrate performance before moving forward in the school (no more social promotions), but the state cannot force students to do the work they will need to do to meet these standards.

Consequently, it requires the full strength of the community, including parents and teachers, to provide students with the kind of encouragement and support they must have to do the important work the schools should be obliged to provide. To ensure that this encouragement and support are provided, many who have been treated historically as outsiders must be brought within the schools. In a word, schools must build communities around the schools rather than expect the schools to serve communities that sometimes do not exist at all.

Part Three

New Norms, New Values, New Directions

Those who lead systemic change need to be armed with every bit of insight available. Even with the most powerful understandings, leading systemic change is a daunting task. The two chapters in this section sum up what I've learned and provide the reader with a more personal view of the future of public education in America.

Chapter Ten

| The Changing Context

In the opening chapter of this book I made reference to Carl Bridenbaugh's notion of the *great mutation,* by which he meant a fundamental shift in the nature of our social arrangements and cultural values. In a book I wrote some years back, *Shaking Up the Schoolhouse,* I described some of these changes under the heading of *seismic shifts.* I will not repeat here what I have already written, but I do want to stipulate that I have not changed my mind about these matters; the fundamental problem confronting public school educators is that the schools are being asked to produce results they have never before produced in a social context that is dramatically different from the context from which the schools emerged. In the present chapter I intend to spell out even further than I did in my previous book or in the introductory chapters to this book the nature of these social changes. I do this because I believe that unless and until schools are designed with these external changes in mind, it is unlikely that the internal changes brought about will be adequate for the task that confronts the schools.

Instrumental and Expressive Organizations

In the effort to understand how schools respond to innovation and change, I have found it useful to categorize organizations according to the values served and the type of functions fulfilled. This results in two broad categories of organizations, which I label *expressive* and *instrumental.*[1]

- Expressive organizations are organizations in which the primary intent is to satisfy the needs of members. Churches, fraternities, and bowling leagues are illustrative of these types of organizations.
- Instrumental organizations are organizations in which the intent is to pursue some set of rationalized goals, produce products, or provide services valued by persons and groups external to the organization. Business corporations, hospitals, military organizations, and most governmental agencies are illustrative of this type of organization.

In expressive organizations, technology (by which I mean, as I noted before, the means of doing the job, whatever the means and the job may be) has very little impact on the processes associated with innovation and change, whereas in instrumental organizations, technology is the heart and soul of change and innovation. There are several reasons this is so:

- Expressive functions—for example, nurturing or providing opportunities for affiliation—do not require technology. Expressive functions are almost totally dependent on the moral commitments of members and the relationships among them.
- Instrumental functions—for example, producing a product or service for the benefit of others—almost always require some known means of doing the job, that is, instrumental functions are dependent on technology.
- Instrumental functions have to do primarily with technical norms (norms that have to do with the way a job gets done) whereas expressive functions are more frequently embedded

---

[1] Sociologists have long used the words *expressive* and *instrumental* to distinguish among types of values being pursued. So far as I can determine, this formulation was first developed by Talcott Parsons and Robert F. Bales in their book *Family, Socialization and Interaction Process* (New York: Free Press, 1955).

in moral norms and aesthetic norms. Therefore science and rationality can play a major role in instrumental organizations. Science and rationality are only marginally related to moral and aesthetic norms. Technology may drive change in instrumental organizations,[2] but in expressive organizations, leaders drive change.

- Innovations that affect technical norms can be introduced into systems through programs and projects, whereas innovations that affect the expressive functions can be introduced only through leadership, for it is only through the actions of moral leaders that moral values can be challenged and worldviews can be altered.

A Matter of Emphasis

All organizations, whether predominantly expressive or predominantly instrumental, must fulfill both expressive and instrumental functions, so there is in reality no pure "type." For example, churches are expressive organizations, yet they must attend to such instrumental concerns as having money to pay salaries, build houses of worship, and so on. But these instrumental concerns are viewed as secondary, and when these concerns become too dominant, members will likely begin to complain that the minister or priest is more concerned with the condition of the church's bank account than with the condition of the members' spiritual lives. Business corporations, in contrast, are predominantly instrumental. The pursuit of rational goals, the production of goods and services, and purposeful adaptation to a changing environment are dominant interests. Technology and changes in technology are central concerns. Instrumental organizations must, however, also attend to the expressive concerns of their members. Indeed, if the

---

[2] Sociologists have long been interested in the linkage between structure and technology and some suggest that new technologies drive structural changes. In addition to C. M. Christensen, *The Innovator's Dilemma: When New Technologies Cause Great Firms to Fail* (Boston: Harvard Business School Press, 1997), which I mentioned earlier, the interested reader might also consult many of the writings of Charles Perrow; see, for example: C. Perrow, *Complex Organizations: A Critical Essay* (Glenview, Ill.: Scott, Foresman, 1972).

recent literature on leadership does not convey any other message, at least these three lessons are clear:

- Leaders in an instrumental organization who are insensitive to that organization's expressive functions will find it more difficult to achieve the instrumental ends they are pursuing than will those who understand the expressive needs of human beings.
- It is expressive concerns having to do with beliefs, values, and commitments, more than instrumental concerns having to do with skills, hardware, and software, that make the installation of disruptive technologies so difficult.
- Leaders who understand the expressive side of the organization they lead and the expressive needs of those they are leading are more likely to be effective in installing disruptive innovations than are leaders who are less attuned to these matters.

Public Schools: From Expressive to Instrumental Organizations

On the one hand, like the family, the public school is properly concerned with the nurture of the young and the induction of new members into the moral order of the larger society, that is to say, with cultural transmission. In this regard, then, the school is a predominantly expressive organization. On the other hand, it is expected that schools will provide the young with the skills they need to succeed not only as citizens and as family members but also as workers, employees, and students in universities, community colleges, and so on. In this sense, schools are instrumental organizations.

When formal schooling began in America, expressive functions were clearly dominant. Indeed, the first schools were established in New England as extensions of the family and the church to ensure that children would be sufficiently literate to read the Bible and thereby able to resist the wiles of that "Old Deluder, Satan." Up through the first half of the twentieth century and to some extent even today, both in custom and in law, the idea that schools are expressive organizations has considerable support. For example, teachers were (and sometimes still are) viewed as substitute parents (in *loco parentis*). It is in this tradition that the idea of the school as a *community* finds much of its sustenance.

At the same time, public funding for schools is increasingly being rationalized and justified in terms of instrumental ends. Though parents may wish to view the schools as extensions of the home and the values of the family and the church, business leaders and nonparent taxpayers are encouraged to support universal free public education for more instrumental reasons, such as a more productive workforce.[3] More important, over the years the instrumental functions of schools have become increasingly prominent, and the role of schools in fulfilling expressive functions has become increasingly problematic.

Although this transformation of America's public schools from quasi-religious community institutions to secular governmental agencies is a subject discussed too little in the academic literature, it is certainly a topic of discussion among many parents, political leaders, and religious leaders, some of whom perceive the ongoing shift as both real and harmful. Among the reasons the schools' instrumental purpose is now emphasized is that for schools to effectively carry out the expressive functions traditionally assigned to them, such as the transmission of culture and values, there needs to be a general consensus regarding those cultural elements and values that are deserving of transmission. The growing ethnic, racial, and religious diversity in American society has made it difficult to find or create such a consensus.

Initially, elites from the dominant culture were able to "solve" the difficulties presented by increased cultural diversity by using the schools as instruments of homogenization. As liberal critics of the 1950s and 1960s regularly observed, the result was that the public schools of America came to be dominated by a white, Protestant, and middle-class view of the world. Furthermore, most civic

---

[3] In the nineteenth century Horace Mann and his colleagues in the common school movement argued for tax-based funding for public schools on two grounds: that the maintenance of a common culture reflecting republican values (as opposed to Jacksonian principles) required a common school promoting a common culture and that the growth of American business and industry depended on a well-educated citizenry. These arguments, in various forms, are still part of the debate over the merit and worth of public education in America.

leaders saw nothing wrong with such dominance. Indeed, one of the reasons for the common school movement, which aimed at providing universal public elementary schools for all children, was the belief that it was essential to promote a common culture; which was to say, a culture based on Anglo-Saxon values reinforced by a Protestant ethic and republican sentiments. Many of those who most strongly supported the rise of the American high school did so in part because they believed that the high school could serve as a mechanism to Americanize the children of the foreign-born.

Sources of Estrangement

There have of course always been tensions between the schools and those who did not share in or aspire to the view of the world the public schools of the nineteenth and early twentieth century were intended to promulgate. Furthermore, these tensions had to do primarily with the way the expressive functions of the school were carried out. Obviously, some groups found—and continue to find—that the compromises they needed to make in order to gain access to an academic education for their child were more than they could tolerate. It was largely because of these tensions that immigrant parents with Catholic backgrounds banded together to create very strong Catholic schools. It is also for this reason that some groups of parents have been willing to forego the promise of a sound academic education in exchange for an institutional promise that their religious values and family values will be upheld and promulgated. There seems little doubt that at least some religion-based academies present such a risk and that at least some parents are willing to assume that risk. For these people, the biblical justification is clear: "For what is a man profited if he shall gain the whole world, and lose his own soul?" The Amish, in fact, renounce higher education as a value and have created their own schools, which operate very much as schools operated in rural communities 150 years ago. And it is also an unwillingness to compromise with public schools' current expressive functions that nowadays makes some minority parents find the idea of charter schools so attractive.

Exacerbating the effects of diversity, or perhaps arising out of diversity, is the fact that identifiable cultural elites in most local environments have experienced a parallel decline. This, combined with the rise of mass media, the emergence of pop culture, and the increasing secularization of society, has moved the debate about matters of taste, morals, ethics, and aesthetics (that is, the debate about the stuff to which expressive functions are addressed) beyond the arena of the local community and the particular values it represents and has encouraged the application of more universal standards in the operation of schools.

Consider the following example. As late as the 1950s, it was common practice in some rural communities in Ohio where a great many parents were practicing Catholics to employ a local priest as the principal of the ostensibly public high school and to hire members of religious orders to teach in this school. The Roman Catholic catechism was a part of the curriculum, and there was a crucifix in every room. In communities with a Protestant majority, it was also commonplace to have religious instruction. Teachers would begin each day with a Bible reading, a salute to the flag, and a prayer (these were called "opening exercises").

Over the past fifty years, actions by the Supreme Court have changed this picture dramatically. Because the Constitution of the United States is silent on the matter of education, people had long assumed that the federal government had no legitimate role in determining what the schools would teach and what values they would promulgate. Indeed, Americans have always prided themselves on the fact that public education was a local matter, subject to local control. The Constitution is not, however, silent on the question of unequal treatment or on the separation of church and state. This fact has opened the door to federal prohibitions that apply to local schools universal norms derived from the Constitution—reframing, for example, the issue of religion and education as an issue of church and state—even in the face of local resistance to these norms. These legal actions have clearly diminished the flexibility school leaders have in responding to the expectation that schools will fulfill expressive functions, especially as these functions have to do with values of concern to religious groups.

The result has been that public school leaders have become increasingly silent on matters of social values, and when they speak, they speak in support of the universal as opposed to the parochial. Even though the need for schools to support universal democratic values is clear, what is equally clear is that the transformation of the schools from community institutions to state agencies has served to reinforce the emphasis schools now place on subjects that serve instrumental ends and to reinforce the decline in support for subjects that serve expressive ends. Put differently, the transformation of schools from community institutions to state agencies has strained the historical alliance among schools, families, and religious organizations: an alliance that once reflected a real or perceived consensus on parochial values. Simultaneously, the increased ability of racial minorities, the handicapped, ethnic minorities, and other groups with distinctive needs and values to use the courts and federal law as a means of imposing universal norms on what have historically been viewed as local institutions also encourages school leaders to attend increasingly to instrumental functions and diminish their attention to functions that are expressive in nature.

Curriculum Impact

It is sometimes overlooked that up to the 1950s some of the most heated debates in education had to do with the proper role of the study of the humanities, including Latin and Greek, the history of the Western world, literature (especially Shakespeare), English grammar, American history, and civics. Today few prominent educators are much concerned about the declining role of Latin in the curriculum, and one sees only occasional commentary about humanities education generally. William Bennett, Diane Ravitch, and Chester Finn notwithstanding, the fact is that the debate today has more to do with less obviously value-laden subjects—subjects like mathematics, science, computer science, and something called *functional literacy*—than it has to do with *cultural literacy*. Indeed, when the idea of cultural literacy is brought up, the first question is likely to be, Whose culture?

In addition the impact of technological changes on the occupational world has been such that the traditional distinctions between vocational studies and academic studies have been blurred. Today academic studies are more likely to be defined in terms of mathematics and science than in terms of history, art, and literature, at least in part because it is assumed that mastery of these subjects is what produces a "world-class workforce." The launching of Sputnik I seems to have been a defining moment in this transition. The first reaction of policymakers was to ensure that

Americans were *scientifically literate*. By 1958, the voices of those concerned that Korean War POWs had defected to the country of their Chinese captors because of inadequate instruction in history were largely drowned out by the voices of those concerned that the Russians were beating us in the space race because of our inadequate instruction in mathematics and science. When the National Commission on Excellence in Education reported to the nation, it was even more concerned with instrumental values.[4] Today, criticism of the ability of schools to fulfill their traditional role in transmitting a common culture is left mainly to college professors in the liberal arts. Journalists and opinion makers are more likely to criticize the schools for failing to achieve instrumental values such as preparing students for the workplace or failing to honor the values of particular subcultures by, for example, the failure to teach black history, women's history, or non-Western literature.

The upshot of all these developments is that public schools are faced with a dilemma. On the one hand they were founded as expressive organizations, and in the view of many cultural conservatives to fail to fulfill these functions is to fail utterly. On the other hand the instrumental demands of the workplace and the secularization of society have created conditions under which schools are found lacking in terms of their ability to carry out their instrumental functions; and this at the same time that they are prohibited from doing those things they would need to do to satisfy the expressive needs they are expected to satisfy.

The Uneasy Relationship Between Schools and Parents

Though it causes some discomfort to educators committed to public schools (and I count myself among them), any reasonable analysis of the relationship between families and schools will surely reveal an almost inherent tension between the organization called public school and parents. Indeed, Willard Waller goes so far as to say that parents and teachers are *natural enemies*. As Waller observes, both parents and teachers have the interests of the child at

---

[4] National Commission on Excellence in Education, *A Nation at Risk* (Washington, D.C.: National Commission on Excellence in Education, 1983).

heart, yet the specific interests they have at heart are often quite different.[5] The parent is concerned about his or her child and the particular values, beliefs, and commitments his or her particular family embraces and wants to uphold. The teacher is concerned about children in general, and the expressive focus of the teacher is apt to be more universal, upholding more general social values and more universal social norms.

The opportunity for conflict here is obvious. The parent who believes and wants his or her child to believe the creationist story is almost certain to be at odds with the teacher or the school that advances the theory of evolution and the claims of science over the claims of faith. The parent who believes that the gay lifestyle is an abomination will have little tolerance for the openly gay teacher or for the teacher who advances the notion that gays are entitled to the same nondiscrimination as are other minorities. More generally, Catholics and Jews are likely to be offended by Protestant prayers and Protestant Bible reading, and atheists are likely to be offended by any prayer at all.

And there are more subtle points of conflict. The teacher necessarily views the expectations he or she has of the student as legitimate, and expects the parent to uphold those expectations, even when they bring discomfort to the parent or the child. Indeed, as Waller notes, for many schools and many teachers, "Parent-teacher work has usually been directed at securing for the school the support of parents, that is, getting parents to see children as teachers see them." Waller then goes on to say: "This is not to say that parent-teacher work of a certain kind might not be very helpful. If parents and teachers could meet often enough and intimately enough to develop primary group attitudes toward each other, and if both parents and teachers might have their say unreservedly, such modifications of school practice and parental

---

[5] Willard Waller presents one of the most clear-eyed views of the relationship between teachers and parents I have ever read, and as he says, "A marked lack of clear thought and plain speaking exists in the literature touching the relations of parents and teachers." For the reader who is willing to approach the topic with an open mind, I recommend Waller's *The Sociology of Teaching* (New York: Wiley, 1967) (Originally published 1932), especially Chapter Six, titled "Parents and Teachers."

upbringing might take place as would revolutionize the life of children everywhere."[6]

The unfortunate fact is that to date, except in very unusual and largely unsustainable circumstances, such relationships between parents and schools do not exist. Because they do not, it is likely that as enabling technological developments emerge, parents, families, informal networks of families, and other community agencies will increasingly be encouraged to meet the instrumental ends of education without benefit of the schools. Furthermore, they will be able to do so without risking the quality of the academic education received by their children.

Until recently, schools—public and private—have been able to maintain a monopoly over academic education primarily because neither parents nor other community agencies were in a position to compete. But this is changing:

- In the past, few parents were sufficiently well educated to warrant the assumption that they could provide a decent academic education to their children. Nowadays many parents are educated at least as well as are their children's teachers. In 1940, 24.5 percent of Americans above the age of twenty-five had a high school education, and only 4.6 percent held a college degree. Today 85 percent have a high school education, and nearly 26 percent have graduated from college.
- With the advent of television, distance learning, and on-line curriculum resources, increasing numbers of parents—including some who are not well educated—are beginning to believe that as providers of academic education, schools may be no better equipped to educate children than is a small group of parents that has the benefit of a well-designed curriculum delivered with support from a wide range of electronic information storing, processing, and communicating devices.

The response of the public school advocate, of course, is that schooling is not simply a matter of academics. Schools do, after all,

---

[6] Waller, *The Sociology of Teaching*, p. 69.

fulfill expressive functions. Unfortunately, for reasons already noted, the ability of schools to fulfill these expressive functions has been seriously eroded. Furthermore, when the expressive values added by the public school are seen as contrary to the hopes and desires of parents, public schools will be increasingly unable to compete with those who take advantage of the ability to separate academic education—as an instrumental end—from expressive education that has nurturance, socialization, and the transmission of values and culture as its primary aims. Parents will simply place their children in environments that reinforce the values they wish to reinforce, and buy academic education from a private provider.

If public schools are to survive and thrive into the late twenty-first century, they must recover their ability to satisfy the expressive needs of the society and at the same time provide high-quality academic experiences. To address this issue, it will be necessary, I think, to reframe the argument. Among other things it will be necessary to entertain the idea that there are three legitimate bases for academic education as well as socialization: first, the home; second, the school; and third, the community at large. It is in defining the proper relationship between and among these three entities that public school educators face their most serious challenges.

The Impact of New Technologies

One of the most fundamental facts confronting those who value public education and want to preserve public schools is the fact that the introduction of electronic means of communicating information, storing information, processing information, and analyzing information has created the possibility of educating people without schooling them. This means that if parents become sufficiently dissatisfied with the way the schools are fulfilling expressive functions, they can remove their children from school without fear of compromising the child's academic education. It also means that those who see schools only in instrumental terms will be increasingly encouraged to turn to less expensive means than schools of delivering what they want and need.

It may well be that education by way of the Internet and television is not the same as education by way of school, but this argument is increasingly unpersuasive to parents who perceive the schools as failing in carrying out expressive functions as the parents would have them carried out while at the same time failing to provide a quality of academic education equal to or better than that they can purchase in the marketplace. As I observed earlier, it is now technologically possible for children to receive a fairly sound academic education without the benefit of school, even if their parents are themselves not very well educated.[7] Leaders who comfort themselves with the argument that non-school-based education is inherently inferior education would, in my view at least, have made good candidates for CEO at Ford at the time when Lee Iacocca was comforting himself and Ford employees with the belief that Japanese cars were inferior and presented no real threat to the American automobile industry. If all one wants from schools is that they fulfill the instrumental functions involved in teaching children to read, write, and cipher, or even to produce a world-class workforce that is literate in the ways of science and competent in mathematics, it may be that the age of schooling is indeed past.

If, however, one believes as I believe that the most fundamental crisis confronting American society is the loss of community and the decline in the quality of civic life, then it is possible to imagine a future for schools, a future that involves transforming schools from organizations that struggle to serve diverse communities, and do this poorly, to organizations central to the building of communities and the enhancement of civic life.

To create such schools, those who lead schools must be prepared to embrace disruptive innovations. To embrace disruptive innovations, schools and school leaders must become much more

---

[7] Of course home-based education has always been available to the educated and the affluent. John Adams spent many hours educating John Quincy Adams and turned to school only to supplement the education he had provided his son. Many others similarly situated did the same. Public schools were designed, in part, to provide the benefits of academic education to children whose parents did not have the talent, money, or inclination to personally provide education for their offspring. As William Bennett and his colleagues at K–12 are trying to demonstrate, however, it is now possible for all students, including the children of the poorly educated, to attain access to a high-quality academic education without attending school. (K–12 is a for-profit corporation that is marketing a comprehensive K–12 curriculum to home schooling parents, using the Internet as a primary means of delivery.)

adept than they now are at bringing about systemic change. To create change-adept organizations, school leaders must understand much better than most now do the nature of the systems they are called on to change and the way actions on one part of a system are likely to affect the operation of other parts. Such understanding cannot come about unless educational leaders embrace more fully than most now do the idea that schools are complex *social* organizations, subject to all the forces that impinge on other complex social organizations, and that consequently there is much that can be learned about schools by looking at what has been learned in other organizational settings.

In sum, what is required is that educators develop what C. Wright Mills referred to as the *sociological imagination,* by which he meant a frame of mind and set of intellectual tools that make it possible to seek explanations in areas that lie outside the direct consciousness of individuals and reside instead in the structure of human relationships: "A quality of mind that will help [us to] use information and to develop reason in order to achieve lucid summations of what is going on in the world and of what might be happening within [ourselves]."[8]

My intention in this book has been to provide readers with some of the ideas and tools they will need if they are to systematically apply the sociological imagination to the redesign of schools.

---

[8] C. W. Mills, *The Sociological Imagination* (New York: Oxford University Press, 1959), p. 5.

Chapter Eleven

The Future of Public Education in America

Americans have always believed in public schools even though they have often been critical of them. Until recently, however, this criticism did not extend to the point where policymakers felt free to consider the possibility of privatizing schooling or even of providing tax dollars to support those who would privatize the schools. This is no longer the case.

Nowadays, those committed to public education are, and feel that they are, embattled. From nearly every front they receive reports on how poorly the schools are doing and on how much better the private schools do at what the public schools spend so much more to do. More and more parents are seeking ways to educate their children outside the context of the traditional public school structure. Sometimes they opt for home schooling, sometimes for private schools, and sometimes for charter schools. Often they ask for, and now many are receiving, vouchers to support their efforts.

In spite of over fifty years of criticism, however, there remains in every community a solid reservoir of goodwill toward public schools and an abiding faith in the proposition that public schools are still our best hope for ensuring that all Americans are well educated and that all American communities are healthy places to live. It is these people to whom educators must turn in the battle to save the public schools. If the public school forces are to win the battle that is now going on, they must be willing to do things many are now uncomfortable with doing. For example, like the radio commentators, journalists, and television evangelists who daily bombard the public with negative stories about public education, they must be prepared to use the electronic media, print media, and every other means at their disposal to shape the debate over the future of public education. *They should not, however, make the mistake of assuming that what is needed is more good news about the schools—that all that is needed is better public relations and a more positive press.* Rather than defending the schools as they now exist, leaders committed to public education need to use every means at their disposal to mobilize the local community on behalf of *better schools,* and they must help the community understand that *better schools* means schools that are radically different from the schools most community members ever attended.

If the effort to save public education is to succeed, public school educators and those who support them must be prepared to be brutally honest with themselves and with others. They cannot afford to whine or hide behind illusions and false claims. Happy talk and self-pity may be comforting, but what is needed now are leaders who can inspire courage rather than quiet surrender and whimpering.

I do not believe that the privatization of education can achieve the ends well-intended proponents (and there are many well-intended proponents of school privatization) believe it will achieve. I fear that the only result of privatization will be the dismantling of the one institution that has the potential to address what may be an even more critical problem than the problem of education— that is, the problem of a declining sense of community and a consequent deterioration in civic capacity and social capital.

The reason I do not believe privatization will provide better education for most children is that the assumption on which both public and private schooling are based is flawed. Both function on the assumption that attendance and compliance are all that are required of students, when the fact is that to educate all children to the level American society now demands, what we need are schools based on the understanding that compliance and attendance are not enough. What we require are commitment and attention. As I have said many times throughout this book, most schools are not designed to produce commitment and attention, though schools are happy to take them if they come their way.

Student engagement, rather than student compliance, must be the goal. To gain student engagement, the communities from which students come must be engaged as well, for without engaged communities the kind of fundamental reforms needed in our schools will never be tolerated, let alone supported.

Put another way, if educators are to be successful in defending public education, they must go on the offensive, and the first step in that offensive is to acknowledge that as they are now organized, public schools are not meeting the expectations Americans have for their schools. Furthermore, without disruptive innovations it is unlikely that they will ever do so. What is needed is an entirely new model or framework for thinking about schooling in America.

I believe public educators possess all the resources and talents necessary to create such a model, but to begin they must step out of the mental world they now inhabit and begin to dream of the world they want to create. In spite of the challenge to create break-the-mold schools, the fact is that most of the innovations offered to date are intended to make the present systems work a little better. Few have had the courage to propose truly *radical* (in the sense of "to the root of") solutions to the problems that confront our schools. Few have demonstrated the kind of imagination needed to create truly novel designs for schooling—designs that would require schools to disrupt present systems and put new systems in their place.

The decision to participate in such an adventure demands a major commitment from all members of the community, not just educators and political leaders. It requires the support of union leaders, business leaders, leaders in the philanthropic community, and leaders of civil rights groups and advocacy organizations. It means a degree of dedication, organization, and discipline that has not always characterized school reform efforts.

Whether or not to join in this bold adventure is a choice the leaders of every community must make. I am confident, however, that with strong, persistent, and committed leadership from school leaders and community leaders, we can indeed reinvent public education in America, and as a by-product, reinvent the communities we inhabit as well.

The problems that beset schooling in America cannot be solved with new standards and new money. In fact, new standards and new money applied to the present systems are as likely to aggravate the problems as they are to solve them. These problems can be solved only when all citizens once again affirm their faith in public education and pledge to do whatever they can do to ensure that public education and the schools that have been entrusted with educating the public will continue to be the beacon on the hill that guides us all through difficult and perilous times. This book has been written for those who want to lead the effort to renew America's lighthouses—the public schools.

Appendix A: Creating Engaging Schoolwork

This appendix describes a framework that can assist teachers as they go about the business of designing engaging work for students. In this book I have discussed the significance of six critical systems in schools and the conditions under which and means by which schools can attempt to install disruptive innovations in those systems. The reason for making such innovative changes is of course so schools and teachers can focus on designing engaging work for students. This appendix summarizes an approach doing so. Readers seeking more information will want to read my 2002 book *Working on the Work: An Action Plan for Teachers, Principals, and Superintendents*. See also the new book by the National Research Council and Institute of Medicine of the National Academies, *Engaging Schools: Fostering High School Students' Motivation to Learn* (2004).

Designing Engaging Schoolwork

If student engagement is the preferred means of educating students, *then the core business of schools and teachers is, or should be, designing intellectual tasks and activities that have those qualities and attributes that are most likely to engage students, and ensuring that these tasks and activities call upon students to learn those things that are considered important.*[1] Furthermore, if engagement is to be central in the schooling process it is essential that teachers learn how to engage students in

---

[1] Conceptually, at least, a curriculum guide should clearly state what it is intended that students know and what they should be able to do as a result of the tasks and activities they undertake in school. Therefore what I suggest here seems very much congruent with the idea of curriculum alignment.

the study of subjects about which students at times do not care and in which they may have no inherent interest. It is also necessary for teachers not only to be responsive to each student's learning style preferences but also to know how to help the student who has a single preferred learning style to develop additional styles. In particular, because much more information is available to those who learn through reading than is available to those who learn only through other means, such as listening, everyone in our culture should be a reader, whether he or she wants to be and whether reading is consistent with his or her preferred learning style. Learning styles, like measured intelligence, can be developed as well as identified. Schools should endeavor to develop a wide range of learning styles, even when the effort produces some discomfort in students. In addition, in doing these things the teacher must keep in mind the fact that some students need, as a condition of embracing high standards, a great deal of assurance that they will not suffer negative consequences if they fail on their initial trials. Many students will not even try to meet a standard unless that assurance is present. Rather, these students will retreat, and some will rebel.

Why might one student find a school task or activity engaging and another student be repelled by it? Why do some school tasks and activities seem engaging to a wide range of students whereas others engage only a few? Along with many colleagues, I have given a great deal of thought to questions like these over the past decade. Out of this thinking has emerged a framework that I call the *working on the work framework*. This framework posits ten separate attributes, or qualities, of school tasks that seem particularly relevant to the motives students bring to the tasks. It is by taking these attributes into account in the design of schoolwork that teachers can hope to increase the rate and frequency of student engagement in their classrooms.

I will discuss each of the following design qualities in some detail:

- Content and substance
- Organization of knowledge
- Protection from negative consequences for initial failures
- Clear and compelling standards
- Product focus
- Affiliation

- Affirmation of performance
- Novelty and variety
- Choice
- Authenticity

Contextual Qualities

Two qualities that must be taken into account when endeavoring to design engaging lessons are the nature of the knowledge and skill to be transmitted, developed, or acquired and the format in which this knowledge is presented to or made accessible to the student. I refer to the first of these as content and substance; the second as organization of knowledge.

Content and Substance

To the extent that a student gets personal enjoyment out of studying a particular subject or developing given skills, these preferences can be used as a source of motivation for undertaking schoolwork.[2] Such preferences are learned. Some students have learned to enjoy the study of history; others have learned that the subject is uninteresting. Some students become excited about the possibility of developing physical skills but have little interest in developing their skills as artists, musicians, or scholars. Others have learned to love music and are less fascinated with developing physical skills.

Learning theorists have had much to say about these differences. Some use brain research to explain why some students

---

[2] It is becoming increasingly popular to criticize the application of words like *work* and *customer* to educational matters. Some seem to assume those who use these words are somehow connected with a cabal that wants to turn schools over to private corporations and make them more businesslike. However, I am simply an old-line pragmatist of the John Dewey persuasion (as distinguished from the Kilpatrick persuasion). To me, *work* is nothing more nor less than purposeful, goal-oriented activity. Similarly, to speak of the student as a *customer* only recognizes the obvious fact that in both private and public schools, students are volunteers, and what they have to volunteer is their attention and their commitment. We can gain their attendance and compliance through bribery and coercion, but we must provide them with work they consider worth doing before they will volunteer their attention and commitment.

respond to some tasks in positive and productive ways and other students respond to the same task in less positive ways. Others, following leads by scholars like Howard Gardner,[3] suggest there is great variance in learning styles and that teachers and curriculum designers would be well advised to take the differences into account. As I just mentioned, I am personally persuaded that learning styles are as much learned as they are innate and that learning styles can be taught as well as responded to. But regardless of the position one takes on this important issue, the fact of wide variance in the ways children learn remains, and anyone who wants to help students learn certain subjects or develop certain skills needs to be aware of these differences and take them into account.

One way this variance has been dealt with is to posit the interest-centered curriculum, attempting to find subjects the student likes or enjoys and then linking them to subjects of less interest to that student. Persons persuaded by brain research or by the line of reasoning presented by Gardner would also suggest designing school-work so it is "brain compatible" and consistent with the learning style of the individual student. This quickly leads to the idea that instruction should be *individualized.* A second strategy is to make a subject more interesting by making it relevant to the real world through connecting it with "real-life" situations or by increasing the entertainment value of the classroom through hands-on experiments and fun projects, activities, and field trips. A third strategy is to ensure that those who teach are persons for whom the student will do whatever work they require, even if that work is meaningless to the student, because the student likes or admires these teachers. There is certainly nothing inherently wrong with using students' present interests to lead them to new interests, there is certainly nothing wrong with the effort to make any subject as interesting as possible, and it is really hard to argue with the notion that all students should have teachers they like and admire. However, each of these strategies has its limits.

Often the result of focusing attention on subjects of interest to students is that instead of linking those interesting subjects to less interesting subjects, the student winds up learning much about the

---

[3] H. Gardner, *Frames of Mind: The Theory of Multiple Intelligences* (New York: Basic Books, 1993).

more interesting subject and little or nothing about the less interesting subject. Goal displacement is as common in the classroom as it is in the boardrooms of school districts and corporations.

The problem with efforts to make tedious content more interesting is that the effort sometimes encourages trivialization, superficial treatment, and lack of intellectual rigor. The fact is that the mastery of any discipline often calls for hard work and the toleration of a certain amount of tedious activity. If the student acquires a real interest in the subject, this interest alone may produce a level of attention and commitment that is sufficient to motivate the student to do the hard work and even endure the necessary tedium. Put differently, when students are personally interested in a subject, they are more likely to become engaged in tasks that result in their learning more about that subject. If, however, students have not learned to love the subject or even to care about it, they are unlikely to give either the attention or the commitment needed to complete the task satisfactorily—*unless* they are able to bring other values to the task. (I will say more much about these other values later in this discussion.)

Strained efforts to entertain students will produce no good results other than relieving boredom and perhaps decreasing rebellion. Of course I am not arguing in support of some educators' tendency to confuse rigor with rigor mortis and to assume that evidence of fun in class is evidence of frivolity. But it is important to recognize that *entertainment* and *engagement* are not synonyms. Students who are not engaged are more likely to need to be entertained than those who are engaged. Moreover, engaged students will do what might otherwise appear to be a trivial task, for example memorizing lists, when they see a link between this task and values that they hold.

The idea of the engaging teacher—as contrasted with the teacher who designs engaging work—has a certain appeal, especially to teachers who are engaging or who try to be. There is, after all, considerable research to support the idea that differences between teachers do make a considerable difference in student

---

[4] See, for example, L. Darling-Hammond, "Teacher Quality and Student Achievement: A Review of State Policy Evidence," *Education Policy Archives*, 2000, *8*(entire issue, 1).

learning.[4] It is, however, an unfortunate fact that educators too often fail to differentiate between teachers who are engaging as persons or as performers and teachers who are skilled at providing work and activities that students find engaging. Failure to make this distinction too often leads to the conclusion that the only way to improve education is to work on the performance of the teachers. This eventually leads to the further, but hopeless, conclusion that the only way to improve the schools is find a means of recruiting to teaching posts in the schools 2.7 million college-educated Americans who are personally engaging and willing to provide heroic personal performances on a routine basis for a relatively modest financial reward.

There are of course some teachers who by force of personality, charm, and wit are able to inspire students to perform, even when the subject is difficult or inherently uninteresting. Heroic teachers do exist, but they cannot be the stuff of which great schools are made. There is simply not enough heroic material to go around. Moreover, though I have no research to support (or challenge) my view, I have some doubts about the overall efficacy of teacher personality as a powerful determinant of student learning. Some— perhaps even many—students will learn more from an engaging teacher. However, even the most engaging teacher will not be engaging to all students and perhaps not even to most students, and even those who find the teacher most engaging are from time to time likely to become disenchanted. In addition, if we examine our own memories of engaging teachers, it often turns out that what made the teacher engaging was not personal actions or attributes but what the teacher encouraged us to do and the care he or she took to ensure that what we were asked to do had meaning and significance in our own lives. The solution to engaging students is to ensure that all teachers know how to create, as a matter of routine practice, schoolwork that engages students. *Schools cannot be made great by great teacher performances. They will be made great only by great student performance.*

If schools are to improve, leaders and reformers must accept the fact that people who have the personal qualities needed to hold any audience spellbound for any length of time are in short supply, and persons who by dint of personality can cause others to do things they might not otherwise do are in short supply as well.

What is in virtually unlimited supply, once teachers figure out how to design them, are tasks, assignments, and activities that students find engaging and from which the students learn those things that teachers and the larger society believe the students should learn.

Organization of Knowledge

In discussing knowledge, I use the word in the broadest and most nontechnical sense possible. *Knowledge* means anything and everything schools intend for the young to learn, including skills and attitudes as well as understandings derived from the academic disciplines. Those who concern themselves with instructional and curriculum design are in fact concerned with organizing knowledge so that it will be optimally accessible and engaging to students. What is sometimes overlooked is that there are occasions on which some forms of knowledge cannot be made engaging. Furthermore, some forms of knowledge are necessarily more difficult to access than are others. Finally, before students can become engaged with some forms of knowledge, they must learn how to learn in the ways these knowledge forms require.[5]

What may be even more important is that ways of learning and ways of knowing may be as much conditioned by cultural and historical circumstances as they are by the way human beings are "wired." For example, 150 years ago, men and women sat with rapt attention and listened to Abraham Lincoln and Stephen Douglas debate for hours on end. There were no electronic amplifiers, so it must have been something of a strain to hear. Yet Lincoln and Douglas were heard, and people did pay attention. And they learned. Today such patience is seldom available in the church, synagogue, or mosque, let alone on the campaign trail or in school. Similarly, in the past it was common to argue from major premise to minor premise and then to a conclusion—in the manner of academic discourse. Journalists and busy managers, however, often put the conclusion first and then provide the facts and arguments for anyone who is interested or who feels the need for them. The result is that many Americans have learned to be

---

[5] This is precisely the point Jerome Bruner made in his now-classic book *The Process of Education* (Boston: Harvard University Press, 1961).

impatient with long and detailed arguments, unless they find the conclusion appealing—and then they want to get to the facts through random access rather than a linear presentation.

It is easy to conclude from such evidence that the attention span of students has diminished and that students are less disciplined than they were in the "good old days." But anyone who believes the attention span of the young has deteriorated should perhaps consider other evidence as well. For example, he or she might study the way adolescents become absorbed in complex, involved, and highly demanding electronic games that require considerable problem solving as well as research and creativity.

The introduction of the electronic age, beginning with the radio and now bringing us the Internet and computers, has changed the basic mode by which people—especially young people—approach the acquisition of knowledge. They no longer need to wade through long documents to get the facts they need. Random access programming makes this effort less necessary. They can also get information from a variety of sources in addition to the spoken and written word—for example, television images, movie images, photographs, and so on. For most students, learning today takes place in a multimedia world where many traditional assumptions about how knowledge is acquired are being turned upside down. Teachers, many of whom learned to learn in a less digital environment, are sometimes unwilling—or unable—to accommodate these emerging learning styles into the way they design work for students.[6]

Unless educators take advantage of the opportunities presented by the electronic revolution, education will increasingly be taken away from schools and turned over to private providers.[7] This is not to say that discovery, hands-on work, and problem solving are always preferred approaches to teaching and learning.

---

[6] Many excellent examples exist of efforts to incorporate understandings such as these into the design of work for students. An excellent source of illustrations is the new publication from the George Lucas Educational Foundation (GLEF) entitled *Edutopia: The New World of Learning* (http://glef.org).

[7] I have made this point several times in this book as well as in other books I have written. I make the point most forcefully in the epilogue to *Shaking Up the Schoolhouse: How to Support and Sustain Educational Innovation* (San Francisco: Jossey-Bass, 2001).

Sometimes lectures are appropriate and sometimes extensive periods of lonely work in the library or on the Internet may be needed. Silence and lack of physical movement do not indicate an absence of learning any more than great activity and mindless babbling indicate deep thought and high levels of learning. Learning is an active process, but thinking is sometimes a sedentary and lonely undertaking.

What proponents of "active learning"—as opposed, I suppose, to passive learning—sometimes miss is the fact that when a student is engaged, what may appear quite passive can be active indeed. When a student is engaged in a task and needs information presented in a lecture to successfully complete it, he or she will likely hear and learn very different things from that lecture than will the student in the next seat who is only attending the class and complying with a requirement. The engaged student is likely to be actively processing what he or she hears in terms of specific meanings he or she brings to the experience, whereas the compliant student will have no context in which to place what he or she is passively receiving. For example, one of the most fascinating lecturers I ever knew was Foster Rhea Dulles, a history professor at The Ohio State University. Dulles assumed that the graduate students in his class were likely to be engaged by intellectual puzzles and problems. Therefore he always began his lecture by posing a problem he was interested in exploring, and he invited his audience to join him in his exploration. Most of the time I was engaged in Dulles's lectures as were most of my colleagues. Dulles's approach may not have been a perfect approach, but it was a long way ahead of the tactics of those whose lectures consisted only of facts, usually presented in a monotone.

Sources of Disengagement

Just as the nature of the content to be taught and the way knowledge is organized can encourage engagement, these same attributes can contribute to disengagement. It is obvious, for example, that students who have learned to dislike the study of history, or any other subject, will likely be disengaged from the study of that subject unless the teacher can find some way *other than interest in the subject* to get them engaged. Similarly, when students are uncomfortable with, unfamiliar with, or otherwise incompatible with a particular instructional strategy, they may disengage. Sometimes this disengagement will be the result of an antipathy to the approach taken and sometimes it will be due to fear that engagement will result in failure.[8] Observations such as these have led me to posit two more qualities about schoolwork that must be present for students to engage. Although they do not act as attractors to the work, their absence can dissuade some students from becoming engaged:

- Protection from negative consequences for initial failures
- Clear and compelling (to the student) standards

Protection from Negative Consequences

In spite of much rhetoric about the need to encourage students to take risks, to be creative, to experiment, and to pursue high standards, schools are amazingly centered on ensuring that punishment always follows failure. Consider, for example, the grading system in the typical school. It is typical for teachers to grade—or otherwise take into account as a part of a grading system—the students' performance on nearly every task of importance. Some go so far as to develop elaborate lists that describe the proportionate weight of each activity for purposes of grading: for example, pop quizzes 10 percent, attendance 10 percent, term paper 30 percent, final exam 30 percent, and so on. Furthermore, it is often the case that among the strongest norms in schools are those dealing with the sanctity of the role of teacher in grading students and the idea that grades, once recorded, should not be changed except to correct a marking or clerical error.

The result of such a system is that student performance is assessed cumulatively. The grade that results says little about what

---

[8] It is not insignificant that although young children tend "to maintain high expectations for success even in the face of repeated failure, older students do not," and that for older students, "failure following high effort appears to carry more negative implications—especially for their self-concept of ability—than failure that results from minimal or no effort"; see L. S. Lumsden, *Student Motivation to Learn,* ERIC Digest No. 92 (Eugene, Oreg.: ERIC Clearinghouse on Educational Management, June 1994) (ED 370 200), p. 1.

the student knew or was able to do at the time the grade was given. Rather, the grade represents an average of what the student knew at various points in time—including the times when he or she was presumably most ignorant about the subject being studied or most unskilled in those areas where skill was to be developed. Whatever failures the student has had along the way are averaged in with whatever successes have accrued. Thus the student who for awhile just could not catch on to fractions or longitude and latitude but who masters these concepts just before the end of the grading period will likely receive a lower grade than will the student who mastered the concepts early on.

Various devices have been developed to get around these difficulties. Some people have advocated doing away with grades altogether and providing in their place detailed progress reports. Portfolio assessment is another strategy. Giving more weight to assignments completed later in the grading period is another strategy. Regardless of the strategies employed, however, it is almost certain that there will be those inside schools and out who will argue that any effort to uncouple grades from punishment for inadequate past performance lowers standards and amounts to grade inflation. The race goes to the swift, as in real life, or so some would say. Teachers may tell the story of the persevering tortoise crossing the finish line ahead of the speedier hare, but in real school the hare gets an A and the tortoise gets a C.

Why is this so? In part it is because schools, like most bureaucracies, are based on the assumption that the best means of gaining compliance is the systematic application of extrinsic rewards and punishments. Those who comply get promoted. Those who fail to comply—whether through lack of skill or lack of will—stay behind. Those who comply gain status in the system; those who fail to comply lose status. Thus it is in real life and thus it should be in school—or so some would argue. A second reason that schools link failure and punishment so tightly is that the traditional function of schools—in addition to developing in some students some degree of academic competence—has been to select and sort students in terms of their likely stations in life. Those who are swift, especially with regard to verbal materials and mathematics, make better "material" for the professional and management classes than do those who are slower and more plodding. As some would have it, "After all, no one is going to baby the laggards once they get out in the real world." This tendency to distinguish between the real world and school is, for me at least, bothersome. What is even more bothersome to me is the assumption that the experiences students have in schools are somehow less *authentic* than "real world" and "hands-on" experiences. First, the assumption that the world of children and youths is somehow less real than the world of adults shows an amazing disrespect for the young. Their world is real, and it is real in its consequences. Second, the failure to understand just how real school life is for children and youths leads to terrible distortions of life in school, and it encourages adults to interact with children who are relative strangers to them in ways that in other settings would be viewed as needlessly punitive and hurtful.

The consequence of this punitive environment is that many students—especially those who have experienced a great deal of failure in their early school experience—begin to adjust their definitions of their own abilities down to a level where they can no longer be punished. Once the student accepts the fact that this level of work is the best he or she can do, and the teacher judges this work to be deserving of, say a D, then the student has become in fact and in self-perception a "D student." Brewster and Fager summarize the matter this way: "students who understand poor performance as a lack of attainable skills, rather than as some innate personal deficiency, are more likely to re-engage themselves in a task and try again. Students whose self-concept is bound up in their history of failure, on the other hand, are less likely to be motivated to learn."[9]

Sensitive teachers can do much to offset the consequences of the punitive environment in which both teachers and students sometimes find themselves, and there are many teachers who do these things. In addition, some programs are designed to dissociate failure due to lack of skill and understanding from punishment, and to view the overcoming of such deficiencies as a normal part of the learning process. The Bay Area Writing Project and many of its local derivatives are illustrative of such an effort. Among other

---

[9] C. Brewster and J. Fager, *Increasing Student Engagement and Motivation: From Time-on-Task to Homework* (Portland, Oreg.: Northwest Regional Laboratory, Oct. 2000), p. 2.

things, the designers of this project recognize that drafts of work are successive approximations and therefore should not be graded. I have, however, heard some teachers report that they felt compelled to violate some of the design principles of this project by, for example, grading rough drafts, in order to have enough grades in the book to justify a final grade. The fact is that much of the punitive nature of schooling is systemic, and about all that individual teachers can do until this system is changed is to ensure that their personal behavior does not reinforce or exacerbate the problem. They can also do much to offset some of the harm the present system does by being especially attentive to and empathetic with those students who are experiencing a great deal of failure even though they are investing effort.

These observations should not be taken as arguments for giving credit for effort, or for grading by different standards students who seem to have less or more academic aptitude. I am simply suggesting that as leaders, teachers need to recognize that students need much more support and encouragement when they are failing than they need when they are experiencing success. Unfortunately, as Skinner and Belmont have observed: "If left to run their typical course, teachers tend to magnify children's initial levels of motivation. This is fine for students who enter the classroom motivationally 'rich'; they will 'get rich.' However, for students whose motivation is low, their typical classroom experiences may result in its further deterioration."[10] Great teachers know this is so, as do other great leaders.

Clear and Compelling Standards

The word *standard* often stirs up images of test scores. Certainly, test scores and other ways of assessing the quality of student performance are connected with the idea of standards in schools, and I do not discount this fact. Here, however, I am more concerned with the standards students hold for themselves than I am with the

---

[10] E. Skinner and M. Belmont, "A Longitudinal Study of Motivation in School: Reciprocal Effects of Teacher Behavior and Student Engagement, unpublished manuscript, University of Rochester, Rochester, New York, 1991, p. 31, quoted in Brewster and Fager, p. 5.

standards adults hold for them and with which adults try to get students to comply. Indeed, unless the standards adults hold for students are somehow communicated to students in ways that are persuasive to them, it is doubtful that these standards can and will have any impact on what students do or what they learn. With regard to the improvement of performance, standards matter only when they are clearly understood by those to whom they apply—in this case students—and when those to whom the standards apply attach meaning and significance to the attainment of the standards. In other words, standards can improve performance only when they are clear to students and compelling as well.

Conversely, when standards are unclear, or when they are clear but not compelling, the lack of clarity and the absence of commitment to the standards can discourage rather than encourage efforts to improve performance in the direction indicated by the standards. For example, students who are not clear on what they are expected to do, especially if they have a history of school failure, are likely to retreat from participation out of self-defense. "If I do not know what it takes to succeed," the student might well be saying, "then why take the risk of failing? Doing nothing is better than doing something that is wrong." When a standard is clear but the student sees little or no prospect of meeting that standard, the prospect of vigorously pursuing activity that will develop the skills and understandings needed to meet the standard is diminished as well. Furthermore, as Brewster and Fager observe:

> Students who are motivated to complete a task only to avoid consequences or to earn a certain grade rarely exert more than the minimum effort necessary to meet their goal. And, when students are focused on comparing themselves with their classmates, rather than on mastering skills at their own rate, they are more easily discouraged and their intrinsic motivation to learn may actually decrease. Brooks et al. (1998) observe that while external rewards sustain productivity, they "decrease interest in the task, thereby diminishing the likelihood that the task will be continued in the future."[11]

---

[11] Brewster and Fager, *Increasing Student Engagement and Motivation*, p. 4; Brewster and Fager are quoting (S. R. Brooks et al., "Improving Elementary Student Engagement in the Learning Process Through Integrated Thematic Instruction" (Master's thesis, Saint Xavier University, 1998), p. 26.

What, then, makes standards compelling to students? Among the more important considerations are the following:[12]

- *The clarity of the standard.* The more certain students are regarding what is expected the more likely they are to be engaged. The less certain they are, the more likely they are to withdraw—especially if they already have a history of failure.
- *The visibility of the performance.* Students are more likely to be committed to a standard when they believe that the performances indicated by the standard are visible (to themselves and to others) and that the performances expected are somehow under their own control—that is, they can do something about the matter. (This is one of the reasons that rubrics are so useful.)
- *The value significant others attach to the standard.* Standards that are clearly valued by persons of significance to the student are more likely to be compelling to the student than are standards that are devalued or not consistently upheld.
- *Consistency of communication.* The importance a student attaches to a standard will vary depending on the frequency with which the standard is communicated to the student and the consistency of the messages the student receives from those to whom he or she refers for guidance and direction (including peers as well as teachers, parents, and others).
- *The investments of others.* Standards likely to be important to students are those in which persons of significance to the student make clear investments as they help the student meet the standards.
- *Personal efficacy.* A student is more likely to embrace a standard and be committed to actions that support meeting that standard when the student believes he or she has the ability to meet it if enough effort is expended.

---

[12] These considerations are my summary of a wide range of research on motivation and evaluation. I have been particularly influenced by the work of S. M. Dornbusch and R. W. Scott, *Evaluation and the Exercise of Authority* (San Francisco: Jossey-Bass, 1975).

It goes almost without saying that when one or more of these qualities are lacking, students—especially those who have already experienced problems with school performance—will be discouraged from embracing the standards their teachers put forward. For example, when the student feels little support from significant adults in his or her life for the active pursuit of a standard and sees little real prospect of meeting the standard, even if he or she tries, it is likely that pressure from peers who are not supportive of the standard will become increasingly compelling. Similarly, where there is a strong anti-intellectual strain in the dominant peer group culture and no off-setting qualities in other areas of school life (for example, highly visible and meaningful celebrations of academic success, faculty engagement in intellectual pursuits that they invite students to share, and so on), it is likely that academic standards will be devalued and engagement in work intended to develop the ability to meet this standard will be low.

The Ubiquity of Context

Context-related design qualities—content and substance, organization of knowledge, protection from negative consequences, and clear and compelling standards—are ubiquitous in the design of engaging work. These first four attributes in the *working on the work framework* are going to come into play in every classroom, every day, whether or not the teacher intends them to do so. Some students will be excited about the subject to be studied and will be easy to engage. Others will be repelled. The teacher's style of presentation, the design of the curriculum, and the pace of the class will meet the needs of some students and cause others considerable distress. Some students will be willing to "go right to work" even though they are likely to fail on the first try, whereas others will stand back until they are assured that failure will not put them at too much risk. It is because these conditions are always present and will affect how students respond to tasks and activities—whether or not the teacher takes them into account—that I refer to these four conditions as *ubiquitous qualities*. They are everywhere present, and teachers who want to be effective in engaging students must take them into account as they design tasks and activities.

Ubiquitous qualities affect learning in the same way that traffic affects driving. Even if you are the only person on the road, the *condition* of traffic still exists—it just happens that on this day driving is easier because there are no other cars. Regardless of what the traffic situation looks like on any given day, the driver must take traffic into account. The more adept the driver is at handling different volumes and types of traffic, the more effective the drive will be. You don't get to choose to ignore the traffic situation when you get into the car. It just *is.* Similarly, content and substance, the way knowledge is organized, fear of failure, and the clarity or ambiguity of standards will have an effect on student engagement regardless of the teacher's intentions. In this matter, teachers have little choice. The only choice they have is how they are going to cope with these qualities as they are presented to them by the students they teach.

Teachers cannot control the predispositions of students toward what teachers want students to learn, nor can they control students' preferred learning styles. Neither can they control the extent to which students need reassurance and guarantees of protection as a condition of pursuing high standards. These are matters that are determined in large measure by the prior experiences of students. The long-term picture may of course be more optimistic. Experiences do continue to add up in students' lives, which means that even though in the short run these qualities cannot be controlled, in the long run they can be altered. For example, if students experience increasing amounts of success, they are likely to need less protection from failure. And if a student becomes engaged in the study of a subject despite not liking it, he or she might eventually come to be sufficiently interested in the subject that this interest itself will serve as a source of engagement. Nevertheless, in the short run the teacher needs to appeal to motives other than those having to do with interest in the subject when this interest does not exist. All the teacher can do is to be aware of students' previous experiences and take them into account while designing tasks and activities for students.

Qualities of Choice

Uncomfortable though it may be for academics to accept, the fact is that academic work is of more interest to academics than it is to the majority of America's citizenry. Nonacademics have other interests and other concerns. This does not mean that nonacademics cannot be brought to do academic work and to pursue tasks that require intellectual rigor, but to encourage them one must be prepared to appeal to interests beyond those served by academic work alone. These interests are covered by the last six qualities in the *working on the work framework:*

- Product focus
- Affiliation
- Affirmation of performance
- Novelty and variety
- Choice
- Authenticity

Product Focus

One way to help students become engaged in academic work is to attach this work to some product, performance, exhibition, or problem of significance to the student. This does not mean a return to the project method nor does it mean that the curriculum must always be organized around problems. What it does mean is that to whatever extent the teacher can identify or create products, performances, exhibitions, or problems that are of significance to students and that will call upon the student to learn what it is intended that the student learn, the likelihood of student engagement is increased. Furthermore, designing such products, performances, exhibitions, and problems is at least as important when students are called on to master low-level knowledge (that is, knowledge best acquired through memorization) as it is when students are expected to engage in such higher-order processes as evaluating and synthesizing. Though it is often assumed that the acquisition of basic skills and the mastery of fundamental facts requires a heavy application of extrinsic rewards and coercion, I do not agree. I also believe that lower-order knowledge gained as a result of engagement will be more profoundly held than will learning that occurs as a result of compliance induced by extrinsic rewards and the threat of negative consequences. Focusing on products, performances, exhibitions, and problems is not, however, the only way of making the routine work associated with acquiring basic skills engaging any more than the project method is the only means of helping students develop the ability to evaluate and synthesize information.

Affiliation

Many students have learned to place considerable value on activities that encourage them to work with others, in other words activities that provide opportunities for affiliation. In band and choral music activities, for example, it is likely that some students are committed and attentive because they value the positive regard of their peers, and a quality performance as a band or chorus member is one means of gaining that regard. Indeed, opportunities for feedback from peers, coaching from peers, and observation by peers are built into the work, and it is the result of these opportunities that appeals to some students. For other students it may simply be the opportunities for camaraderie that keep them engaged in this work. The band director who fails to provide opportunities to realize the latter value may well find engagement deteriorating among those who place high value on affiliation. The point here of course is that for some students affiliation is a powerful motivating force.

There is a caution, however; for some students affiliation is, or may become, a negative value. Few teachers have failed to hear the complaint that *group work* simply holds some students back or slows them down. If this is so, it is because the group work is not properly designed. Indeed, some tasks assigned to groups are really not group tasks—they are tasks that could be done by one person if given enough time. Group tasks cannot be accomplished by one person; they require cooperative action and coordination of effort. It is, for example, impossible for one person to sing both bass and soprano at the same time or to simultaneously play as quarterback and center on a football team. Similarly, if one student is assigned the role of researcher, another the role of writer, another the role of editor, and still another the role of presenter, and if the teacher monitors the work to ensure that each person carries out the functions assigned to his or her role, academic group work might both play to strengths and develop new strengths as well. Furthermore, defining tasks in this way tends to encourage students to become invested in the success of their peers because they are dependent on them.

Affirmation of Performance

In some team sports functional interdependence is almost totally lacking, yet the presence of other team members often has a powerful effect on each person's level of engagement. For example, swimming, golf, and tennis, with the exception of relays and tennis doubles, are sports that provide little interdependence other than statistical interdependence. Each player is solely responsible for what he or she accomplishes and is not beholden to others for those accomplishments. The reason the presence of a team is important is that it introduces to the activity yet another value that is sometimes important to student engagement—affirmation of the significance of the quality of the student's performance. For example, on a golf team, even though each golfer scores independently, the success of each team member is of real concern to every other team member for the simple reason that it is the score of the total team that wins the match. This encourages each team member to be invested in the success of all other team members and to indicate this investment in ways that *affirm* the significance of all the contributions, from that of the lowest performer to that of the highest performer.[13]

Engagement is likely to increase when students perceive that the quality of their performance is of consequence to others who are important to them. Thus the extent to which teachers can build into tasks and activities an assurance that the quality of each participant's performance is important to every other participant will

---

[13] In a now-classic study William Foote Whyte reported the counterintuitive finding that among street gangs bowling scores varied with status in the group. When a person's group status increased, the person's bowling scores also increased. When group status declined, bowling scores declined. Apparently having one's importance to the group affirmed had a direct impact on performance; see W. F. Whyte, *Street Corner Society: The Social Structure of an Italian Slum* (Chicago: University of Chicago Press, 1943). If this finding could be generalized, it would have important implications for the design of schoolwork. As it is, it remains a piece of anecdotal evidence to support the commonsense notion that people perform better when they think what they are doing makes a difference and matters to others whose judgments are of value. As Dornbusch and Scott, *Evaluation and the Exercise of Authority,* have shown, evaluations are more powerful when done by people who count in the life of the person being evaluated.

clearly affect the likelihood of student engagement. Furthermore, the more frequently others who are significant to the student, such as parents, are put in a position to see the student perform or read or present a detailed description of what he or she has accomplished (as opposed to reading or hearing a teacher's evaluation of the task), the more likely it is that the power of affirmation as a motive force for engagement will be realized.

Novelty and Variety

Though it is true that people resist change, they also like and need a certain degree of novelty and variety in their lives. In fact some psychiatrists see an overly heavy insistence on routine as an indicator of mental illness or approaching senility. Novelty not only introduces some degree of excitement into an activity but also tends to fasten the student's attention, because newness, in itself, calls upon the student to develop new skills or to employ established skills in new ways. For example, during the 1980s—and to some extent even now—the introduction of computers into classrooms increased student engagement in learning tasks simply because these tasks were often designed so that students had to use this novel device of the computer to accomplish what it was intended that they accomplish. Some students paid attention and were committed to tasks that allowed them to use computers when under other circumstances these same students would have done their work only if other incentives were offered.

As students become more accustomed to computers and computer uses are routinized, the novelty wears off. Once this occurs, the opportunity to use a computer will be no more motivating than the opportunity to use a pen or pencil. However, the computer may continue to be a source of novelty if the content available through electronic means is novel.

Choice

Children and adolescents, like adults, are more likely to find a task or activity engaging when they feel they have some choice in the work they do or at least in how they go about the work. Obviously, there are some tasks in which little choice is possible. When this is the case, the teacher must attend to enhancing other design qualities in order to engage the student. When it is possible to introduce choice, however, the likelihood of engagement is increased. Choice can be made available in many ways. For example, the teacher might construct group work so that students can choose their work partners—though all partners must work on the same task. Or the teacher might assign partners and give the groups a choice in the product of a task.

The critical point is that students are more likely to find schoolwork compelling when they feel they have some control over the nature of their own participation. Compelling work is essential to engagement. Though the indiscriminate use of choice can introduce frivolity and shallowness and can lead to the confusion of entertainment with engagement, the fact is that lack of choice can also lead to carelessness, decreases in attention, and feelings of estrangement from the task or activity one is called on to do.[14]

Authenticity

The word *authentic* is second only to the word *relevant* in terms of the confusion differences in meaning can introduce into a conversation about teaching and learning. For some the word *authentic* has to do with experiences based in or oriented toward the "real world out there," meaning beyond the doors of classrooms and schools. Such usage assumes that what goes on in school is not real and that the worlds of students—as students construct them—are not real. As I discussed earlier, I reject this meaning. When teachers are considering building authenticity into the tasks and activities provided for students, it is important that they appreciate that for many students, life beyond the classroom is lacking in authenticity; it is school life that is real. For students, authenticity has to

---

[14] A great deal of research has been done on this matter in industrial settings. Lack of choice and lack of feelings of control are increasingly coming to be understood as sources of poor quality work in factories. One does not have to think of the school as a factory to see that there might be some lessons here to be learned by educators.

do with *that which is real to the student*. For some students the idea that they should be concerned with reading books is simply not within their reality. The football game on Friday night is real. Conversations in the hallway are real. The way parents respond to schoolwork taken home is real. Personal embarrassment is real.

Realities such as these must be of concern to teachers who would use authenticity as a means of increasing engagement. They must attend carefully to the world in which their students live their present lives at least as much as they attend to the world they anticipate these students will inhabit after leaving school.

This is not to say that the outside world and anticipated futures should play no role in the decisions made by teachers, for these factors should play a role indeed. But for most students reality has less to do with the world of adults than it has to do with the world of children and adolescents. Both school and the adult world outside of school are sometimes seen by students as disconnected from their reality.[15] As Willard Waller observed long ago, one of the most serious challenges confronting the teacher is that of developing sufficient empathy with the world of students that he or she can "understand [student] roles and live vividly roles of his own not wholly incompatible with the roles of [students]."[16] At the same time, the teacher must maintain his or her standing and perspective as an adult, even though, as Waller also observed, it is difficult for the teacher to take the world of students seriously without so identifying with the children that an adult perspective gets lost. Or, worse, to protect themselves from this overidentification with the world of children, some teachers interpose an "immense distance" between themselves and students, and then "the teacher-pupil relationship becomes one of dominance and subordination in its strictest form."[17]

---

[15] See, for example, P. Hersch, *A Tribe Apart: A Journey into the Heart of American Adolescence* (New York: Fawcett Columbine, 1998).

[16] W. Waller, *The Sociology of Teaching* (New York: Wiley, 1967) (Originally published 1932), p. 60.

[17] Waller, *The Sociology of Teaching*, p. 59.

A Summary

If the activities and tasks that students are expected to undertake in school or initiate in response to encouragement from teachers and school leaders are to be engaging, they must contain qualities that respond to the motives and values students bring to those tasks and activities. In this discussion and elsewhere in my writings, I have identified ten of these qualities. Four of these qualities—content and substance, the way knowledge is organized, clear and compelling standards, and the creation of a psychologically safe learning environment—are ubiquitous. Teachers must take them into account, and if the teacher fails to take them into account they will still have an impact—either positive or negative—on engagement.

Six other qualities—product focus, affiliation, affirmation of performance, novelty and variety, choice, and authenticity—are available for teachers to exploit, but teachers must consciously introduce these qualities into the design of the work or they will not be present. The art and science of teaching is to be found in designing school tasks and activities in such a way that the number of students who are engaged in the tasks and activities that students are provided or encouraged to undertake is optimized. The most serious conversations teachers can have center on the ways these qualities can be most effectively built into lessons and units of schoolwork. The most productive action research a group of teachers could pursue might be research that sheds light on how each of these qualities affects the way their own students respond to and adapt to the schoolwork their teachers provide.

Appendix B: Creating a Learning Community to Transform Schools

A definition: a *learning community* is a group of persons who are bound together by the pursuit of common questions, problems, or issues. They have developed clear norms and procedures that ensure that this pursuit goes forward in a way that honors the ideas of mutualism, collegiality, trust, loyalty, and friendship while showing a bias for hard-nosed analysis and concrete action.

Among the conditions necessary to establish and maintain a learning community committed to transforming schools into engagement-focused systems are the following:

- The existence of a common agenda or common set of questions about which all members care passionately and that they are willing to pursue even at the risk of some personal sacrifice and discomfort. Among these questions are the following:

  How can schools and classrooms be organized to support teachers more effectively in creating engaging work for students and to encourage students to become engaged in the work they are provided?

  How can engagement be identified, measured, and differentiated from compliance produced by the promise of extrinsic rewards or the threat of unpleasant consequences?

  What elements that teachers control can they build into the tasks they assign to students or the activities they encourage students to undertake that increase student engagement? Do the effects of these elements vary across grade levels, the subject being taught, the season of the year, and so on?

What evidence is there that students who do tasks because they are engaged develop more profound understanding of what they learn than do those who are simply compliant? What evidence is there that engaged students learn more and retain what they learn longer than those who are simply compliant?

What do teachers and school principals need in order to ensure that they can and will focus effectively on creating engaging work for students and school environments that encourage student engagement in academic tasks?

- The existence of a common framework and vocabulary to facilitate discussion and analysis and a commitment by members of the group to use these frameworks and this language in a disciplined way. (The framework presented in Appendix A is illustrative.)
- School leaders, beginning with the school board and the superintendent, who understand that the creation of an environment supportive of giving engagement a central focus will require bringing about change in many of the systems that shape behavior in schools—for example, evaluation systems, induction systems, and power and authority systems. These leaders must be prepared to lead in providing support to the disruptive activities that will necessarily accompany these changes.
- The development of trust and norms of reciprocity among all members of the group and the systematic induction of new members into the group, including induction into the questions, processes, and norms that the community upholds.

As learning communities come into existence and become fully functional, they will, of course, put their own stamp on the requirements listed here, which are intended as a starting point.

Bibliography

American Institutes for Research. *An Educators' Guide to Schoolwide Reform.* Arlington, Va.: Educational Research Service, 1999.

Becker, H., Greer, B., Hughes, E. C., and Straus, A. *Boys in White: Student Culture in Medical School.* Chicago: University of Chicago Press, 1961.

Blau, P. *Exchange and Power in Social Life.* Piscataway, N.J.: Transaction, 1986.

Bloom, B. S., and Krathwohl, D. R. *Taxonomy of Behavioral Objectives: The Classification of Educational Goals by a Committee of College and University Examiners: Handbook I. The Cognitive Domain.* White Plains, N.Y.: Longman, 1956.

Brewster, C., and Fager, J. *Increasing Student Engagement and Motivation: From Time-on-Task to Homework.* Portland, Oreg.: Northwest Regional Laboratory, Oct. 2000.

Bridenbaugh, C. "The Great Mutation." *American Historical Review,* 1963, *68*(2), 315–331.

Brooks, S. R., Freiburger, S. M., and Grotheer, D. R. "Improving Elementary Student Engagement in the Learning Process Through Integrated Thematic Instruction." Master's thesis, Saint Xavier University, 1998.

Bruner, J. *The Process of Education.* Boston: Harvard University Press, 1961.

Bryk, A. S., and Schneider, B. *Trust in Schools: A Core Resource for Improvement.* New York: Russell Sage Foundation, 2002.

Burkett, E. *Another Planet: A Year in the Life of a Suburban School.* New York: HarperCollins, 2002.

Christensen, C. M. *The Innovator's Dilemma: When New Technologies Cause Great Firms to Fail.* Boston: Harvard Business School Press, 1997.

Chubb, J. E., and Moe, T. M. *Politics, Markets, and America's Schools.* Washington, D.C.: Brookings Institution, 1990.

Cochran-Smith, M., and Lytle, S. L. *Inside/Outside: Teacher Research and Knowledge.* New York: Teachers College Press, 1993.

Coleman, J. S. *The Adolescent Society: The Social Life of the Teenager and Its Impact on Education.* New York: Free Press, 1961.

Collins, J. *Good to Great: Why Some Companies Make the Leap . . . and Others Don't.* New York: HarperCollins, 2001.

Corwin, R. G. *A Sociology of Education: Emerging Patterns of Class, Status, and Power in Public Schools.* Upper Saddle River, N.J.: Appleton-Century-Crofts, 1965.

Corwin, R. G. "Education and the Sociology of Complex Organizations." In D. Hansen and J. Gerstl (eds.), *On Education: Sociological Perspectives.* New York: Wiley, 1967.

"Council Minutes from January 2003," *Educational Researcher,* June–July 2003, *32*(5), 39–45.

Darling-Hammond, L. "Teacher Quality and Student Achievement: A Review of State Policy Evidence." *Education Policy Archives,* 2000, *8*(entire issue, 1).

Deal, T., and Kennedy, A. *Corporate Cultures: The Rites and Rituals of Corporate Life.* Reading, Mass.: Addison-Wesley, 1982.

Dev, P. C. "Intrinsic Motivation and Academic Achievement: What Does Their Relationship Imply for the Classroom Teacher?" *Remedial and Special Education,* 1997, *18*(1), 12–19.

Dewey, J. *How We Think.* New York: Dover, 1997. (Originally published 1909.)

Dornbusch, S. M., and Scott, R. W. *Evaluation and the Exercise of Authority.* San Francisco: Jossey-Bass, 1975.

Dreeben, R. S. *On What Is Learned in School.* Reading, Mass.: Addison-Wesley, 1968.

Dreeben, R. S. *The Nature of Teaching and Schools: Schools and the Work of Teachers.* Glenview, Ill.: Scott, Foresman, 1970.

Drucker, P. *Managing for Results.* New York: HarperCollins, 1964.

Drucker, P. *Management: Tasks, Practices, Responsibilities.* New York: Harper-Collins, 1974.

Durkheim, É. *The Rules of Sociological Method.* New York: Free Press, 1966. (Originally published 1895.)

Etzioni, A. *A Comparative Analysis of Complex Organizations: On Power, Involvement and Their Correlates.* New York: Free Press, 1961.

Fullan, M. *Leading in a Culture of Change.* San Francisco: Jossey-Bass, 2001.

Fullan, M. *The Moral Imperative of School Leadership.* Thousand Oaks, Calif.: Corwin Press, 2003.

Gardner, H. *Frames of Mind: The Theory of Multiple Intelligences.* New York: Basic Books, 1993.

George Lucas Educational Foundation (GLEF). *Edutopia: The New World of Learning.* [http://glef.org].

Gerzon, M. *A House Divided: Six Belief Systems Struggling for America's Soul.* New York: Putnam, 1996.

Glasser, W. *Schools Without Failure.* New York: HarperCollins, 1969.

Goodwin, B. *Digging Deeper: Where Does the Public Stand on Standards-Based*

Education? Issues Brief. Aurora, Colo.: Mid-continent Research for Education and Learning, 2003.

Graff, G. *Clueless in Academia: How Schooling Obscures the Life of the Mind.* New Haven, Conn.: Yale University Press, 2003.

Herriot, R. E., and Gross, N. (eds.). *The Dynamics of Planned Educational Change.* Berkeley, Calif.: McCutchan, 1979.

Hersch, P. *A Tribe Apart: A Journey into the Heart of American Adolescence.* New York: Fawcett Columbine, 1998.

Hess, F. M. "Public Schools and the Public Interest." *School Administrator,* Sept. 2002, pp. 28–31.

H. H. Hickam, *Rocket Boys: A Memoir.* New York: Delacorte Press, 1998.

Hofstadter, R. *Anti-Intellectualism in American Life.* New York: Random House, 1966.

Homans, G. *The Human Group.* Piscataway, N.J.: Transaction, 2001. (Originally published 1950.)

House, E. *Evaluating with Validity.* Thousand Oaks, Calif.: Sage, 1980.

Humes, E. *School of Dreams: Making the Grade at a Top American High School.* Orlando: Harcourt, 2003.

Jencks, C. *Inequality: A Reassessment of the Effect of Family and Schooling in America.* New York: Harper Colophon Books, 1972.

Kanter, R. M. *Rosabeth Moss Kanter on the Frontiers of Management.* Boston: Harvard Business School Press, 1997.

Kohn, A. "Only for My Kid: How Privileged Parents Undermine School Reform." *Phi Delta Kappan,* Apr. 1998, pp. 568–577.

Kohn, A. "Fighting the Tests: A Practical Guide to Rescuing Our Schools." *Phi Delta Kappan,* Jan. 2001, pp. 348–357.

Kotter, J. P. *Leading Change.* Boston: Harvard Business School Press, 1996.

Larabee, D. F. "The Peculiar Problems of Preparing Educational Researchers." *Educational Researcher,* May 2003, pp. 13–21.

Little, J. W., and McLaughlin, M. W. (eds.). *Teachers' Work: Individuals, Colleagues, and Context.* New York: Teachers College Press, 1993.

Lortie, D. C. *Schoolteacher: A Sociological Study.* Chicago: University of Chicago Press, 1975.

Lumsden, L. S. *Student Motivation to Learn.* ERIC Digest No. 92. Eugene, Oreg.: ERIC Clearinghouse on Educational Management, June 1994. (ED 370 200)

Matthews, D. *Is There a Public for Public Schools?* Dayton, Ohio: Kettering Foundation Press, 1996.

McAdams, D. *Fighting to Save Our Urban Schools . . . and Winning: Lessons from Houston.* New York: Teachers College Press, 2000.

Meier, D. "The Road to Trust." *The American School Board Journal,* Sept. 2003.

Merton, R. K. *Social Theory and Social Structure.* New York: Free Press, 1968.

Merton, R. K. "The Ambivalence of Scientists." In R. K. Merton, *Sociological Ambivalence and Other Essays*. New York: Free Press, 1976.

Meyer, J. W., and Rowan, B. "Institutionalized Organizations: Formal Structures as Myths and Ceremony." *American Journal of Sociology*, 1977, *83*(2), 340–363.

Meyer J. W., and Rowan, B. "The Structure of Educational Organizations." In J. V. Baldridge and T. Deal (eds.), *The Dynamics of Organizational Change in Education*. Berkeley, Calif.: McCutchan, 1983.

Mills, C. W. *The Sociological Imagination*. New York: Oxford University Press, 1959.

Mosenthal, P. B. "Understanding Engagement: Historical and Political Contexts." In J. T. Guthrie and D. E. Alvermar (eds.), *Engaged Reading: Processes, Practices and Policy Implications*. New York: Teachers College Press, 1999.

National Commission on Excellence in Education. *A Nation at Risk*. Washington, D.C.: National Commission on Excellence in Education, 1983.

The National Dialogue on Standards-Based Education. Newsroom. [www.nationaldialogue.org], July 21, 2003.

National Research Council and Institute of Medicine of the National Academies. *Engaging Schools: Fostering High School Students' Motivation to Learn*. Washington, D.C.: National Academies Press, 2004.

Parsons, T., and Bales, R. F. *Family, Socialization and Interaction Process*. New York: Free Press, 1955.

Perrow, C. *Complex Organizations: A Critical Essay*. Glenview, Ill.: Scott, Foresman, 1972.

Pope, D. C. *Doing School: How We Are Creating a Generation of Stressed Out, Materialistic and Miseducated Students*. New Haven, Conn.: Yale University Press, 2003.

Putnam, R. D. *Bowling Alone: The Collapse and Revival of American Community*. New York: Simon & Schuster, 2000.

Ravitch, D. *Left Back: A Century of Failed School Reforms*. New York: Simon & Schuster, 2000.

Resnick, L. B., and Hall, M. W. "Learning Organizations for Sustainable Education Reform." *Daedalus*, 1998, *127*(4), 89–118.

Sarason, S. *The Culture of the School and the Problem of Change*. New York: Teachers College Press, 1996.

Sarason, S. "Some Features of a Flawed Educational System." *Daedalus*, 1998, *127*(4), 1–12.

Sarason, S. (ed.). "Education Yesterday, Education Tomorrow." Special Issue. *Daedalus*, 1998, *127*(4).

Schlechty, P. C. "The Psychological Bias of American Educators." Ball State University, Occasional Papers, 1967.

Schlechty, P. C. "A Survey of Parent Attitudes Toward the Virginia Beach Year-Round School Pilot Program: Final Report, 1974." Unpublished report.

Schlechty, P. C. *Teaching and Social Behavior: Toward an Organizational Theory of Instruction.* Needham Heights, Mass.: Allyn & Bacon, 1976.

Schlechty, P. C. "Career Ladders: A Good Idea Going Awry." In T. J. Sergiovanni (ed.), *Schooling for Tomorrow.* Needham Heights, Mass.: Allyn & Bacon, 1989.

Schlechty, P. C. "Going Native." Paper presented to the American Educational Research Association, Boston, 1990.

Schlechty, P. C. *Reform in Teacher Education: A Sociological View.* Washington, D.C.: American Association of Colleges for Teacher Education, 1990.

Schlechty, P. C. *Schools for the 21st Century: Leadership Imperatives for Educational Reform.* San Francisco: Jossey-Bass, 1990.

Schlechty, P. C. "Education Services as a Regulated Monopoly." *Education Week,* Apr. 10, 1991, p. 36.

Schlechty, P. C. *Inventing Better Schools: An Action Plan for Educational Reform.* San Francisco: Jossey-Bass, 1997.

Schlechty, P. C. *Shaking Up the Schoolhouse: How to Support and Sustain Educational Innovation.* San Francisco: Jossey-Bass, 2001.

Schlechty, P. C. *Working on the Work: An Action Plan for Teachers, Principals, and Superintendents.* San Francisco: Jossey-Bass, 2002.

Schlechty, P. C., Crowell, D., Whitford, B. L., and Joslin A. "Understanding and Managing Staff Development in an Urban School System." Final Report on NIE contract 400-79-0056, 1983.

Schlechty, P. C., and Whitford, B. L. "The Organizational Context of School Systems and the Functions of Staff Development." In G. Griffin (ed.), *Staff Development: Eighty-Second Yearbook of the National Society for the Study of Education:* Part II. Chicago: University of Chicago Press, 1983.

Senge, P. M. *The Fifth Discipline: The Art and Practice of the Learning Organization.* New York: Doubleday, Currency, 1990.

Stone, C. N., Henig, J. R., Jones, B. D., and Pierannunzi, C. *Building Civic Capacity: The Politics of Reforming Urban Schools.* Lawrence: University of Kansas Press, 2001.

Waller, W. *The Sociology of Teaching.* New York: Wiley, 1967. (Originally published 1932.)

Whyte, W. F. *Street Corner Society: The Social Structure of an Italian Slum.* Chicago: University of Chicago Press, 1943.

Williams, R. M., Jr. *American Society: A Sociological Interpretation* (3rd ed.). New York: Knopf, 1972.

Wood, G. *A Time to Learn.* New York: Dutton, 1998.

Index

89–91, 108, 108n, 136–137; state and local power eroded by, 191

Normative order: compliance with norms and, 49–53; defined, xiv, 20; effects of observed differences in, 36; understanding knowledge basis of, 100–102; use of term, 31, 31n

Norms: adaptations to, accompanying innovation, 40–43, 41n; coherence between various types of, 23, 33–34, 36–37; of continuous improvement, 39–40, 127–128, 134–136; of evasion, 53–54, 140; necessity of conformity to, 38; preachment, practice, and pretense framework and, 23–26; questions about, 35–37; social, 20; sources of variance in compliance with, 46–58; specialty, 29, 50–52, 131–132; types of, 21–23; variation in enforcement of, 20–21, 36, 63, 131

Novelty, in engaging schoolwork, 237

O

Open meeting laws, 123

Operational standards, 141, 142

Organizational set, 168–169, 187

Organizations: critical systems of, xiv; instrumental vs. expressive, 199–201; learning, 88; social, 212

Ought norms, 24, 35–36

P

Paradigm shift, needed in educational system, 16–17

Parents: activist, superintendent's strategy with, 150, 176; declining school participation by, 179; as guarantors, 184–187; involved in children's education, 24, 25; as partners, 183–184, 189–190; privileged, and school reform, 106; redefining boundaries of, 180–182; relationship between public schools and, 207–210; relationship between teachers and, 207–209, 208n; and year-round school program, 171

Partners, parents as, 183–184, 189–190

Passive compliance. *See* Ritual compliance

Pay-for-performance systems, 40, 59

Performance, affirmation of, and engaging schoolwork, 236–237, 236n

Performance visibility, in evaluation systems, 137–139

Performance-based accreditation, 135

Performance-based pay, 134

Personal characteristics, as consideration in recruitment, 81–83

Personnel selection, school board role in, 53–54

Persuading, vs. convincing, 89–93

Pioneers, 125, 129

Portfolio assessment, 227

Power: coercive and remunerative, 133–134; influence vs., 111–112. *See also* Power and authority systems

Power and authority systems, 111–132; common efforts at reforming, 119–124, 120n; concepts relevant to, 111–112; defined, xiv; disruptive innovations resisted by, 112–118; new funding generated by, 118–119; with norms of continuous improvement, 127–128; questions about, 128–132; rewards available under, 125–127, 129, 130

Practices: gap between theory and, 104–106; and norms, 24

Preachments: and norms, 24; questions about, 35–36; ritual enforcement of, 53–54

Pretenses: and change, 26; and norms, 24–25, 24n; question about, 36. *See also* Cultural fictions

Primary schools. *See* Elementary schools

Principals: changed role of, with engagement, 18; high school, oganizational set for, 169; lesson plan requirements of, 55–56; time spent with teachers by, 50–51. *See also* Educators

122–124; of comprehensive high schools, 62; of social systems, 47–49
Universities: importation of knowledge from, 98–100; teacher education programs of, 78–79, 83
Urban/suburban separation, denial of reality to maintain, 30–31
Urbanski, A., 34
U.S. Marine Corps, induction system, 72

V

Values: cultural, vs. reality, 26; of instrumental vs. expressive organizations, 199–201, 200n; and standardized testing, 164
Variety, in engaging schoolwork, 237

W

Waller, W., 25, 31n, 51, 57, 105, 175, 207–208, 208n, 239
Whyte, W. F., 236
Williams, R. M., Jr., 21, 24n, 49n, 53
Work: in education, 219n; group, 235; knowledge, 88; valuing of, 15–16. *See also* Engaging schoolwork
Working on the work framework, 218
Working on the Work (Schlechty), 217

Y

Year-round school program, 171

Z

Zero tolerance policies, 21

Other Books by Phillip C. Schlechty

Working on the Work
An Action Plan for Teachers, Principals, and Superintendents

ISBN: 0-7879-6165-5   Paperback

www.josseybass.com

"Any teacher who is interested in providing an authentically engaging classroom should embrace and utilize Phil Schlechty's WOW philosophy. It is an invaluable guide for teachers to become leaders and designers of quality lessons that facilitate student engagement and success."

—Kristin Barton, teacher, Gardenhill Elementary, La Mirada, California

"Once again Dr. Schlechty provides a must-read to the professional educator who is serious about improving and sustaining public education in our country."

—Ann Denlinger, superintendent, Durham Public Schools, Chapel Hill, North Carolina

If student performance is to be improved, says Phillip Schlechty, there are at least three ways to approach the problem: 1) work on the students, 2) work on the teachers, or 3) work on the work. Unfortunately, the first two have thus far produced unimpressive results. The key to improving education, Schlechty believes, lies in the third alternative: to provide better quality work for students—work that is engaging and that enables students to learn what they need in order to succeed in the world.

In this practical companion to the author's popular books, *Shaking Up the Schoolhouse* and *Inventing Better Schools,* Schlechty, one of America's most renowned school reformers, presents the Working on the Work (WOW) framework—an outline for improving student performance by improving the quality of schoolwork. Field-tested in schools across the country, the WOW framework describes the twelve essential components of a WOW school and suggests ways to improve the quality of content, organization of knowledge, measurement of achievement, nurturance of creativity, and novelty and variety of tasks. Schlechty offers practical guidelines for redesigning classroom activity so that more students are highly engaged in schoolwork, developing clear and compelling standards for assessing student work, and making clear connections between what students are doing and what they are expected to produce. He also discusses the roles of teachers, principals, and superintendents—and how they individually and collectively play a part in the WOW process.

Other Books by Phillip C. Schlechty

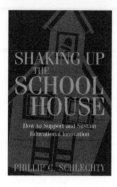

Shaking Up the Schoolhouse

How to Support and Sustain Educational Innovation

ISBN: 0-7879-7213-4   Paperback

www.josseybass.com

Grow into a skillful leader of lasting change! Drawing from decades of experience and from actual cases, you'll learn the essential characteristics of change-adept organizations and gain a practical framework for overcoming obstacles in the learning experience, from reviewing the competition to improving student engagement through more effective standards.

Praise for *Shaking Up the Schoolhouse*

"*Shaking Up the Schoolhouse* is all about empowering leaders so they can improve schools. This book is a must-read for policymakers at any level and for those who think and care about school improvement."

—Paul D. Houston, executive director,
American Association of School Administrators

"Schlechty's recommendations to school board members, central office staff, union leaders, principals, teachers, parents, and state legislators make this an important resource for creating schools in which all staff and students are learning and performing at high levels. Schlechty's suggestions are wonderful dialogue starters for educators searching for ways to make dramatic improvement in schools."

—Dennis Sparks, executive director, National Staff Development Council

"I have worked with Phil Schlechty for over twenty years and I continue to learn from him. *Shaking Up the Schoolhouse* is filled with sound suggestions for school leaders, as well as practical suggestions for parents and politicians. Those familiar with Schlechty's work will find fresh and new insights in these pages."

—Gerry House, president and CEO, Institute for Student Achievement,
and former Superintendent of the Year

"Schlechty's solution to improving public education is straightforward: focus on the quality of students' work. Engaging and loaded with ideas, *Shaking Up the Schoolhouse* brings together experience and theory in a single volume of wisdom."

—Betty Lou Whitford, professor of education and director of the National Center
for Restructuring Education, Schools, and Teaching,
Teachers College, Columbia University

Other Books by Phillip C. Schlechty

Inventing Better Schools
An Action Plan
for Educational Reform

ISBN: 0-7879-5610-4   Paperback
www.josseybass.com

Winner of the National Staff Development Counsel's 1998 Outstanding Staff Development Book Award

"Schlechty offers a clear and concise vision of systemic change to address the problems with education."
— *The School Administrator*

In this powerful wake-up call to educators, Phillip Schlechty argues that schools must change or become obsolete—and that central to this change is a rethinking of old rules, roles, and relationships. *Inventing Better Schools* offers a plan of attack that is thoughtful, practical, and full of step-by-step advice. Schlechty shows both educators and parents how to envision reform and design quality educational systems. He explains how the visioning process must be rooted in real shared beliefs, how mission statements must unpack visions into concrete goals that are connected to action, and how the results of reform can be usefully assessed. He points out that reinventing schools must be looked upon as a continual process, and he provides leaders with the tools to negotiate their way through it.

Drawing on the author's vast experience in the day-to-day work of implementing school reform, *Inventing Better Schools* offers new approaches for setting standards and ensuring accountability—and includes samples of actual mission statements and strategic plans of successful school districts.

"Schlechty marshals readers through the ideas-to-action labyrinth of improving schools .... A worthy successor to his earlier work."
—*The American School Board Journal*

"A book filled with hope. . . . Not all reformers in the country will agree with Schlechty's solutions or even the problems, but they will be the richer for having read what he has to say on the subject."
—*Louisville Courier-Journal*

"Schlechty adds a refreshing voice to the ongoing how-to-fix-our-schools debate. . . . Highly recommended."
—*Library Journal*

Schools for the 21st Century
Leadership Imperatives for Educational Reform

ISBN: 1-55542-366-3   Paperback
www.josseybass.com

"Schlechty's common-sense approach to restructuring is combined with a strategic planner's vision and the translation of beliefs into action. . . . A wide audience, including principals and superintendents, can find in this book practical outlines for restructuring, and a distinctive and focused view of their role in the educational systems of the twenty-first century."

—*The School Administrator*

"Schlechty offers no quick fixes, nor does he recommend steps prescribed by outsiders. Rather, he works closely with business and community leaders, as well as school boards and school personnel, in making real changes. When he works in my home state of Arkansas, Schlechty always insists that those who begin a restructuring effort accept the necessity of a long-term commitment. Warning that the effort to improve schools should be neither a stopgap nor a piecemeal process, he emphasizes that there will have to be a break in business as usual in public schools."

—from the foreword by Bill Clinton

While the economy and the work force have changed drastically in the last century, public education has lagged far behind. In order to prepare our children for a future of constant change, the structure and fundamental purposes of our schools must be reexamined. One of our most clear-thinking advocates for educational reform looks at curricula, teaching roles, grading systems, classroom schedules, as well as the history, culture, and structure of our public schools. Schlechty provides an adaptable framework for the kind of change schools must accommodate if they are to meet the challenges of the next century.